Digital Psychological Warfare

Tarnveer Singh

Digital Psychological Warfare

Weaponisation of Digital Platforms

palgrave
macmillan

Tarnveer Singh
Cyber Wisdom Ltd
Birmingham, Staffordshire, UK

ISBN 978-3-032-15293-0 ISBN 978-3-032-15294-7 (eBook)
https://doi.org/10.1007/978-3-032-15294-7

Cover credit: Alex Linch shutterstock.com

This Palgrave Macmillan imprint is published by the registered company Springer Nature Switzerland AG
The registered company address is: Gewerbestrasse 11, 6330 Cham, Switzerland

Preface

In an age where digital technologies permeate every aspect of human life—from com-munication and commerce to governance and warfare—the battlefield has expanded beyond physical terrain into the psychological domain. *Digital Psychological Warfare* arrives at a criti-cal juncture, offering a timely and incisive exploration of how digital tools are weaponised to influence, manipulate, and destabilise individuals, communities, and nations.

This book does not merely catalogue the tactics of psychological operations in cyber-space; it interrogates the deeper structures that enable them. From algorithmic persuasion and disinformation campaigns to behavioural profiling and cognitive overload, the author unpacks the mechanisms through which digital systems exploit vulnerabilities in human perception, emo-tion, and decision-making. The result is a chilling yet essential account of how power is exer-cised invisibly—through screens, feeds, and networks—often without the target's aware-ness.

What distinguishes this volume is its interdisciplinary lens. Drawing from cybersecurity, psychology, media studies, and ethics, the author constructs a framework for understanding dig-ital psychological warfare not just as a technical phenomenon, but as a socio-political and ethi-cal crisis. The book challenges readers to reconsider the boundaries between propaganda and influence, surveillance and engagement, freedom and control. It reveals how digital platforms—originally designed for connection and convenience—can be repurposed for coercion, polarisa-tion, and psychological harm.

Importantly, this work does not treat its subject matter with alarmism or fatalism. Instead, it offers a rigorous and balanced analysis, grounded in evidence and informed by a commitment to resilience and ethical governance. The author proposes strategies for digital hygiene, cogni-tive defence, and institutional accountability, empowering readers to recognise and resist ma-nipulative digital practices. Whether through education, regulation, or technological redesign, the book advocates for a collective response to a threat that is as pervasive as it is insidious.

For policymakers, technologists, educators, and security professionals, *Digital Psycho-logical Warfare* serves as both a warning and a guide. It illuminates the psychological dimen-sions of cyber conflict and calls for a new kind of literacy—one that equips individuals to navi-gate digital environments with critical awareness and emotional intelligence. It also underscores the need for ethical leadership in the design and deployment of digital systems, lest we sacrifice autonomy and truth at the altar of efficiency and engagement.

As digital influence operations grow more sophisticated and globalised, the insights in this book become not only relevant but urgent. The stakes are no longer confined to elections or public opinion—they extend to mental health, democratic integrity, and societal cohesion. This book invites us to confront uncomfortable truths, to question the narratives we consume, and to reclaim agency in a world increasingly shaped by unseen forces.

This book encourages the reader to read deeply, reflect critically, and act responsibly. Because in the digital age, psychological warfare is not a distant threat—it is a present reality. And understanding it is the first step toward defending against it.

Staffordshire, UK Tarnveer Singh

Contents

About the Author

Tarnveer Singh is an award-winning Chief Information Security Officer who has worked for many decades in security and consulting roles. Tarnveer has significant experience leading information security and digital transformation. Tarnveer has been a keynote speaker at seminars and conferences discussing cyber security, technology leadership and digital transformation. He is a Fellow of the Chartered Institute of Information Security and Fellow of the British Computer Society.

Tarnveer is a recognised author and expert on cybersecurity and emerging technologies. He offers coaching and mentoring on technology leadership. He has been recognised for his thought leadership and as a technology influencer. He is on a mission to spread greater awareness of technology and ethics.

CHAPTER 1

Our Psychological Vulnerabilities

People are on all sides of technologies, either as representatives of technology platforms and implementers or on the receiving end as platform users. Each individual brings their own psychology, their own biases and motivations whether it is big technology firms, who in some instances, prioritise financial gains over the real harms caused or users who are susceptible to potential manipulation on these platforms.

Have you ever been near an unattended phone? Have you heard the sounds it makes each time it gets a notification? It rings, it pings, and chirps. How does it make you feel? Antsy? Anxious?

The phone may not even be yours but it has you under its control. The rings and pings are not even yours. It doesn't matter… The *conditioning* has been there for years. Someone else is ringing the bell and it's been happening for so long we don't realise how deeply the hooks have been set. Rings a bell?

We like to believe we are civilised and that we are masters of our own destinies. Yet we are no more sophisticated than Pavlov's dogs, allowing ourselves to be conditioned. As soon as a cell phone, laptop, or smartwatch makes a noise it begins producing mental and physical reactions in us. Our heart rates increase and our skin tingles. We become increasingly antsy with each and every second we don't look at the screen.

It is with some irony that we find ourselves in this predicament, no less conditioned than Pavlov's dogs. If it isn't our devices controlling us,

T. Singh, *Digital Psychological Warfare*,
https://doi.org/10.1007/978-3-032-15294-7_1

it is the people behind them. Whether they be the big tech firms or the organised political groups abusing their platforms. All it ever takes is a *dog whistle*, political shorthand for a phrase that may sound innocuous to some people, but communicates something far more insidious to their targeted audience. This is just one tactic used to manipulate and stoke prejudice. As soon as we hear suggestive or even racially charged language it invokes emotions in all of us.

Enriques and Peterson (2024) propose a framework based on *Consumer Vulnerability Theory* to explain the effects of state-sponsored propaganda on citizens' propensity to become vulnerable consumers by manipulating their beliefs. *Vulnerability* leads citizens to employ coping strategies that help achieve the propagandist's goals.[1]

Davidson and Martellozzo (2013) argue *online vulnerabilities* refer to individuals' capacity to experience detriments to their psychological, reputational, or physical well-being as a result of engaging in online activities).[2] Buglass et al. (2017) contend individuals who use social media excessively may be more susceptible to fears, worries, and anxieties.[3]

Tell me lies. Tell me sweet little lies. We favour the comfort of conviction over the discomfort of doubt. We like *populists* because they promote extremely simplistic solutions to complex problems in a highly emotional manner. The term opportunism would be more accurate. The ideas of populists tend to be based on age-old myth, tropes, and perceived grievances rather than reality.

Ahmed et al. (2024) insist vulnerability depends on how individuals interact with social media. For example, online practices such as self-disclosure and amassing large unmanageable networks contribute to online vulnerability. Scholars theorise that these self-promoting online behaviours are users' attempts to regulate psychological needs deficits of social control, connectivity, and belonging.[4]

We fulfil these psychological needs deficits when propagandists offer us humour and nostalgia, even if it encourages hatred towards others. Populists tell us how we belong in a majority group and help us feel comfortable within that social identity. They communicate threats and perceived grievances by stereotyping minority groups who have little or no power.[5] This creates a seductive '*us vs them*' narrative. Should we as the majority of society take responsibility for the natural outcomes of our decisions? Or is it more convenient to simply blame minority groups for all of society's ills? It is far easier to slip into the comfort of our group and blame everyone outside it. We love generalisations because we have our own biases.

Judge (2024) contends antiliberal populists exploit *identity biopolitics* to drive support for their political programme.[6] Later in this book we will discuss the case studies of the Internet Research Agency and Cambridge Analytica during the 2016 general election in the USA to demonstrate the symbiosis between social media and antiliberal populism. Stereotypes help us simplify and categorise the world and its discourse into simple shorthand we can understand. Modern life has made us time poor. The twenty-four hour news cycle means we are overloaded with information, much of which is propaganda. We like crude messages communicated in a highly emotional way as we rely on snap judgements. We prefer simpler ideas than those ideas that require greater thought. They say knowledge is power but wisdom comes from accepting uncertainty and what we don't know.

Sarno and Black (2024) argue human factors play a big role in our susceptibility to misinformation. A much bigger proportion of society is vulnerable than would care to admit. We know vast numbers of people of every background are caught out by phishing emails and scam text messages and invariably the same people are caught out by fake news.[7]

Sultan et al. (2024) confirm it is not simply people of a specific demographic that fall victim to misinformation.[8] Faragó et al. (2024) suggest some research suggests adolescence can play a role in naivety; however, their own research suggests otherwise.[9]

Lu et al. (2024) argue emotional appeals contained in fake news explain why older people have high levels of consumption as it confirms preconceptions based on surface-level analytical reasoning.[10]

Ziemer and Rothmund (2024) contend an individuals' susceptibility to misinformation is often based on *superficial information processing* and *selective information processing*. *Superficial processing* is well encapsulated in the framework of classical reasoning where information processing is shaped by two modes that differ in the amount of cognitive effort put into the processing: in effortful processing, information is systematically scrutinised to deliberatively arrive at conclusions. In effortless processing, information is scrutinised in a more superficial way to arrive at conclusions using cognitive shortcuts or heuristics.[11]

Selective processing or motivated reasoning suggests information processing is selective, non-truth convergent, and driven by goals that are distinct of accuracy motivation. Motivated reasoning is the consequence of experiencing high levels of defence motivation due to cognitive dissonance, resistance to change, or identity threat.[12]

Individuals motivated to defend their personal or social identity are more inclined to believe information in line with existing, identity-relevant beliefs and less inclined to believe information to the contrary. Motivated reasoning is a major cause of misinformation susceptibility and a major psychological barrier to combat misinformation.[13]

Singh and Goel (2024) argue we are surrounded by a plethora of information that requires much mental effort, referred to as *cognitive load*. Cognitive load has become pivotal, adding to the psychological vulnerabilities of users and increasing the likelihood of being susceptible to misinformation.[14]

Kaufman et al. (2024) argue the formation of false beliefs is heavily influenced by exposure to misinformation, but lack of access to high-quality information is not necessarily the primary precursor.[15] A range of cognitive, social, and affective factors plays a crucial role in the formation of false beliefs.[16]

Antolis (2024) contends *Cognitive factors*, such as the use of intuitive thinking and memory failures, can contribute to the belief in misinformation. Theoretical accounts of the *continued influence effect (CIE)* draw upon models of memory in which information is organised in interconnected networks, and the availability of information is determined by its level of activation.[17]

One perspective suggests that the CIE arises when a correction is not sufficiently encoded and integrated with the misinformation in the memory network. An alternative account proposes that the CIE occurs due to the selective retrieval of misinformation, even when corrective information is present in memory.

Social factors, such as reliance on source cues to determine truth, can influence the formation of false beliefs. Source credibility, the perceived trustworthiness and expertise of the sources providing the misinformation and correction, is a crucial socio-affective factor. Individuals are more likely to be persuaded by and accept advice from similar or like-minded others.[18]

There is evidence that source cues on social media influence how individuals judge information veracity. People may judge misinformation as more likely to be true if it is attributed to sources that have previously published attitudinally congruent news.

Ghergut-Babii (2024) proposes a framework called the 'misbelief funnel', which describes the progression of individuals from experiencing emotional triggers to relying on alternative media sources that reinforce their existing beliefs. The author discusses the role of cognitive biases, personality traits, and social factors in shaping conspiracy theory beliefs.[19]

Affective factors, such as the influence of mood on credulity, can contribute to the formation of false beliefs. A person's worldview, their values, and belief system that ground their personal and sociocultural identity, can render corrections ineffective or even backfire.[20]

Emotion is another socio-affective factor that influences the CIE. Corrections can produce psychological discomfort, motivating individuals to disregard the correction to reduce the feeling of discomfort. Momentary emotion, regardless of its type or valence, has been found to predict increased belief in misinformation and decreased discernment between real and fake news.[21] Increased negative emotionality has been associated with higher perceived credibility of fake news.

The *illusory truth effect*, also known as the illusion of truth, is a *cognitive bias* that describes how repeated exposure to false information can lead people to believe it is true.[22] This effect occurs even when individuals initially know the information is false. The familiarity created by repetition increases processing fluency, making the information feel more truthful.

According to the processing fluency account, when information is repeated, it becomes easier to process mentally.[23] Over time, people learn to associate this fluent processing with truthfulness, even if the information is inaccurate. Consequently, repeated misinformation is perceived as more truthful than new information.

The illusory truth effect is further supported by research on habituation and repetition suppression effects. As the number of repetitions increases, there are exponential decreases in associated behavioural and neural responses. This suggests that the increases in processing fluency become incrementally smaller with each repetition. Correspondingly, the increases in perceived truth also become progressively smaller beyond a certain number of repetitions.[24]

Heuristics are mental shortcuts or rules of thumb that people use to make quick judgements, especially when dealing with large amounts of information.[25] While heuristics can be useful for efficient decision-making, they can also lead to incorrect conclusions and contribute to the belief in misinformation. Lelo (2024) argues situations of disinformation as a heuristic notion that draws attention to the instances where falsehoods sound relevant.[26]

One example is the *social endorsement heuristic*, where people judge the trustworthiness of information based on whether someone they trust has endorsed or shared it. However, this heuristic is not a reliable indicator of truth, as trusted individuals can also spread misinformation unintentionally.

MacLean et al. (2024) contend that *Cognitive dissonance* occurs through the psychological discomfort experienced when encountering information that contradicts one's existing beliefs. To alleviate this dissonance, individuals may reject credible information that challenges their beliefs, leading them to maintain false beliefs instead.[27]

Riazi and Livan (2024) conclude Cognitive dissonance can contribute to the persistence of misinformation, as people may be motivated to dismiss corrections or fact-checks that contradict their previously held beliefs. Cognitive dissonance can make it difficult to change deeply rooted false beliefs, even in the face of overwhelming evidence.[28]

Source Credibility plays a crucial role in influencing belief formation. In general, messages are more persuasive and seem more truthful when they come from information sources perceived as credible rather than non-credible.[29] People tend to trust human information sources more if they perceive the source as attractive, powerful, and similar to themselves.

However, these source judgements can be imperfect. Individuals tend to believe in-group members more than out-group members, weigh opinions equally regardless of the competence of those expressing them, and overestimate how much their beliefs overlap with others', leading to a perception of false consensus.

Mende et al. (2024) argue experts and political elites are *trusted* by many and have the power to shape public perceptions. Therefore, it can be especially damaging when leaders make false claims. False claims that were made about public health threats like COVID-19 by political leaders reduced the perceived threat of the virus and the perceived efficacy of counter measures, decreasing adherence to public health measures.[30]

The credibility of a correction source also matters for misinformation reliance after a correction, although perhaps less than the credibility of the misinformation source. The effectiveness of factual corrections might depend more on the perceived trustworthiness rather than the perceived expertise of the correction source, although perceived expertise might matter more in science-related contexts like health misinformation.

Westney et al. (2024) conclude that trust in social media post owners was a pivotal factor in social media users becoming vulnerable to the persistent spread of disinformation on COVID-19.[31]

Mo et al. (2024) identified psychological traits that lead to social media users' susceptibility to health misinformation in the case of COVID-19. They found psychological traits played a part in vulnerability to misinformation. These traits, such as high health-consciousness and the reliance on information popularity-based pathways emerged as pivotal factors influencing susceptibility to health misinformation.[32]

Group identity is taken personally. An individual's worldview, values, and belief system that ground their personal and sociocultural identity can influence their susceptibility to misinformation. Corrections attacking a person's worldview can be ineffective or even backfire, as they may be experienced as an attack on one's identity. This can trigger a chain of appraisals and emotional responses that hinder information revision.[33]

For example, if a message is perceived as an identity threat (e.g., a correction that vaccine risks do not outweigh disease risks might be seen as a threat by someone identifying as an anti-vaxxer), it can lead to intense negative emotions. These emotions can motivate strategies such as discrediting the correction source, ignoring the evidence, or selectively focusing on worldview-bolstering evidence.

Research suggests that vulnerable caste groups are more prone to believing and sharing misinformation, with caste awareness reinforcing group identity and reducing the ability to discern misinformation.[34] Additionally, vulnerable groups exhibit a preference for social media platforms that either conceal their identity or feature a closed network structure.

Emotion and *persuasion* are powerful. Misleading content that spreads rapidly and widely on the internet often contains emotional appeals, which can increase persuasion. For example, messages aiming to generate fear of harm can successfully change attitudes, intentions, and behaviours under certain conditions if recipients feel they can act effectively to avoid the harm. Moreover, according to a preprint that has not been peer-reviewed, 'happy thoughts' are more believable than neutral ones. People seem to understand the association between emotion and persuasion, and naturally shift towards more emotional language when attempting to convince others. For instance, anti-vaccination activists frequently use emotional language. Emotion can be persuasive because it distracts readers from potentially more diagnostic cues, such as source credibility. In one study, participants read positive, neutral, and negative headlines about the actions of specific people; social judgements about the people featured in the headlines were strongly determined by the emotional valence of the headline but unaffected by the trustworthiness of the news source.

Mood effects have an important role. Inferences about information are also affected by one's own emotional state. People tend to ask themselves 'How do I feel about this claim?', which can lead to influences of a person's mood on claim evaluation. Using feelings as information can leave people susceptible to deception, and encouraging people to 'rely on their emotions' increases their vulnerability to misinformation. Likewise, some specific emotional states, such as a happy mood, can make people more vulnerable to deception[35] and the illusory truth effect. Thus, one functional feature of a sad mood might be that it reduces gullibility. Anger has also been shown to promote belief in politically concordant misinformation as well as COVID-19 misinformation. Finally, social exclusion, which is likely to induce a negative mood, can increase susceptibility to conspiratorial content.

Familiarity and *repetition* have a major influence on beliefs. Repeated exposure to misinformation can lead individuals to believe it is true, even when they initially know the information is false.[36] This phenomenon is known as the illusory truth effect or the illusion of truth. Repetition increases processing fluency, making the information feel more truthful.[37] According to the processing fluency account, when information is repeated, it becomes easier to process mentally, and people learn to associate this fluent processing with truthfulness over time.

The illusory truth effect is further supported by research on habituation and repetition suppression effects. As the number of repetitions increases, there are exponential decreases in associated behavioural and neural responses. This suggests that the increases in processing fluency become incrementally smaller with each repetition. Correspondingly, the increases in perceived truth also become progressively smaller beyond a certain number of repetitions.

Memory distortion due to misinformation has been linked to faulty reconstructive processes during *memory retrieval* and the reactivation of brain regions involved in the initial encoding of misleading details (cortical reinstatement). Exposure to even subtle forms of misleading information can significantly alter memory for past events.

Research has shown that warning participants about the threat of misinformation can modulate cortical reinstatement during memory retrieval and reduce misinformation errors. Warned participants demonstrated increased activity in visual regions associated with the original source of information and decreased activity in auditory regions associated with the misleading source of information. Stronger visual reactivation was associated with reduced susceptibility to misinformation, whereas stronger auditory reactivation was associated with increased susceptibility to misinformation. These findings suggest that a simple warning can modulate reconstructive processes during memory retrieval and reduce memory errors due to misinformation.

Group dynamics can be pivotal. *Emotions* play a significant role in shaping group dynamics and influencing the spread of misinformation. News agencies, politicians, and creators of fake news leverage emotional appeals to attract attention and increase engagement on digital and social media.[38] Algorithms on social media platforms are optimised to promote content that provokes strong emotional reactions, as this increases user engagement. Negative moral-emotional messages about groups that individuals dislike seem to be particularly effective in driving engagement.

Humans are inherently social beings, and content that reinforces group identity, enhances the status of one's in-group, or diminishes the status of an out-group can be highly motivating. This dynamic is evident in polarised conversations surrounding topics like climate change on social media. On one side, there are social movements and political parties advocating for urgent action against climate change, while on the other side, climate scepticism and denial are more prevalent among far-right, populist, or libertarian groups that oppose economic regulation and benefit from anti-elite rhetoric.

Polarisation in discussions between opposing sides often intensify around events like climate protests or the release of climate change reports, fuelling the spread of misinformation. Political polarisation further exacerbates the dissemination of misinformation.

Echo chambers exacerbate and entrench opinions. Due to the attention-grabbing nature of outrageous content and the motivation of individuals with stronger opinions to persuade others, extreme voices and toxic content tend to be more visible on social media. Individuals with nuanced views who can relate to both sides of a debate are less visible, and the majority of individuals who generally agree with a nuanced perspective but are not interested enough to participate in discussions are entirely invisible.

This phenomenon creates an illusion of stronger polarisation on digital media than what exists in society, fuelling hate and misunderstanding between opposing groups. Individuals are more likely to encounter and engage with content that aligns with their existing beliefs, leading to the formation of echo chambers where misinformation can spread unchallenged.

Additionally, research suggests that exposure to fake news can make intense communication within groups counterproductive.[39] However, it may also prompt diversification among group members in terms of their information-spreading abilities, as a potential adaptive response to mitigate the effects of misinformation.

Emotion and *misinformation* are powerful tools. Misleading content that spreads rapidly and widely on the internet often contains emotional appeals, which can increase persuasion. For example, messages aiming to generate fear of harm can successfully change attitudes, intentions, and behaviours under certain conditions if recipients feel they can act effectively to avoid the harm.

Emotional manipulation through highly charged language, imagery, and appeals to fear or anger can trigger strong emotional responses and drive engagement. *Fear* and *anger* have profound influence. People seem to understand the association between emotion and persuasion, and naturally shift towards more emotional language when attempting to convince others. For instance, anti-vaccination activists frequently use emotional language. Emotion can be persuasive because it distracts readers from potentially more diagnostic cues, such as source credibility. In one study, participants read positive, neutral, and negative headlines about the actions of specific people; social judgements about the people featured in the headlines were strongly determined by the emotional valence of the headline but unaffected by the trustworthiness of the news source.

Čavojová et al. (2024) argue anger has also been shown to promote belief in politically concordant misinformation as well as COVID-19 misinformation. They also contend consistency with one's beliefs is the best indicator of trust in fake news and willingness to share such news.[40]

Inferences about information are also affected by one's own emotional state. People tend to ask themselves 'How do I feel about this claim?', which can lead to influences of a person's mood on claim evaluation.

Using feelings as information can leave people susceptible to deception, and encouraging people to 'rely on their emotions' increases their vulnerability to misinformation.

Likewise, some specific emotional states, such as a happy mood, can make people more vulnerable to deception and the illusory truth effect. Thus, one functional feature of a sad mood might be that it reduces gullibility. Finally, social exclusion, which is likely to induce a negative mood, can increase susceptibility to conspiratorial content.

Raising global awareness about the prevalence and impact of fake news should be a key objective in tackling the problem of misinformation.[41] It is crucial to establish ongoing measurement and communication of the circulation of fake news across various platforms, its estimated reach, and its impact. Additionally, understanding the underlying patterns can make the identification of fake news easier and more reliable at an early stage, and this knowledge should be made available to all stakeholders, including through special APIs that can programmatically estimate the probability of a given story being unreliable.

The proposed 'Fake News Evaluation Network' focuses on retrospective, large-scale analysis of fake news with the intent to quantify the problem, extract patterns, and share the derived knowledge with all involved parties. This solution emphasises measuring the level of responsibility of news providers, publishers, and social media platforms in an attempt to educate, raise global awareness, and influence the corporate social responsibility strategies of online media companies.

Gavurova et al. (2024) conclude that leading social platforms exert diverse pressures on society's negative processes, causing detrimental effects on individuals and communities. To adequately capture the impact of various social anomalies, it is essential to continue developing systems and conceptual frameworks for assessing different aspects of people's lives, including impact to their quality of life.[42]

Big Technology platform providers like Google, Meta, and Twitter/X are biased towards their own financial motivations and are comfortable relying on algorithms which are created for scale and profit, not human rights and democracy. They are run as utopian dictatorships that ruthlessly dodge responsibility for the harms their platforms create.

Despite countless suicides, radicalisation and other social harms caused by their platforms, big tech firms like Google, Twitter/X, or Meta push back against accountability using the same tactics employed previously by tobacco companies, prioritising profits over public health, particularly the health of the youngest users.

Technology and *regulation* could help provide solutions. The objective is to quantify the problem and raise global awareness by systematically taking snapshots of content that is assessed and labelled by humans. Newly identified content is unified and linked to its 'master copy', other related 'stories', and any relevant factual information and metadata. It is then compared against the already labelled content to estimate the 'degree of deviation from reality' using 'fact-checked versions of the same story' and known patterns.

Furthermore, the platform can offer APIs to expose the patterns and knowledge extracted from the ongoing analysis of content, enabling third parties to predict the trustworthiness of new content at the time of publishing or sharing. Social media platforms must also contribute by educating their users and demonstrating real social responsibility through meaningful actions towards a better-informed society.

Companies could consume special APIs to cross check content at the time of sharing and notify users if the content is already flagged or if there are signals of limited trustworthiness, while leaving the sharing decision to the user. Retrospectively, social platforms could notify users who have already engaged with verified fake stories (e.g., liked, shared, saved, commented on, or consumed) and explain how to avoid such content in the future.

The reality is the majority of internet users will not consider measures to reduce their own susceptibility to disinformation, bias, and manipulation. However, recommendations are shared for those who wish to improve their own resilience as well as for regulators, technologists, and ethicists.

Building *cognitive resistance* is vital. Developing *critical thinking* skills is crucial for building cognitive resistance against misinformation and disinformation. Critical thinkers possess the ability to raise vital questions, gather and assess relevant information, come to well-reasoned conclusions, think open-mindedly within alternative systems of thought, and communicate effectively to find solutions to complex problems.[43]

A study by Stanford University recommends applying a different mindset to web-based publications, one that takes into account how easy it is for anyone to impersonate legitimate resources and post false information. The recommended approach is not to validate information by looking at the website or its materials, but rather to access external unrelated sources to evaluate the website's sponsoring organisation and the content on that website.

The risk of being caught up in groupthink and misleading or false information on the web tends to be directly related to the viewer's analytic reflection skills. Individuals who scored higher on a Cognitive Reflection Test (CRT), designed to measure analytic reflection skills, tended to rely on more traditional and reliable sources of news and information, shared higher quality content from more credible sources, and engaged with weightier subjects like politics.

It is important to note that critical thinking is a skill that can be learned, regardless of an individual's age or education level. Hundreds of studies over many decades have shown that critical thinking can be developed through proper education and training, even for those with lower levels of formal education or innate intelligence.

Raising awareness on cognitive biases and their potential negative impact on decision-making can help mitigate the influence of misinformation. Researchers have proposed various awareness-training techniques to initiate the exploration of debiasing techniques applicable in real-life settings and achieve lasting improvement in decision-making.[44]

One approach is to *educate* individuals about misleading argumentation techniques, which has been shown to reduce the influence of those techniques.[45] For example, the 'the science is uncertain' argument has been used by tobacco companies and other groups to mislead the public and spread misinformation.

Simply being aware of *confirmation bias* might help individuals be more cautious about making up their minds quickly on important issues and be more open to opinions that differ from their own.

Education and awareness training can help improve society's general reasoning ability and thereby reduce potential biases typically arising from the use of naive theories – knowledge structures with a causal or explanatory component.

Siebert and Siebert[46] proposed an awareness-training (AT) technique that illustrates the potential negative impact of the bias blind spot (BPB) using hypothetical real-life situations or damaging medical hoaxes, such as the alleged relationship between the MMR vaccination and autism.[47] The AT technique involves raising misinformation recipients' awareness of BPB and its potential negative impact on their opinions when exposed to misinformation.

Overall, awareness-training interventions have been found to be effective in mitigating various cognitive biases, such as the bias blind spot, confirmation bias, fundamental attribution error, anchoring bias, representativeness bias, and social correction bias.

Building *emotional resilience* is important. *Emotions* play a crucial role in influencing an individual's susceptibility to disinformation. Studies have shown that those who recognised a news story and believed it experienced stronger emotional responses to the content. In all countries, the data revealed a significant link between emotion and behavioural engagement, such as clicking on the link or sharing the story with others.[48] The data showed that emotional impact was a key driver in engagement, with 78% of those who felt very 'fearful', 70% of those who were very 'surprised', and 84% who were very 'excited' saying they would have interacted with the story in some way.

Misinformation conveying negative emotions such as fear or anger might be particularly likely to evoke a continued influence effect. This influence might be due to a general negativity bias or more specific emotional influences. For example, misinformation damaging the reputation of a political candidate might spark outrage or contempt, which might promote continued influence of this misinformation (particularly among non-supporters).

Countering disinformation that seeks to fuel fear or anger can benefit from a downward adjustment of emotional arousal. For instance, refutations of vaccine misinformation can reduce anti-vaccination attitudes by mitigating misinformation-induced anger.

Rodrigo et al. (2024) suggest *Mindfulness techniques* can help individuals process information effectively by enabling the evaluation of new information in a manner that creates greater sensitivity to one's environment.[49] Mindfulness is not only associated with attentional capabilities but also with the ability to process others' emotional experiences, known as interoceptive awareness.[50] Such awareness informs individuals to be aware, behave, and respond attentively to others, facilitating prosocial and positive emotions in ethical approaches towards communication.

Mindfulness can be used to augment individuals' information processing in a manner that prompts increased self-control and subsequent positive behaviours, ethical awareness, reasoning, and conduct. Having a trait mindfulness can help individuals build digital resilience as they pay closer attention to the information they are being exposed to and form an awareness to evaluate information.

Mindfulness intervention has a positive effect on attention focus, self-regulation, and subjective well-being, and is proven to mitigate negative emotional effects and even alter mind patterns.[51] Studies have shown that mindfulness training can improve trait mindfulness effectively, especially in facets of describing, acting awareness, and non-judgement, and mitigate the negative effect from bad information coverage.

In experiments, mindfulness training groups significantly reduced negative affect, indicating that mindfulness intervention could decrease subjective distress and negative emotion caused by reading negative news. The underlying mechanism is that mindfulness practice increases individuals' attention focus and awareness of their emotional states, thus improving attention control and switching, rumination, and emotion regulation.

Regulators should require manufacturers of technologies to have appropriate security controls in place from the outset and educate users on how to use technology wisely. Browser extensions and apps like Adblock Plus, Domain Whitelist, Website Whitelist, and Whitelist Manager can help users protect themselves from harmful ads and websites that spread disinformation. Adblock Plus, for instance, blocks advertisements and websites through filtering lists, while allowing users to whitelist ads that meet 'acceptable ads' standards. Users can further adjust settings to block even these whitelisted ads.

These tools not only block ads but also prevent requests to sites not included in the user's whitelist, effectively shielding them from potentially harmful or disinformation-spreading websites. By carefully curating their whitelists, users can create a safer online environment and reduce exposure to misinformation.

Ziemer and Rothmund (2024) argue *fact-checking tools* can help counter disinformation.[52] Several web-based tools have been developed to assist in verifying information and debunking misinformation. ClaimBuster, for example, is an automated fact-checking tool that relies on natural language processing and machine learning to identify factual and false information. It is available as a web application and a Slack app.

Climate Feedback is another web-based tool that allows scientists to annotate articles, providing additional context and drawing attention to inaccuracies, resulting in a credibility score for the content. Emergent.Info tracks and verifies or debunks online rumours and conspiracies, with staff reviewing and determining the veracity of claims suggested by individuals.

Tools like Exifdata, ExifTool, Forensically, HackerFactor, Get-Metadata Viewer, and Metapicz provide metadata information about images, including source, timestamp, creation, and modification details, which can aid in verifying their authenticity.[53] The Reveal Image Verification Assistant and YouTube Data Viewer specifically focus on image and video verification, respectively, offering features like tampering detection, metadata analysis, and reverse image search.[54]

Additionally, browser extensions like Newstrition provide information about news sources and rate the accuracy of news stories, helping users identify reliable information.[55]

While these tools can be valuable resources in combating misinformation, it is important to note that their accuracy and effectiveness may be limited by factors such as the quality of training data and the potential for bias. Human expertise and intervention may still be necessary, particularly for more sophisticated forms of misinformation like deepfakes.

Alon et al. (2024) contend that *Digital Media Literacy* courses are vital.[56] Evidence-driven educational programmes have proven effective in helping people discern the reliability of information sources, distinguish facts from opinions, resist emotional manipulation, and become responsible digital citizens.[57] Research from the RAND Corporation and others shows that media and information literacy improve critical thinking, awareness of media bias, and the desire to consume quality news – all of which help combat misinformation. Even brief exposure to media literacy training can improve competencies such as better understanding news credibility or evaluating biases. Notably, media literacy has a stronger impact than political knowledge on the ability to evaluate the accuracy of political messages, regardless of an individual's political opinion. Digital media literacy has been found to reduce the perceived accuracy of false news, and training remains effective when delivered in different ways and by different groups.

Tamboer et al. (2024) conducted research on adolescents and found digital media literacy courses successfully stimulated their self-efficacy in identifying fake news.[58] The impact of media literacy training is long-lasting. A year and a half after adults underwent a programme from IREX (a nonprofit organisation), they continued to be 25% more likely to check multiple news sources and 13% more likely to discern between disinformation and objective reporting. In Jordan and Serbia, participants in IREX's training improved their media literacy skills by up to 97%. Media literacy programmes can also be affordably and extensively delivered through schools, as demonstrated by the positive results in Finland and Sweden, where media literacy has been incorporated into their education systems for decades. In Britain, youth who received training in schools showed an improvement in media literacy skills.

Several states in the USA, such as California, have recognised the importance of media literacy education and have mandated public schools to teach these skills.[59] California's Assembly Bill 873, which passed with bipartisan support, requires public schools to instruct media literacy, including recognising falsified data, identifying fake news, and generating responsible internet content. The bill aims to help students become more responsible digital citizens, understand online safety and privacy, and engage in civil dialogue.

Rather than offering media literacy as a standalone course, the bill requires schools to incorporate media and digital literacy lessons into existing core subjects, making the integration more feasible for teachers and budgets. The true value of the bill lies in drawing attention to the importance of media literacy as an issue. By making media literacy education a priority, California aims to equip students with the skills necessary to navigate the digital world responsibly and critically.

Orosz et al. (2024) argue training and empowering an individual within a family as a means to challenge disinformation can be effective.[60]

Teaching critical analysis is vital, especially in schools, colleges, and universities. As scientific misinformation proliferates, it is imperative for science teachers to help students use critical thinking to examine claims not based on science.[61] Social science research offers teachers experimentally tested methods to help students identify misinformation, such as educating them about misleading argumentation techniques, which has been shown to reduce the influence of those techniques.

One example of a misleading argument is the 'the science is uncertain' claim, which has been used by tobacco companies and other groups to mislead the public and spread misinformation. Teachers should educate students on how to investigate suspicious 'scientific' claims they encounter in the media by using the Purpose, Author, Relevance, Currency, and Sources (PARCS) framework:

> *Purpose:* Is someone trying to sell you something, create an emotional reaction, or provide accurate information?
> *Author:* Who made the claim, and what qualifications do they have?
> *Relevance:* Does the claim apply to you?

Currency: When was the information published?
Sources: Are there good references, and do well-qualified people agree with the claim or hold another view?

Even after teaching students the facts about topics like evolution, climate change, or pseudoscientific claims, some students may still accept claims that scientists reject. In such cases, the National Science Teachers Association guidelines state that science teachers should be non-judgemental about students' personal beliefs and focus on promoting critical thinking and teaching what scientists have concluded and why.

Additionally, research suggests that it is possible to 'inoculate' public attitudes against real-world misinformation by providing accurate information about the overwhelming expert consensus on issues like climate change. Surprisingly, many science teachers are unaware of the strong consensus among experts on topics like climate change, making it difficult for them to teach about it effectively.

References

1. Enriques, S. and Peterson, M., 2024. A Consumer Vulnerability Perspective on State-Sponsored Propaganda. *Journal of Macromarketing*, p. 02761467241256578.
2. Davidson, J. and Martellozzo, E., 2013. Exploring young people's use of social networking sites and digital media in the internet safety context: A comparison of the UK and Bahrain. *Information, Communication & Society*, *16*(9), pp. 1456–1476.
3. Buglass, S.L., Binder, J.F., Betts, L.R. and Underwood, J.D., 2017. Motivators of online vulnerability: The impact of social network site use and FOMO. *Computers in Human Behavior*, *66*, pp. 248–255.
4. Ahmed, S., Bee, A. W. T., Masood, M., & Wei, T. H. (2024). You have been blocked: Exploring the psychological, personality, and cognitive traits of blocking misinformation sources on social media. *Telematics and Informatics*, *89*, 102123.
5. Sarcinschi, A., 2024. Discussing hybrid warfare via social psychology: The Case of Disinformation and propaganda exploiting minority groups. *Strategies XXI: The Complex and Dynamic Nature of the Security Environment*, pp. 61–74.

6. Judge, B., 2024. The birth of identity biopolitics: How social media serves antiliberal populism. *New Media & Society*, *26*(6), pp. 3273–3289.
7. Sarno, D.M. and Black, J., 2024. Who gets caught in the Web of lies?: Understanding susceptibility to phishing emails, fake news headlines, and scam text messages. *Human Factors*, *66*(6), pp. 1742–1753.
8. Sultan, M., Tump, A.N., Ehmann, N., Lorenz-Spreen, P., Hertwig, R., Gollwitzer, A. and Kurvers, R., 2024. Susceptibility to Online Misinformation: A Systematic Meta-Analysis of Demographic and Psychological Factors.
9. Faragó, L., Orosz, G., Paskuj, B. and Krekó, P., 2024. Analytic adolescents prevail over fake news–A large-scale preregistered study. *Personality and Individual Differences*, *229*, p. 112747.
10. Lu, X., Jiang, J., Head, M., Dalmer, N. and Flynn, T., 2024. Older Adults' Consumption of Fake News–An Interoceptive Perspective.
11. Ziemer, C.T. and Rothmund, T., 2024. Psychological underpinnings of misinformation countermeasures: A systematic scoping review. *Journal of Media Psychology: Theories, Methods, and Applications*.
12. Jonas, E., McGregor, I., Klackl, J., Agroskin, D., Fritsche, I., Holbrook, C., Nash, K., Proulx, T., & Quirin, M. (2014). Threat and defense: From anxiety to approach. In M. P. Zanna, & J. M. Olson (Eds.), *Advances in experimental social psychology* (Vol. *49*, pp. 219–286). Elsevier. https://doi.org/10.1016/B978-0-12-800052-6.00004-4.
13. van Bavel, J. J., Harris, E. A., Pärnamets, P., Rathje, S., Doell, K. C., & Tucker, J. A. (2021). Political psychology in the digital (mis)information age: A model of news belief and sharing. *Social Issues and Policy Review*, *15*(1), 84–113. https://doi.org/10.1111/sipr.12077.
14. Singh, S. and Goel, S., 2024. The Impact of Cognitive Load on Belief in Fake News and Real News.
15. Kaufman, R., Broukhim, A. and Haupt, M., 2024. WARNING This Contains Misinformation: The Effect of Cognitive Factors, Beliefs, and Personality on Misinformation Warning Tag Attitudes. *arXiv preprint arXiv:2407.02710*.
16. https://www.nature.com/articles/s44159-021-00006-y.

17. Antoliš, K., 2024. Disinformation Supported by Artificial Intelligence from Dynamic Research to Holistic Solutions. *Public Security and Public Order*, (35), pp. 11–23.
18. https://www.nature.com/articles/s41598-024-54030-y.
19. Gherguț-Babii, A.N., 2024, January. The Misbelief Funnel: A Framework for the Factors that Influence the Belief in Conspiracy Theories. In *Argumentum: Journal the Seminar of Discursive Logic, Argumentation Theory & Rhetoric* (Vol. 22, No. 1).
20. Singh, T., & Zheng, S.Y. (2025). *The Psychology of Cybersecurity*. Routledge.
21. https://www.ncbi.nlm.nih.gov/pmc/articles/PMC8224890/.
22. https://thedecisionlab.com/biases/illusory-truth-effect.
23. https://cognitiveresearchjournal.springeropen.com/articles/10.1186/s41235-021-00301-5.
24. Singh, T. (2025). *Cybersecurity, Psychology and People Hacking*. Palgrave Macmillan.
25. https://firstdraftnews.org/articles/the-psychology-of-misinformation-why-were-vulnerable/.
26. Lelo, T., 2024. Introducing a praxeological framework for studying disinformation. *Communication Theory*, *34*(1), pp. 18–28.
27. MacLean, P., Cahillane, M. and Smy, V., 2024. Lifting the lid on manipulative website contents: A framework mapping contextual and informational feature combinations against associated social cognitive vulnerabilities. *Social and Personality Psychology Compass*, *18*(2), p. e12947.
28. Riazi, D. and Livan, G., 2024. Public and private beliefs under disinformation in social networks. *Physica A: Statistical Mechanics and its Applications*, *637*, p. 129621.
29. https://www.nature.com/articles/s44159-021-00006-y.
30. Mende, M., Ubal, V.O., Cozac, M., Vallen, B. and Berry, C., 2024. Fighting infodemics: labels as antidotes to mis-and disinformation?!. *Journal of Public Policy & Marketing*, *43*(1), pp. 31–52.
31. Westney, Z.V., Hur, I., Wang, L. and Sun, J., 2024. Examining the effects of disinformation and trust on social media users' COVID-19 vaccine decision-making. *Information Technology & People*, *37*(3), pp. 1334–1359.
32. Mo, Z., Guo, Y. and Pan, D., 2024. Why are social media users susceptible to health misinformation? A perspective from complexity theory. *Aslib Journal of Information Management*.

33. Singh, Tarnveer, Cybersecurity And Human Factors: Keeping Information Safe (July 16, 2024). Available at SSRN: https://ssrn.com/abstract=4896153 or http://dx.doi.org/10.2139/ssrn.4896153.
34. https://papers.ssrn.com/sol3/Delivery.cfm/SSRN_ID4704493_code6201479.pdf?abstractid=4595215.
35. https://cognitiveresearchjournal.springeropen.com/articles/10.1186/s41235-020-00252-3.
36. https://www.ncbi.nlm.nih.gov/pmc/articles/PMC8116821/.
37. https://www.ncbi.nlm.nih.gov/pmc/articles/PMC7502729/.
38. https://www.stockholmresilience.org/news--events/climate-misinformation/chapter-4-emotions-and-group-dynamics-around-misinformation-on-social-media.html.
39. https://appliednetsci.springeropen.com/articles/10.1007/s41109-019-0227-z.
40. Čavojová, V., Lorko, M. and Šrol, J., 2024. Reasoning versus prior beliefs: The case of COVID-19 fake news. *Applied Cognitive Psychology*, *38*(2), p. e4194.
41. https://www.theinnovationmode.com/the-innovation-blog/misinformation-online-a-solution-powered-by-state-of-the-art-tech.
42. Gavurova, B., Moravec, V., Hynek, N., Miovsky, M., Polishchuk, V., Gabrhelik, R., Bartak, M., Petruzelka, B. and Stastna, L., 2024. The impact of digital disinformation on quality of life: a fuzzy model assessment. *Technological and Economic Development of Economy*, *30*(4), pp. 1120–1145.
43. https://mobroadband.org/critical-thinking-and-the-internet-developing-skills-to-counter-online-disinformation-confirmation-bias-algorithms/.
44. Singh, T. (2025). Digital Resilience, Cybersecurity and Supply Chains (1st ed.). Routledge. https://doi.org/10.4324/9781003604969.
45. https://www.nsta.org/using-critical-thinking-counter-misinformation.
46. https://www.apa.org/topics/journalism-facts/misinformation-belief-action.
47. https://www.ncbi.nlm.nih.gov/pmc/articles/PMC10871482/.
48. https://www.cardiff.ac.uk/news/view/2499631-recognition,-belief-and-an-emotional-response-to-disinformation-are-key-factors-in-it-being-shared-on-social-media,-study-finds.

49. Rodrigo, P., Arakpogun, E.O., Vu, M.C., Olan, F. and Djafarova, E., 2024. Can you be mindful? The effectiveness of mindfulness-driven interventions in enhancing the digital resilience to fake news on COVID-19. *Information Systems Frontiers*, *26*(2), pp. 501–521.
50. https://link.springer.com/article/10.1007/s10796-022-10258-5.
51. https://www.ncbi.nlm.nih.gov/pmc/articles/PMC9950779/.
52. Ziemer, C.T. and Rothmund, T., 2024. Psychological underpinnings of misinformation countermeasures: A systematic scoping review. *Journal of Media Psychology: Theories, Methods, and Applications*.
53. https://onlinelibrary.wiley.com/doi/full/10.1111/joes.12604.
54. https://cognitiveresearchjournal.springeropen.com/articles/10.1186/s41235-021-00292-3.
55. https://www.hybridcoe.fi/wp-content/uploads/2023/11/20231108-Hybrid-CoE-SA-34-Identity-as-a-tool-for-disinformation-WEB.pdf.
56. Alon, A.T., Rahimi, I.D. and Tahar, H., 2024. Fighting fake news on social media: a comparative evaluation of digital literacy interventions. *Current Psychology*, pp. 1–19.
57. https://ssir.org/articles/entry/strengthen_media_literacy_to_win_the_fight_against_misinformation.
58. Tamboer, S.L., Vlaanderen, A., Bevelander, K.E. and Kleemans, M., 2024. Do You Know What Fake News Is? An Exploration of and Intervention to Increase Youth's Fake News Literacy. *Youth & Society*, *56*(4), pp. 774–792.
59. https://www.theguardian.com/education/2023/dec/05/california-media-literacy-class-schools-misinformation.
60. Orosz, G., Faragó, L., Paskuj, B., Rakovics, Z., Sam-Mine, D., Audemard, G., Modeliar, M.S. and Krekó, P., 2024. Softly empowering a prosocial expert in the family: lasting effects of a counter-misinformation intervention in an informational autocracy. *Scientific Reports*, *14*(1), p. 11763.
61. https://www.nsta.org/using-critical-thinking-counter-misinformation.

CHAPTER 2

Information Warfare and Cyber Propaganda

In its simplest form, ***disinformation*** refers to lies spread consciously with an explicit – often political – objective.[1] It is distinct from misinformation, as disinformation is purposeful, usually originating from the source of the lie, while those who unknowingly propagate the lie become carriers of misinformation. In other words, misinformation can be the product of a successful disinformation campaign.

Disinformation is a term that has been frequently used in recent times due to its widespread nature.[2] However, it is not a new phenomenon, as the long history of disinformation predates modern technology and has been widely used by political figures and governments since ancient times to help them achieve their goals through manipulation.

Around 2000 years ago, during the end of the Roman Republic, the alliance known as the Second Triumvirate was crumbling down. Octavian claimed to have obtained Antonius' will (though there is still debate among historians if the will was real or forged), which contained inflammatory accusations against Antonius, including plans to leave Roman territories to his children with Cleopatra. Octavian read the will aloud in the Senate and completely shifted the public's perception of Antonius, ultimately costing him his power and his life, as both Antonius and Cleopatra committed suicide, leaving Octavian as Rome's sole ruler. This illustrates how disinformation can prey on people's emotions and prejudices, as Octavian masterfully manipulated the Roman public by framing

T. Singh, *Digital Psychological Warfare*,
https://doi.org/10.1007/978-3-032-15294-7_2

Antonius as a lovestruck man who was 'under the spell' of Cleopatra, tapping into existing Roman biases against the wealth and perceived decadence of the East, as well as suspicions about powerful women.

The invention of the Gutenberg printing press in 1493 dramatically amplified the dissemination of disinformation and misinformation,[3] ultimately delivering the first large-scale news hoax – 'The Great Moon Hoax' of 1835.[4] In this hoax, *The New York Sun* published a series of articles describing fantastic animals such as unicorns, two-legged beavers, and even flying bat-men on the Moon, falsely claiming the discoveries were made by a well-known astronomer at the time. These made-up stories were very popular, and sales of the paper shot up as readers wanted to find out about this amazing 'discovery'.

The practice of disinformation has had its place in every civilisation, but its fundamental purpose of achieving political change limited its use throughout antiquity and into the dynastic age when autocratic figures controlled the distribution of information. Even prominent campaigns of the early seventeenth century, such as those waged by Habsburg supporters during the Thirty Years' War, were examples of localised attempts to consolidate domestic power by controlling one's own information environment. Such intrastate politics are a far cry from interstate campaigns designed to erode the legitimacy of distant ruling parties by altering public perception.

Political deception as a strategy has grown in use over time. In ancient Rome, around 2000 years ago, during the end of the Roman Republic, the alliance known as the Second Triumvirate was crumbling down. Octavian claimed to have obtained Antonius' will (though there is still debate among historians if the will was real or forged), which contained inflammatory accusations against Antonius, including plans to leave Roman territories to his children with Cleopatra. Octavian read the will aloud in the Senate and completely shifted the public's perception of Antonius, ultimately costing him his power and his life, as both Antonius and Cleopatra committed suicide, leaving Octavian as Rome's sole ruler. This illustrates how disinformation can prey on people's emotions and prejudices, as Octavian masterfully manipulated the Roman public by framing Antonius as a lovestruck man who was 'under the spell' of Cleopatra, tapping into existing Roman biases against the wealth and perceived decadence of the East, as well as suspicions about powerful women.

The Donation of Constantine, now recognised as a forgery, was widely used in Medieval times to support papal claims of political authority.[5]

As far back as ancient Egypt, the pharaohs were careful to make records only of their military 'victories', thus leaving historians to infer their defeats from reading about a series of victories that started at the outskirts of Egypt and moved successively closer to the ruler's capital.

Augustus deceived everyone in Rome into thinking the Republic was still alive. While orchestrating this deception, he was amassing more power and wealth for himself than anyone in history.

A recent example of such an attempt comes from the Malaysia Airlines Flight (MH17) shot down over eastern Ukraine. While a preliminary investigation implicated pro-Russian forces, a Russian government funded media organisation suggested that the plane had been shot down by Ukraine in a failed attempt to assassinate Vladimir Putin. A poll conducted a week after the event found that 80% of Russians believed the crash was indeed caused by the Ukrainian military, and only three per cent blamed pro-Russian forces. Just before Putin was to attend a G20 summit in Australia, Russian state television broadcast a purportedly leaked, spy-satellite image of a Ukrainian fighter jet firing a missile at a passenger plane over Donetsk, though the photo was later revealed to be a poorly doctored image from Google Earth.

Less than a month later in an annual address to Russian Parliament, Putin claimed Crimea, recently annexed by Russia against the wishes of Ukraine, holds the status of a Russian Holy Land, comparing it to the sacredness the Temple Mount in Jerusalem holds for Muslims and Jews. Putin bases his claim on a legend that Grand Prince Vladmir was baptised in Crimea during the tenth century. However, this legend is not supported by historical evidence, which instead indicates Vladmir was baptised before he captured Crimea. Moreover, the Grand Prince's capital was Kiev – presently Ukraine's capital – so it is doubtful how much such a claim would support the notion that Crimea is more Russian than Ukrainian, even if it were true. Tactics and techniques used by political groups continue to grow in sophistication.

Propaganda is a type of psychological warfare that involves spreading information from biased or unverifiable sources.[6] Propaganda can be used to frame conflicts in a certain way, or to make people feel a certain way about something. Techniques are methods used by political groups to manipulate public opinion and sway beliefs in their favour.[7] These techniques are often based on socio-psychological research and can be classified as logical fallacies or abusive power tactics.

Common propaganda techniques employed include name calling or stereotyping. This gives a person or idea a negative label to make the audience reject them without examining the evidence.[8] Virtue words involve using vague, positive words to make something appear acceptable without scrutiny. Deification involves making an idea appear sacred or above criticism, portraying opposing views as blasphemous. Transfer involves using respected symbols or authorities to make an idea seem more legitimate. Testimonial involves citing a respected or hated celebrity's endorsement of an idea to convince the audience. Plain folks is the approach of portraying an idea as popular among ordinary people to increase its appeal. Bandwagon relies on claiming that everyone accepts an idea to persuade others to follow suit. Artificial dichotomy involves presenting only two sides of an issue when more perspectives exist.

Political groups may engage in *information warfare (IW),* which involves manipulating information to achieve political objectives.[9] Tactics include galvanising support through the internet, altering public perceptions through multimedia techniques, and decreasing domestic support for controversial actions. Governments may face challenges in shaping public opinion amid ambiguity and uncertainty in the IW realm.

Political groups can exploit various media channels to disseminate propaganda and disinformation. Newspapers can selectively report stories, choose biased headlines, and endorse specific parties during elections.[10] Television and radio news are required to be fair and balanced, but the internet allows the spread of inaccurate information with fewer restrictions. Political parties can use online platforms to interact with voters, share information, and respond to concerns.

New media outlets provide unprecedented access to information and enable ordinary citizens to scrutinise public officials, bringing issues to prominence that may be overlooked by mainstream journalists.[11] However, the ease of producing and distributing content online has also facilitated the spread of fake news and emotional appeals that shape public opinion more than objective facts.

Political groups may employ psychological manipulation tactics to influence voters' motives, reasoning, and behavior.[12] These tactics can undermine the consent on which democratic legitimacy depends. Tarnishing opponents with innuendoes or baseless investigations. Concealing intended policies until elected. Appealing to prejudices like xenophobia. Gerrymandering electoral districts. Attaching 'poison pills' to legislation. Arranging vote sequences to favour desired outcomes.

Psychological operations (PSYOP) are operations aimed at conveying selected information to influence the behaviour of governments, organisations, and foreign powers.[13] The purpose is to induce behaviour favourable to US objectives through persuasion, deception, and credible threats.

PSYOP can undermine an adversary's decision-making process, degrade their ability to conduct military operations, and lower morale, potentially leading to surrender. Tactics include disseminating white (overt), grey (ambiguous source), or black (covert) products through various media channels like loudspeakers, leaflets, radio, television, and social media.

While PSYOP forces are forbidden from targeting US citizens, they have been used extensively in military operations like those in Somalia to shape domestic support. The 'Battle of the Narratives' is an emerging field of strategic PSYOP, involving cognitive warfare in the information environment.

Political groups may employ *espionage* and *sabotage* tactics as part of their disinformation campaigns.[14] German Interior Minister Nancy Faeser warned of growing threats from foreign adversaries like Russia, China, and Iran, who are waging intense campaigns involving *espionage, cyberattacks, and disinformation operations*.

The physical sabotage campaign is part of a broader strategy that includes propaganda, increased espionage, and efforts to sow doubts about military prospects and divisions within alliances. This 'war with the West' involves covert operations, fake social media accounts, and pro-Western narratives to undermine adversaries.[15]

In the South and East China Seas, both the USA and China have engaged in 'cognitive warfare', involving displays of force, staged photographs, and the sharing of disinformation.[16]

The impact of political deception on society is damaging. Disinformation can manipulate citizens, creating distrust in international norms, institutions, or democratically agreed strategies.[17] It can disrupt elections or fuel disbelief in key challenges such as climate change. By repeatedly exposing people to false information, political groups can stimulate them to act, exploiting online recommendations, reviews, and social endorsement cues like 'likes' and 'shares'.[18]

Political elites can increase the circulation of false signals suggesting one social group is threatened by another, exaggerating 'out-group' threats. For example, some conservative Republicans in the USA have traded in signals of threats from ethnic minority and immigrant communities to encourage White in-group identity for political benefit.

Undermining democratic institutions is a key ploy. Disinformation undermines human rights and many elements of good democracy, but counter-disinformation measures can also prejudicially impact human rights and democracy. It threatens freedom of thought, the right to privacy, the right to democratic participation, and economic, social, and cultural rights. It diminishes broader indicators of democratic quality by distorting free and fair elections, fomenting digital violence and repression.

With *conspiracy theories* and disinformation on the rise in media and politics, trust in society, institutions that inform us, and the democratic process itself is at risk. A sense of responsibility for the everyday information shared may diminish, and deceitful politicians may escape scrutiny by claiming truths are false, falsehoods are true, and nothing can be proved.

Deception can involve withholding information, switching topics, strategic ambiguity, diversions, deflections, or generating conditional, counterfactual versions of events to make belief in false interpretations more comfortable.

Major disinformation campaigns have had significant impact on the course of history. During *World War II*, German propaganda emphasised the prowess of the German army and contrasted it with the British and Allied armies, who were depicted as cowards and butchers, or brave but misguided. Russian troops were presented as dehumanised beasts and killers who attacked without fear of death.[19] After the Nazi loss at Stalingrad in February 1943, Goebbels admitted recent losses and argued for total war in his famous Sportpalast speech. While the new strategy prolonged the war, Goebbels recognised that his efforts were failing, noting, 'Enemy propaganda is beginning to have an uncomfortably noticeable effect on the German people. Anglo-American leaflets are now no longer carelessly thrown aside but are read attentively; British broadcasts have a grateful audience'.

The radio broadcasts were the handiwork of the British Political Warfare Executive (P.W.E.), created by Winston Churchill in 1941 to disseminate propaganda that would damage enemy morale. The British Broadcasting Company's foreign language broadcasts became a key element in the Allied campaign for German loyalties. By 1945, the British had established more than 40 clandestine pseudo-German radio stations using powerful American transmitters. The P.W.E. also delivered subversive messages to the German people through so-called Black propaganda, printed postcards, and leaflets dropped behind enemy lines.

In the USA, the Office of War Information (O.W.I.) was the source of such propaganda. After the Japanese attack at Pearl Harbor, most Americans were convinced to support the war, but Roosevelt created the O.W.I. in 1942 to boost wartime production at home and undermine enemy morale in Europe, Asia, and Africa. O.W.I photographers documented aspects of homefront life and culture, such as women in the workforce and 'subversive activities' like the Los Angeles zoot suit riots.

Inexpensive, accessible, and ever-present in schools, factories, and store windows, posters helped mobilise Americans to war. A representative poster encouraged Americans to 'Stop this Monster that Stops at Nothing. PRODUCE to the Limit!' depicting a monster with two heads, one Nazi, one Japanese, clutching the Statue of Liberty in one hand and fending off American advances with the other.

While most propaganda aimed to boost patriotism, some took on racist overtones. Director Frank Capra produced seven films called Why We Fight, which portrayed Germany, Italy, and Japan as nations of inhuman murderers. As World War II progressed, the O.W.I. had a hand in Hollywood, which churned out patriotic films such as Yankee Doodle Dandy (1942) with James Cagney, Pin-Up Girl (1944) with Betty Grable as a USO entertainer, and Anchors Aweigh (1945) with Gene Kelly as a dancing sailor. Even cartoon characters got into the act, with Warner Brothers sending Popeye and Bugs Bunny to fight the Japanese, while Disney released a short showing Donald Duck incapacitating Hitler with a ripe tomato.

During the *Cold War*, the USA and the Soviet Union refined covert methods of political intervention and conflict, making use of proxy wars, election interference, and disinformation campaigns to advance their respective interests.[20] Throughout the Cold War, the USA and USSR competed in an arms race of fictions, attempting to cultivate ideological support internationally and domestically.

In response to sophisticated and widespread Soviet disinformation, the USA created the Active Measures Working Group (AMWG), which operated using a 'Report-Analyse-Publicize' strategy that prioritised overt disinformation and successfully challenged Soviet active measures in the 1980s.

Exploiting US race relations and disseminating disinformation about pandemics were major methods of Soviet disinformation during the later stages of the Cold War.[21] The Kremlin aimed to discredit the US government, delegitimise its institutions, disorient and polarise American society, and cast doubt on the true account of events to undermine the country's effective functioning as a democracy.

Soviet active measures involving US race relations during the civil-rights era took two forms: commissioning hate crimes and forging race-based hate letters, both with the strategic aim of dividing American society. Following riots in 1965, the KGB paid American agents to paint swastikas on synagogues and desecrate Jewish cemeteries, falsely claiming they were the work of Black activist groups. The KGB also typed hundreds of anonymous letters containing virulent racist diatribes, purportedly from White supremacists and 'normal' Americans, and sent them to African missions at the United Nations.

Another strain of Soviet disinformation was to discredit the US government by alleging that it was developing biological weapons capable of causing pandemics. After the Korean War, the KGB disseminated disinformation that the US military had unleashed germ warfare in China and North Korea. In operation INFEKTION, the KGB spread disinformation that AIDS had been manufactured by the US military at Fort Detrick – the same conspiracy theory that appeared during the COVID-19 pandemic. The KGB's strategic aim was to discredit the US government domestically and internationally, cause Americans to lose faith in public health, and destroy Washington's ability to claim the moral high ground when it came to Soviet human rights abuses.

In January 2024, some US voters in New Hampshire received automated phone messages in which President Joe Biden's voice urged them not to vote in the state's Democratic Party primary election, though it wasn't actually Biden; the message had been generated by artificial intelligence (AI).[22] The rise of such AI fakery has made more people concerned about the effect of misinformation on elections, particularly in 2024, when more than 50 countries will have held elections, including high-profile polls in the USA, UK, India, South Africa, and Mexico, totalling more than 2 billion potential voters.

The 2024 election in India was plagued by *deepfakes*, from deceased political figures making speeches to Bollywood actors giving fake endorsements to political parties. In Slovakia, fake audio of a parliamentary candidate talking about buying votes and plans to raise the beer price was released on the eve of the September 2023 election. AI is likely to increase the volume of misinformation because it lowers the level of technical skill needed to create credible content.

Voters are already fairly savvy – they know that campaigning tactics often include *distortions* and *untruths*, which can feature *misinformation (inaccurate, false, and misleading information) or disinformation (details deliberately designed to be misleading).*[23] Unfortunately, recent research shows the lack of clarity in defining misinformation and disinformation is a problem, with no consensus, making it harder to chart the scale of the issue.

Researchers often fail to provide clear definitions and do not carefully compare different types of disinformation, adding uncertainty to evidence examining its effect on voting behaviour. Studies have shown low effects of fake news on persuading voters, leading some researchers to argue that the panic about fake news is overblown. Other studies have looked at the potential influence of disinformation by asking people how they intended to vote and whether they believed specific pieces of disinformation, but it's hard to establish a reliable causal influence of fake news on voting.

Political affiliation doesn't seem to matter, as people tend to rate fake news as accurate when it's in line with their own political beliefs. For instance, in the 2016 US presidential elections, both Hillary Clinton and Donald Trump supporters were equally likely to rate fake news about their opposition as accurate. Undecided voters may be more or less susceptible to political fake news, but accurately profiling them is difficult, as people are cautious in revealing their voting intentions and reasons.

Ultimately, most research suggests that fake news is more likely to enhance existing beliefs and views rather than radically change voting intentions of the undecided. Disinformation, such as political propaganda, likely has some influence on voting, but assigning it too high an influence denies people's agency in making free voting choices. Studies show that people are aware that manipulative methods are used on them but still judge that they can maintain an ability to make their own choice when voting.

There have been significant technological advances in spreading disinformation. The invention of the Gutenberg printing press in 1493 dramatically amplified the dissemination of disinformation and misinformation,[24] ultimately delivering the first large-scale news hoax – 'The Great Moon Hoax' of 1835.

As one-to-many communications developed in the twentieth century, especially with the advent of radio and television, satirical news evolved, sometimes being mistaken as the real thing in news consumers' minds.

The arrival of the internet in the late twentieth century, followed by social media in the twenty-first century, dramatically multiplied the risks of misinformation, disinformation, propaganda, and hoaxes. Both errors and fraudulent content now go viral through peer-to-peer distribution (many-to-many communication), while news satire is regularly misunderstood and re-shared as straight news by unwitting social media users.

Social media has increasingly grown in power and influence and has acted as a medium to accelerate sociopolitical movements.[25] Network effects enhance participation in social media platforms which in turn spread information (good or bad) at a faster pace compared to traditional media. Furthermore, due to a massive surge in online content consumption primarily through social media, both business organisations and political parties have begun to share content that is ambiguous or fake[26] to influence online users and their decisions for financial and political gains.[27]

Social media's enormous impact is unmistakable. Facebook sees approximately 300 million new photos uploaded daily, while six thousand Tweets are sent every second.[28] The manipulation of social media platforms has also spread widely, and such platforms have been used to promote instability, spread political conflict, and call for violence. Researchers believe that organised social media misinformation campaigns have operated in at least 81 countries, a trend that continues to grow yearly, with a sizable number of manipulation efforts by states and private corporations.

A robust social media ecosystem refers to a substantial proportion of the public who are regularly on social media. This activity sparks large, dense networks facilitating the rapid spread of information. These platforms vary in format, regulation, online culture, and popularity. Given their role in spreading information and SMM, non-mainstream or regionally popular formats like Telegram, Gab, and messaging apps like WhatsApp and Viber are also included in this category. Some social media platforms, such as VK (Russian Federation) or TikTok (China), are also believed to share user data with authoritarian governments.

Algorithm manipulation is common. Despite differences in social media platforms, the 'attention economy' is a crucial aspect. Researchers have noted that a person's attention is a scarce resource, and social media tech companies rely on keeping users' attention to drive revenue. Tech companies have a range of techniques, such as using '*friends*', '*likes*', '*subscriptions*', and other quantifiable measures to secure users' attention, which in turn strengthen the social media ecosystem and create a focused, engaged audience for advertisers.

Trolling and harassment is widespread leading to deliberate provoking and antagonising individuals targeted online to disrupt conversations and create a hostile environment. The public valuation of tech companies is tied to their number of users, and without sustained public outcry, companies are often slow to crack down on misinformation that may risk driving away users. Some companies have directly addressed *troll factories, shell accounts, bots*, or other amplifiers of misinformation by establishing special response protocols, but these actions are influenced by revenue concerns generated from the attention economy.

Platforms' structure and algorithms also have an essential role in spreading misinformation. Platform architecture is a conceptual blueprint that describes how the ecosystem is partitioned into a relatively stable platform and a complementary set of modules that are encouraged to vary, and the design rules binding on both. Business models of these platforms are based upon maximising user engagement. For example, in the case of Facebook or Twitter, the user feed is based on their existing beliefs or preferences. User feeds provide users with similar content that matches their existing beliefs, thus contributing to the echo chamber effect.

Platform architecture makes the transmission and retransmission of misinformation easier. For instance, WhatsApp has a one-touch forward option that enables users to forward messages simultaneously to multiple users.[29] Earlier, a WhatsApp user could forward a message to 250 groups or users at a time, which as a measure for controlling the spread of misinformation was limited to five members in 2019. WhatsApp claimed that globally this restriction reduced message forwarding by 25%.

Modern technologies are amplifying *cognitive biases* in harmful ways.[30] Search engines direct users to sites that inflame their suspicions, and social media connects them with like-minded people, feeding their fears. Bots – automated social media accounts that impersonate humans – enable misguided or malevolent actors to take advantage of these vulnerabilities.

Search engines and social media platforms provide personalised recommendations based on the vast amounts of data they have about users' past preferences. They prioritise information in users' feeds that they are most likely to agree with – no matter how fringe – and shield them from information that might change their minds, making users easy targets for polarisation.

Experiments on Twitter indicate that information is transmitted via 'complex contagion': when users are repeatedly exposed to an idea, typically from many sources, they are more likely to adopt and reshare it. Programmers who design the algorithms for ranking content on social media assume that the 'wisdom of crowds' will quickly identify high-quality items; they use popularity as a proxy for quality. Analysis of vast amounts of anonymous data about clicks shows that all platforms – social media, search engines, and news sites – preferentially serve up information from a narrow subset of popular sources, even when users want to share the best information, the algorithms end up misleading them.

Bots also influence users by pretending to represent people from their in-group. A bot only has to follow, like, and retweet someone in an online community to quickly infiltrate it. Simulations show that these bots can effectively suppress the entire ecosystem's information quality by infiltrating only a small fraction of the network. Bots can also accelerate the formation of echo chambers by suggesting other inauthentic accounts to be followed, a technique known as creating 'follow trains'.

Polarisation is a social phenomenon characterised by the fragmentation of society into antagonistic factions with vehemently opposed values and identities that impede cooperation and the pursuit of a common good.[31] The threat is significant, and democracies globally are under siege and reeling from the impact of polarised societies. According to the latest World Economic Forum study on global risks, societal polarisation is not just one of the world's top 10 present concerns, but also a long-term threat over the next decade.

Public trust is being eroded faster than ever. The long-standing problem of political misinformation drew public attention in the aftermath of the 2016 US presidential election.[32] Scholars, journalists, and politicians expressed alarm that the spread of fake news could destabilise political institutions and delegitimise media organisations. To the extent that fake news can undermine the public's confidence in mainstream media, it may not only leave its consumers misinformed, but also make them more vulnerable when disaster strikes.

The content of false news stories can influence our confidence in the media. Cynical coverage and tabloid-style focus on scandal can erode citizen trust in news organisations. Those are characteristics typical of many fake news stories as their producers aim to increase audience engagement through sensational and divisive content. Fake news can also discredit the press directly by accusing them of bias, complicity, and incompetence – or indirectly by contradicting a range of claims made by mainstream media. The very existence of online misinformation resembling a journalistic product can diminish the credibility of legitimate news.

Méndez-Muros et al. (2024) argue natural disasters or other sensitive times of unpredictability and surprise generate a climate of uncertainty in the population, making them ripe for targeting with disinformation. These are crisis situations that cause the management of public and governmental institutions to be questioned, diminish citizens' trust in the media, and reinforce anonymity in social networks. Digital algorithms create a scenario plagued by fake news and levels of virilisation of rumours never before contemplated.[33]

Research suggests that negative or biased reporting can reduce political trust and increase cynicism and apathy. Financially motivated fake news outlets produce sensational content often aiming to generate more views by appealing to partisan bias, triggering negative emotions, and fuelling political arguments. Scandal and incivility in current affairs coverage can draw and hold public attention while at the same time lowering political trust.

An NPR survey conducted earlier this year found that 64% of the American population believes that US democracy is in crisis and is at risk of failing.[34] A Quinnipiac University survey reveals that 76% of respondents think political instability within the country is a bigger danger to the USA than external adversaries. Amazingly, this suggests that Americans recognise that they are a bigger threat to their own democracy than any other potential external threat. Sadly, according to this poll, over half of Americans (53%) expect political divisions in the country to worsen over their lifetime rather than get better.

The phenomenon of polarisation has impeded pandemic response in countries, slowed consensus on critical global issues such as climate change, and continues to challenge the resilience of societies, resulting in a catastrophic loss of diversity in the social fabric. Not only does polarisation increase the likelihood of violence in societies, but violent demonstrations may exacerbate polarisation and divide individuals along partisan lines.

Information technology and social media, in particular, play a crucial role in fostering polarisation, with a spillover effect on offline violence and protests. These platforms are not merely spaces of public discourse, but also raise concerns over free speech, particularly when they contribute to the online amplification of the most radical and polarising content. Debates on free speech on platforms predominantly revolve around disinformation and hate speech, both of which are considered to exacerbate polarisation.

New research from Aalto University and the University of Helsinki investigated how real-world shocks affect online discussions, using the Ukraine war and Finland's NATO accession to understand how disinformation reinforces polarisation.[35] By analysing retweeting patterns, they found three separate user groups before the invasion: a pro-NATO group, a left-wing anti-NATO group, and a conspiracy-charged anti-NATO group. After the invasion, the left-wing anti-NATO group members broke out of their retweeting bubble and connected with the pro-NATO group despite their difference in partisanship, while the conspiracy-charged anti-NATO group mostly remained a separate cluster.

'An external threat can bridge partisan divides, but bubbles upheld by conspiracy theories and disinformation may persist even under dramatic external threats', says Ylä-Anttila. 'The continuity of these bubbles is likely explained by the notion that people within disinformation bubbles have limited communication with others outside their bubble, which tends to reinforce their prior beliefs'. People who have strong, non-mainstream opinions are often more likely to hold on to their beliefs and are more prone to confirmation bias, meaning that they're more likely to disregard information that is contrary to their own beliefs.

Social media's enormous impact is unmistakable. Facebook sees approximately 300 million new photos uploaded daily, while six thousand Tweets are sent every second.[36] The manipulation of social media platforms has also spread widely, and such platforms have been used to promote instability, spread political conflict, and call for violence. Researchers believe that organised social media misinformation campaigns have operated in at least 81 countries, a trend that continues to grow yearly, with a sizable number of manipulation efforts by states and private corporations.

A robust social media ecosystem refers to a substantial proportion of the public who are regularly on social media. This activity sparks large, dense networks facilitating the rapid spread of information. These platforms vary in format, regulation, online culture, and popularity. Given their role in spreading information and SMM, non-mainstream or regionally popular formats like Telegram, Gab, and messaging apps like WhatsApp and Viber are also included in this category. Some social media platforms, such as VK (Russian Federation) or TikTok (China), are also believed to share user data with authoritarian governments.

Social media platforms have become a privileged channel for spreading news, information exchange, and fact-checking.[37] However, automated accounts known as social bots contribute significantly to this process of information diffusion. Worryingly, research has demonstrated that these automated accounts are particularly efficient in spreading low-credibility content and amplifying their visibility.[38]

Automated social media accounts, known as bots, have been shown to spread disinformation and manipulate online discussions.[39] A study on the behaviour of retweet bots on Twitter during the first impeachment of US President Donald Trump found that although bots represent 1% of all users, they generate over 31% of all impeachment-related tweets.

The study also revealed that bots share more disinformation but use less toxic language than other users. Among supporters of the QAnon conspiracy theory, a popular disinformation campaign, bots have a prevalence near 10%. The follower network of QAnon supporters exhibits a hierarchical structure, with bots acting as central hubs surrounded by isolated humans.

Using the generalised harmonic influence centrality measure, researchers quantified the bot impact and found a greater number of pro-Trump bots. However, on a per-bot basis, anti-Trump and pro-Trump bots have similar impact, while QAnon bots have less impact. This lower impact is due to the homophily of the QAnon follower network, suggesting that this disinformation is spread mostly within online echo chambers.

Studies show that social bots account for 9% to 15% of total active Twitter users on average. These bots evolve over time, making it challenging for Twitter admins, tech-savvy users, or cutting-edge applications to distinguish them from legitimate users. Social bots target influential people, bombarding them with hateful content and influencing public opinion during noteworthy events. They even interact with genuine users according to their political affiliations.

Remarkably, researchers have observed the existence of formations of bots shared by a group of human-operated accounts, a phenomenon not previously reported in literature. These 'bot squads' retweet messages from two or more strong hubs, aiming to increase the visibility of their tweets. Notably, 89% of the original tweets from these bot squads contain URLs, with 97% of those URLs referring to a website blacklisted as a source of political disinformation.

Despite differences in social media platforms, the 'attention economy' is a crucial aspect. Researchers have noted that a person's attention is a scarce resource, and social media tech companies rely on keeping users' attention to drive revenue.[40] Tech companies have a range of techniques, such as using 'friends', 'likes', 'subscriptions', and other quantifiable measures to secure users' attention, which in turn strengthen the social media ecosystem and create a focused, engaged audience for advertisers.

Information technology and social media, in particular, play a crucial role in fostering polarisation, with a spillover effect on offline violence and protests. These platforms are not merely spaces of public discourse but also raise concerns over free speech, particularly when they contribute to the online amplification of the most radical and polarising content.

Politics remains a favoured breeding ground for disinformation and hate speech. While social media and online platforms have played a pivotal role in amplifying the spread of disinformation and hate speech, recent reports reveal the rampant misuse of these platforms by governments and political parties in over eighty countries engaged in political disinformation campaigns.

Debates on free speech on platforms predominantly revolve around disinformation and hate speech, both of which are considered to exacerbate polarisation.

Fake news websites are rife. Disinformation actors pose as reputable news sources to gain legitimacy and influence public debate.[41] One trend involves established news brands spreading disinformation, with notorious cases like France Soir or the role of mainstream media in electoral disinformation during the US elections.

Another trend involves online 'media' outlets posing as credible sources to spread disinformation, such as coordinated disinformation campaigns in the case of the MH17 takedown in Ukraine. Some once-reputable sources rebrand as disinformation spreaders, resting on their past credibility.

Polarised mainstream media hold greater responsibility in sharing disinformation than malign foreign actors. Excessively factional media play an active role in spreading disinformation. Media outlets spreading disinformation go as far as obtaining recognition as registered newspapers.

Disinforming actors steal the identities of genuine journalists, exploiting their reputation to spread disinformation. Online media outlets coordinate with Russian intelligence to mislead criminal court trials and spoof on reputable media to operate intra-EU disinformation campaigns. They also use fake personas to recruit freelance journalists.

Additionally, media outlets are used for domestic influence operations to silence opposition and hire real freelance journalists to push hidden agendas. Some media outlets franchise their malign activities to front media organisations and military factions.

What follows is a short interview conducted with a victim of troll factory abuse. This helped the author to emphasise the impact that this form of online abuse has and generated guidance provided in this chapter.

Author: Thank you for agreeing to speak with me today. I understand this has been a challenging time for you. Can you share a bit about what happened and how you became a target of online trolls?

Victim: Thank you for having me. It started about six months ago when I posted a series of articles on social media discussing the state of the nation and how politicians need to do more on mental health awareness. Out of nowhere, I began receiving an onslaught of abusive messages. At first, I thought it was just a few trolls, but it quickly escalated. The messages were malicious, personal, and often targeted my reputation.

Author: That sounds incredibly difficult. How did these attacks affect your daily life and mental health?

Victim: It was devastating. The constant barrage of hate took a toll on my mental health. I started feeling anxious, depressed, and isolated. It was hard to focus on work or enjoy everyday activities. The fear of being judged or attacked publicly was overwhelming. My reputation took a hit as well; some people believed the false accusations and lies spread by the trolls.

Author: Online abuse can be incredibly damaging. How did you cope with the situation and what steps did you take to protect yourself?

Victim: At first, I tried to ignore the trolls, hoping they would lose interest. But as the attacks continued, I realised I needed a more proactive approach. I started by reporting the abusive accounts to the social media platforms, though the response was often slow. I also reached out to friends and family for support, which helped me feel less alone. Eventually, I sought professional help from a therapist to manage my anxiety and depression. I also consulted with a lawyer to explore legal options for protecting my reputation.

Author: It's important to have a support system and take legal action when necessary. How do you think social media platforms and society can better address the issue of online trolling?

Victim: Social media platforms need to take stronger and swifter actions against abusive accounts. They should implement more effective algorithms to detect and prevent harassment. Society as a whole needs to promote a culture of empathy and respect online. We should educate people about the impact of their words and encourage them to think before they post. There should also be more resources available for victims of online abuse, including legal support and mental health services.

Author: It's clear that the experience had a profound impact on your mental health. Can you delve a bit deeper into the psychological effects you faced as a result of the targeted abuse from the troll factory?

Victim: The psychological impact was significant and multifaceted. Initially, I felt a constant sense of anxiety and dread. Every time I logged into my social media accounts or checked my email, I braced myself for more hateful messages. It felt like I was under siege, and there was no escape.

Author: That sounds incredibly overwhelming. Were there specific aspects of the abuse that made it feel particularly personal and targeted?

Victim: Yes, the trolls didn't just send generic hate messages. They somehow managed to dig up personal information about me, my family, and my career. They referenced my past experiences, used my photos, and even targeted my friends and colleagues. It was clear that this wasn't random; they had done their homework to make their attacks as personal and hurtful as possible.

Author: That's truly invasive. How did this personalised nature of the abuse affect you mentally and emotionally?

Victim: It was incredibly isolating. I started to doubt myself and my worth. The personal nature of the attacks made me feel exposed and vulnerable. I became paranoid, questioning who I could trust and whether my personal information was safe anywhere. The constant fear and anxiety led to sleepless nights and a decline in my overall well-being. I also experienced bouts of depression, feeling as if there was no way to rebuild my reputation or escape the negativity.

Author: It's heartbreaking to hear how deeply this affected you. Did you notice any changes in your behaviour or relationships as a result of the abuse?

Victim: Definitely. I became more withdrawn and hesitant to engage in social activities. I avoided posting anything online and distanced myself from social media. My relationships also suffered. I pushed away friends and family because I didn't want them to become targets as well. My work performance declined because I couldn't focus, and the stress was overwhelming.

Author: It's understandable that you'd want to protect those around you. How did you begin to rebuild your confidence and sense of security after such a traumatic experience?

Victim: Rebuilding took time and a lot of effort. Seeking professional help was crucial. My therapist helped me develop coping strategies to manage my anxiety and rebuild my self-esteem. I also worked on re-establishing my boundaries, both online and offline. Gradually, I began to re-engage with trusted friends and family, which helped me feel less isolated. I also took steps to enhance my digital security, such as using stronger passwords and being more cautious about the information I shared online.

Author: It's inspiring to hear how you took proactive steps to recover. What advice would you give to others who might be going through a similar experience with targeted online abuse?

Victim: Firstly, reach out for support. Whether it's friends, family, or professionals, having a support network can make a huge difference. Document and report the abuse to the relevant platforms and authorities. If necessary, seek legal advice. Take control of your online presence by enhancing your digital security and being mindful of what you share. Most importantly, focus on self-care and give yourself time to heal. Remember, the abuse is a reflection of the attackers, not you. The trolls' goal is to make you feel powerless, but by seeking help and taking action, you can regain control.

Author: Thank you for sharing your story and insights. Your experience highlights the importance of addressing online abuse and supporting those affected. I wish you continued strength and resilience.

Victim: Thank you for giving me the opportunity to speak. I hope my story can help others who are going through similar situations.

References

1. https://thestrategybridge.org/the-bridge/2020/1/14/the-evolution-of-disinformation-how-public-opinion-became-proxy.
2. https://cyabra.com/blog/evolution-of-disinformation-tactics/.
3. https://www.icfj.org/sites/default/files/2018-07/A%20Short%20Guide%20to%20History%20of%20Fake%20News%20and%20Disinformation_ICFJ%20Final.pdf.
4. https://www.bbc.co.uk/bitesize/articles/zwcgn9q.

5. https://hac.bard.edu/amor-mundi/political-lies-altering-facts-and-rewriting-history-2015-02-09.
6. https://www.britannica.com/topic/psychological-warfare.
7. https://en.wikipedia.org/wiki/Propaganda_techniques.
8. https://www.uvm.edu/~jleonard/AGRI183/propoaganda.html.
9. https://www.rand.org/pubs/monograph_reports/MR661.html.
10. https://www.bbc.co.uk/bitesize/guides/zqhmjty/revision/1.
11. https://www.bbvaopenmind.com/en/articles/the-new-media-s-role-in-politics/.
12. https://philarchive.org/archive/NOGMIP.
13. https://en.wikipedia.org/wiki/Psychological_operations_(United_States).
14. https://www.politico.eu/article/espionage-cyber-attack-reach-new-dimension-germany-interior-minister-warns-nancy-faeser/.
15. https://www.rusi.org/news-and-comment/in-the-news/russias-brazen-and-intensifying-sabotage-campaign-across-europe.
16. https://en.wikipedia.org/wiki/Psychological_warfare.
17. https://www.europarl.europa.eu/RegData/etudes/STUD/2021/653635/EXPO_STU(2021)653635_EN.pdf.
18. https://www.gresham.ac.uk/watch-now/breaking-democracy.
19. https://www.pbs.org/wgbh/americanexperience/features/goebbels-propaganda/.
20. https://www.wilsoncenter.org/publication/formative-battles-cold-war-disinformation-campaigns-and-mitigation-strategies.
21. https://tnsr.org/2022/09/whats-old-is-new-again-cold-war-lessons-for-countering-disinformation/.
22. https://www.nature.com/articles/d41586-024-01696-z.
23. https://blogs.lse.ac.uk/medialse/2024/02/05/disinformation-is-often-blamed-for-swaying-elections-the-research-says-something-else/.
24. https://www.icfj.org/sites/default/files/2018-07/A%20Short%20Guide%20to%20History%20of%20Fake%20News%20and%20Disinformation_ICFJ%20Final.pdf.
25. https://www.ncbi.nlm.nih.gov/pmc/articles/PMC8853081/.
26. https://www.ned.org/wp-content/uploads/2018/06/How-Disinformation-Impacts-Politics-and-Publics.pdf.
27. https://www.marubeni.com/en/research/potomac/backnumber/19.html.

28. https://www.stimson.org/2022/social-media-misinformation-and-the-prevention-of-political-instability-and-mass-atrocities/.
29. https://www.sciencedirect.com/topics/social-sciences/information-warfare.
30. https://www.scientificamerican.com/article/information-overload-helps-fake-news-spread-and-social-media-knows-it/.
31. https://www.ncbi.nlm.nih.gov/pmc/articles/PMC10106894/.
32. https://misinforeview.hks.harvard.edu/article/misinformation-in-action-fake-news-exposure-is-linked-to-lower-trust-in-media-higher-trust-in-government-when-your-side-is-in-power/.
33. Méndez-Muros, S., Alonso-González, M. and Pérez-Curiel, C., 2024. Disinformation and Fact-Checking in the Face of Natural Disasters: A Case Study on Turkey–Syria Earthquakes. *Societies*, *14*(4), p. 43.
34. https://www.brookings.edu/articles/misinformation-is-eroding-the-publics-confidence-in-democracy/.
35. https://phys.org/news/2024-01-disinformation-polarisation-society.html.
36. https://www.stimson.org/2022/social-media-misinformation-and-the-prevention-of-political-instability-and-mass-atrocities/.
37. https://www.nature.com/articles/s42005-020-0340-4.
38. https://www.ncbi.nlm.nih.gov/pmc/articles/PMC9910783/.
39. https://www.ncbi.nlm.nih.gov/pmc/articles/PMC10166499/.
40. https://www.ncbi.nlm.nih.gov/pmc/articles/PMC10106894/.
41. https://www.disinfo.eu/publications/the-role-of-media-in-producing-and-spreading-disinformation-campaigns/.

CHAPTER 3

Cognitive Warfare and Fake News in the Post-Truth Era

Cognitive warfare is a type of information warfare that aims to weaken an adversary's rationality and public trust in open information sources.[1] This can be done by spreading fake news, manipulating perceptions, and exploiting psychological vulnerabilities. Stories that are not true or are meant to be misleading are used to make money, change views and opinions, and make us question who we can trust.[2]

Propaganda has been used in wars throughout history to try and change people's views. In 1898, some newspapers blamed the Spanish for the sinking of the USS Maine in Cuba, using artist's illustrations of a dramatic explosion to convince readers, despite a lack of evidence. Closer to home, in 1917 during the First World War, British newspapers ran a gruesome story claiming that the Germans were extracting fat from the bodies of dead soldiers to make soap and margarine, which was spread by the British government to persuade readers that the Germans were a barbaric enemy.

Post-Truth refers to circumstances where objective facts are less influential in shaping public opinion than appeals to emotion and personal belief.[3] It denotes a predicament in which political speech is increasingly detached from the factual infrastructure, compromising our ability to react to events and engage in democratic opinion-formation. Post-truth politics is characterised by the repeated assertion of talking points to

T. Singh, *Digital Psychological Warfare*,
https://doi.org/10.1007/978-3-032-15294-7_3

which factual rebuttals are ignored, with debate framed largely by appeals to emotion disconnected from policy details.[4]

Most potent examples of post-truth politics involve outright lies about verifiable facts being used for various political purposes towards adversaries and supporters alike. Such claims are not primarily attempts to convince or persuade but rather to create confusion, anger, and disorientation, with the main impact being hijacking attention rather than letting the best argument win. The political image of a post-truth politician is built around unpredictability, carelessness to detail, and the systematic use of blatant lies, aiming to attract attention, confuse, and perplex rather than persuade or convince.

The discussion on post-truth politics in recent years has suffered from a lack of shared conceptual understanding, with different authors using the term differently without acknowledging competing definitions. While the term was used academically before 2016, it gained prominence that year due to its proliferation in events like the US presidential election and Brexit referendum, often used to signal a distinctive kind of politics.[5]

Some scholars argue that post-truth has similarities with past debates about relativism, postmodernity, and dishonesty in politics, while others insist it is specifically concerned with twenty-first century communication technologies and cultural practices.[6] A breakdown in institutional authority for truth-telling, ushered by new media, user-generated content, editing technologies, and a saturating promotional culture, has resulted in confusion and games of truth-telling.

Populist movements and their use of social media are often held responsible for post-truth politics, providing opportunities for individuals to shape media consumption around their opinions and for populist leaders to encourage them. Populist politicians' reliance on assertions without factual basis creates a false worldview, not to convince elites but to reinforce prejudices among potential supporters, using repetitive dominant motifs devoid of evidence as a rhetorical device.

Fake News can originate from various sources, some intentionally created to deceive, while others stem from errors, mistakes, or misinterpretations.[7] López et al. (2024) argue deliberate fake news is crafted and disseminated with the intent of generating maximum engagement, often driven by financial motives. However, non-deliberate misinformation, inadvertently released by individuals or groups, can spread just as rapidly and cause significant psychological harm.[8]

Wu et al. (2024) conclude from their research that heuristic and systematic processing can synergistically influence belief in fake news when the cues are message and situational factors. Status-seeking motives favoured by social media tend to exacerbate belief in fake news.[9]

The proliferation of technology and the growth of social media have contributed significantly in enabling the propagation of fake news. Research indicates that false information frequently spreads faster than factual news online. Social media users play a pivotal role in this dissemination by liking, sharing, and engaging with posts containing misinformation.

Online fake news can also be amplified through the use of bots, which are computer algorithms designed to automatically generate content and interact with humans on social media, potentially influencing their behaviour. Additionally, the phenomenon of circular reporting, where one source publishes misinformation that is subsequently picked up and cited by other news outlets, perpetuates the cycle of misinformation.

Fake news encompasses a broad spectrum, including hoaxes, misinformation, urban legends, satire, propaganda, and more.[10] To better understand its complexities, it can be categorised into types.[11]

False stories are entirely fabricated with no basis in truth, intentionally created to mislead or generate revenue through clicks. This category includes fake news websites or 'imposter sites' designed to resemble credible sources. Misleading stories contain no established baseline for truth but promote a specific agenda. These stories often take a small factual element and distort it to fit a particular narrative, aiming to provoke strong reactions.

Biased stories contain truthful elements but selectively omit or emphasise certain facts to serve a particular agenda or gain attention. Manipulated content or imagery is that which has been altered, doctored, or photoshopped to misrepresent reality. Humorous stories are purposefully fake with no intention to cause harm but have the potential to be misinterpreted as real. False connections are headlines or visuals that misrepresent or falsely connect unrelated events or issues. False context is where genuine content is shared with misleading contextual information. Imposter content is where genuine sources impersonated or misrepresented.

It's important to note that not all fake news is intentionally deceptive; some forms, like satire or parody, are meant to be humorous but can be misinterpreted when shared out of context.

Psychological impact must be considered. Cognitive biases are psychological processes that make our brains more susceptible to believing things that aren't true, affecting our judgement when trying to determine facts from fallacies.[12] Examples of cognitive biases include familiarity bias. Social media operates on the 'high volume = believability' principle. If we hear something often enough, our brain will want to believe it is true. Availability bias is where our brains tend to believe things that are easiest to remember. This is why sensational stories easily spread. The easier it is for our brain to retrieve a memory, the more believable it will seem. Confirmation bias reflects our natural tendency is to seek out and believe information that supports our existing beliefs and expectations.

When we connect in person or online/social media, we are regularly set up to fall into one of these cognitive biases, influencing our judgement to share information, verified or not.

Social conformity is a key factor. Cognitive biases originate from how the brain processes the vast amount of information encountered daily. The brain can deal with only a finite amount of information, and too many incoming stimuli can cause information overload.[13] This has serious implications for the quality of information on social media, where steep competition for users' limited attention means some ideas go viral despite their low quality – even when people prefer to share high-quality content.

One cognitive shortcut happens when deciding whether to share a story on one's social media feed. People are heavily affected by the emotional connotations of a headline, even though that's not a good indicator of an article's accuracy. More important is who wrote the piece.

Another source of bias comes from society itself. When people connect directly with their peers, the social biases that guide their selection of friends come to influence the information they see. Research has shown that it is possible to determine a Twitter user's political leanings by simply looking at the partisan preferences of their friends.

The tendency to evaluate information more favourably if it comes from within one's own social circles creates *echo chambers* ripe for manipulation, either consciously or unintentionally. This helps explain why so many online conversations devolve into 'us versus them' confrontations.

Studies have found that after exposure to others' comments critical of a fake news article, individuals' attitudes, propensity to make positive comments, and intentions to share the fake news were lower than after exposure to supportive comments.[14] Furthermore, disclaimers from social media companies alerting users that news might be fake do not lower attitudes, positive comments, and sharing intentions as much as critical comments from other users.

Soetekouw and Angelopoulos (2024) argue training social media and technology users to recognise fake news is vital. They found a direct positive relationship between age and level of education on the one hand and ability to detect fake news on the other, which has implications for future research. They contend that there is potential in training protocols to counter the effects of fake news, as a scalable solution that empowers users and addresses concerns about the time-consuming nature of fact-checking.[15]

Educational initiatives with youngsters can be helpful in combating the spread of fake news. Organisations like the BBC have developed a range of classroom resources aimed at enhancing digital literacy and equipping students with the skills to identify and stop fake news.[16] These resources are designed for secondary school students, covering topics such as distinguishing fact from fiction, understanding how fake news is presented, and recognising the historical use of propaganda.

The BBC Bitesize – Fact or Fake? collection provides interactive materials to help 11–16 year-olds spot and stop fake news. The 'Digital Literacy: Fake news' short film explores the phenomenon and highlights the importance of distinguishing it from real news. Additionally, the 'Making the News: How fake news is presented' film examines how online news stories can be manipulated and questions their trustworthiness.

Beyond classroom resources, the BBC also offers the 'BBC Young Reporter - Recognising fake news' collection, suitable for 11–18 year-olds, to help students differentiate between real and fake information. Live lessons, such as the 'BBC News - Live Lesson', provide interactive sessions on fake news, false information, and how to sort fact from fiction.

Educational initiatives like these aim to develop digital resilience and equip young people with the critical thinking skills necessary to navigate the digital landscape and make informed decisions about the information they encounter.

Hammond et al. (2023) contend that developing digital resilience in youngsters should be a collective endeavour involving children at an individual level, parents/carers within home environments, youth workers, civil society, teachers, and schools at a community level, along with governments, policymakers, the education system, Big Tech platforms, and internet corporations at a societal level.[17] Vissenberg et al. (2022)

caution against relying on digital literacy as a reliable facilitator in young people's well-being.[18]

Governments and regulatory bodies worldwide are exploring various measures to combat the spread of fake news and disinformation online. One approach involves imposing a 'duty of care' on online platforms, holding them accountable for harmful content on their platforms.[19] The British Government's proposed Online Safety Bill (OSB) aims to grant the broadcasting regulator Ofcom new powers to act as a regulator in this regard, potentially covering deepfakes, fake news, and disinformation.

The European Union (EU) has drafted the Digital Services Act (DSA) and Digital Markets Act (DMA), which build on existing e-commerce rules to force online platforms to take more responsibility for the content they serve to users. Notably, the DMA relies on competition law-like remedies to make platforms more transparent, interoperable, and accountable, allowing users to take their data to other platforms and incentivising a more responsive market. Additionally, the DSA will require audits of algorithms used by the largest platforms to prevent them from automatically leading users to the most vicious and misleading content for financial gain.

However, some experts caution that new regulations aimed at curbing 'false' or 'fake' content could have a chilling effect on free speech.[20] Instead, they suggest that governments should focus on encouraging the enforcement of existing laws and terms of service agreements developed by companies to deal with harmful forms of content.

Regulatory measures also aim to improve transparency in political advertising by verifying the identities of individuals and organisations purchasing advertisements on social media and allowing users to see why they are being targeted by specific messages. Some legislation requires social media companies to create public archives of all advertisements bought and sold, holding political parties accountable for any dark advertisements they purchase during campaigns.

While artificial intelligence (AI) has shown promise in flagging, blocking, and removing harmful content in areas like child protection and terrorism, experts argue that automating responses to fake news can be challenging due to the subjective nature of 'truth'. However, AI can potentially identify indicators of fake news, such as content that individuals share without actually clicking through to read. Ultimately, human review should remain a part of the content moderation process to ensure a balance between combating misinformation and preserving free speech.

The media plays a pivotal role in combating the spread of fake news and disinformation. News organisations must focus on providing high-quality journalism that builds public trust and attracts larger audiences.[21] It is crucial for them to call out fake news and disinformation without legitimising them. The news industry should clearly differentiate itself from fake news sources, demonstrating to the public that they should seek out real news to understand the world around them.

Many participants agreed that digital platforms have an obligation to address the problem of fake news. Recently announced strategies by platforms like Facebook, Google, and Twitter include improved systems for users to flag suspected false information, partnerships with third-party fact-checking organisations, and greater policing of actors who misrepresent themselves on social media. However, some participants were wary of platforms downgrading individual news providers in their algorithms, viewing it as a step towards censorship.[22]

Governments should promote news literacy and strong professional journalism within their societies. They should avoid crackdowns on the news media's ability to cover news, as such activities limit freedom of expression and hamper journalists' ability to report on political developments. Additionally, governments should refrain from censoring content or making online platforms liable for misinformation, as this could curb free expression and discourage people from sharing political opinions for fear of censorship.

Instead of censorship, governments should focus on encouraging the enforcement of existing laws and terms of service agreements developed by companies to deal with harmful forms of content. Regulatory measures could also improve transparency in political advertising by verifying the identities of individuals and organisations purchasing advertisements on social media and allowing users to see why they are being targeted by specific messages.

While artificial intelligence (AI) has shown promise in flagging, blocking, and removing harmful content, experts argue that automating responses to fake news can be challenging due to the subjective nature of 'truth'. Human review should remain a part of the content moderation process to ensure a balance between combating misinformation and preserving free speech.

Governments should prioritise funding efforts to enhance news literacy, especially for young people. Educational institutions should make informing people about news literacy a high priority. Along with media freedom, governments should make efforts to boost media literacy among citizens, which should act as a counter-surveillance measure against fake news perpetrators, especially in times of crisis.[23]

False information is dangerous because of its ability to generate emotion, affect public opinion and electoral discourse. According to David Lazer, 'such situations can enable discriminatory and inflammatory ideas to enter public discourse and be treated as fact. Once embedded, such ideas can in turn be used to create scapegoats, to normalise prejudices, to harden us-versus-them mentalities and even, in extreme cases, to catalyse and justify violence'.[24]

From a theoretical perspective, two contrasting perspectives exist regarding the role of emotion in belief in misinformation. The motivated cognition account argues that analytic thinking, rather than emotional responses, are primarily to blame. By this account, people reason like lawyers rather than scientists, using their reasoning abilities to protect their identities and ideological commitments rather than to uncover the truth.[25]

On the other hand, the classical reasoning account argues that reasoning and analytic thinking typically help uncover the truth of news content.[26] By this account, individuals engaging in reasoning and reflection are less likely to mistake fake news as accurate.

Prior research has also focused on the roles of individuals' emotional experiences when engaging in accuracy judgements. Different emotions have been suggested to differentially impact judgement in general, as well as perceptions of political fake news in particular. For instance, anger has been suggested to promote politically aligned motivated belief in misinformation, whereas anxiety has been posited to increase belief in politically discordant fake news due to increased general feelings of doubt.

Recent polling data demonstrate how harmful these practices have become to the reputations of reputable platforms. According to the Reuters Institute for the Study of Journalism, only 24% of Americans today believe social media sites 'do a good job separating fact from fiction, compared to 40 percent for the news media'. That demonstrates how much these developments have hurt public discourse.

Studies have found that momentary emotion, regardless of the specific type or valence, predicted increased belief in fake news and decreased discernment between real and fake news.[27] Inducing emotional processing increased belief in fake news and decreased truth discernment, regardless of headline concordance.

Pseudo-profound bullshit receptivity and the tendency to overclaim were positively correlated with perceived accuracy of fake news and negatively correlated with the tendency to think analytically. Bullshit receptivity was associated with more fake and real news sharing on social media. Increased negative emotionality was also associated with higher fake news credibility.

Taken together, the results suggest that emotion in general, regardless of the specific type of emotion, predicts increased belief in fake news. Furthermore, nearly every type of emotion appears to have a significant interaction with type of news, indicating an effect of emotion on differentiating real from fake news.

In the ever-evolving landscape of news and information, it is crucial to rely on trustworthy sources to stay informed while avoiding misinformation and disinformation.[28] Identifying reliable sources involves evaluating their credibility, accuracy, and objectivity.

Prioritise news from reputable journalists and official news outlets, as they are held accountable for their reporting and adhere to rigorous fact-checking processes. Examine the track record of the source by reviewing their previous work. Reliable sources typically report facts without bias or personal opinions. Cross-reference the information across multiple credible sources. If the same details are corroborated by other reputable outlets, it increases the likelihood of accuracy. Look for sources that provide clear evidence and cite their sources, allowing you to verify the information independently. Be cautious of claims that seem too outlandish or sensational to be true, as they may be designed to attract attention rather than convey facts.

Building a curated list of trusted sources across various platforms (news websites, radio, TV, etc.) and perspectives can help you escape filter bubbles and access a diverse range of reliable information.[29]

Even reputable news outlets can inadvertently publish inaccurate information or require corrections due to the fast-paced nature of digital reporting.[30] To combat this, fact-checking websites dedicated to verifying claims and refuting inaccuracies can serve as valuable resources. Some popular fact-checking sites include PolitiFact, ProPublica, Snopes, and The Sunlight Foundation.

When evaluating fact-checking sites, we must examine their verification process and the sources they use to validate claims. Assess whether they provide additional context and evidence to help you make informed decisions. Understand their process for refuting statements deemed false or misleading. Cross check the information across multiple fact-checking sites for added credibility. Be aware of any potential biases, as some fact-checkers may lean towards specific political ideologies.

Utilising a combination of trusted news sources and reputable fact-checking websites can help you navigate the complex landscape of information and separate facts from fiction.

Protecting children is vital. If a child has fallen for false information, it's important to approach the situation with empathy and understanding. They might feel embarrassed, so take the time to review the misinformation with them in a non-judgemental manner.[31] Discuss what made them think it was real, and then show them the signs that it was false. This exercise can help them critically assess information in the future.

If a child shares misinformation with others, encourage them to take ownership of their mistake. If it was shared on social media, they could make a follow-up post acknowledging that the previous information was false. Additionally, they should share the correct information and delete the misinformation where possible.

In severe cases, such as scams or impacts on body image, children might need additional support. This could involve talking with a counsellor or seeking support from their school. The platforms or apps the child uses likely have policies on misleading content. While some policies are more robust than others, it's essential to report any misinformation or misleading content encountered. Even if unsure, the moderation team can assess the content and make an informed decision.

Bias is an important factor where people tend to for snap judgements based on little information. Recognising and acknowledging our own biases and microaggressions is often more challenging than identifying them in others.[32] However, when we choose to become aware of our shortcomings, we can use this knowledge to inform our behaviour and correct discriminatory tendencies.

Paying attention to your thoughts and examining your beliefs can help identify the assumptions you currently hold. For example, do you believe that people will always speak up when they disagree? Do you think showing emotions or crying at work is a sign of weakness? How do you feel when someone misses a deadline? Do you automatically assume they are unproductive or incapable, or can you extend empathy and listen to their reasons?

The key is to slow down and investigate your beliefs and assumptions so that you can see the other person for who they truly are. When someone challenges these long-held beliefs and values, it can be uncomfortable. Instead of getting defensive, pay attention to your immediate reaction, take a breath, and try to approach the situation from a place of curiosity and positive intent.

Your mistakes are not dead-ends but opportunities to learn and improve. These discussions can open you up to seeking feedback from others, who can become catalysts to help you uncover your biases. Reach out to a diverse group of peers to understand how they perceive you and what you can do better. People with different perspectives and opinions are more likely to provide insightful feedback.

Cultivating a diverse network is a great way to embrace diverse perspectives. When examining your network, if you find that many of your friends and colleagues share similar backgrounds, privileges, and social capital, it can turn into an echo chamber where people share similar thoughts and opinions.

Implicit bias refers to an automatic or unconscious tendency to associate particular characteristics with particular groups.[33] It is not malicious but can lead to disparate treatment of individuals and groups. Journalism has not been immune to this phenomenon, with research showing that female politicians are treated differently in news stories and by voters than male politicians, while Black families are overly associated with crime and Muslims with terrorism by media outlets convinced they treat every group fairly.

A journalist who fails to recognise their blind spots can unintentionally distort the meaning of their reporting. Not understanding a country's racial history can unwittingly convince even the best journalists to write about minority groups in ways that can lead to harmful racial stereotypes or exclude them from coverage altogether.

While implicit bias is not malicious, it can blind people to others' realities. Hiring reform is only part of the solution; internal practices must also change. Newsrooms should begin aggregating data about their coverage decisions, including tracking how many stories are told about a particular area, who is usually included as sources, and studying it.

No reputable journalistic outfit can credibly claim ignorance about blind spots that affect coverage. It is a choice to try to tackle blind spots or leave them as is, whether the bias is implicit or explicit.

The traditional media, comprising broadcast and print outlets, have long been the primary source of news and information for society.[34] These professional media organisations employ rigorous processes to authenticate and verify information before disseminating it to their audiences. However, the rise of social media platforms has introduced a new dynamic, allowing unprocessed and uncertified information to reach multitudes of people rapidly.

While social media offers the ability to share information instantly and reach a broader audience, it also presents a significant challenge in discerning credible sources from misinformation or fake news. Most users lack the means to assess the credibility of information shared on these platforms, especially when the original source is obscured through repeated sharing across networks.

Furthermore, the potential for intentional misuse of social media to spread misinformation, rumours, and fabricated news stories is a growing concern. Fake news, defined as deliberate misinformation spread through traditional or online media, often exploits the viral nature of social media to gain traction and engagement.

Public perception is constantly evolving. According to the Eurobarometer (2022) survey, 75% of respondents claimed that television remains one of their most used forms of media to access news, followed by online news platforms (43%) and radio (39%).[35] Unsurprisingly, there were socio-demographic and cross-country variations, with older respondents relying more on traditional media like television and print, while younger participants were more likely to use social media platforms, blogs, and video platforms.

When it comes to trust in news media, citizens expressed more confidence in traditional broadcast and print media, including their online presence, than in online news platforms and social media channels. Specifically, 49% of respondents in the European Union (EU) claimed that publicly owned TV and radio stations, including their online versions, constitute trusted news sources, followed by the written press at 39%. In contrast, privately owned TV and radio stations were mentioned by only 27% of participants as trusted media sources.

However, younger respondents expressed a preference for online news platforms and social media channels, considering them more trusted sources than mainstream broadcast and print media. Levels of trust also differed notably across the EU, with some countries like Finland exhibiting high trust in public TV and radio stations (73%), while others like Hungary and Poland showed very low trust in their public media outlets (22% and 23%, respectively.

Interestingly, in certain countries, including Bulgaria, Latvia, Lithuania, Hungary, and Poland, respondents expressed more confidence in individuals they followed on social media than in privately owned TV, radio, or print press.

Increasingly persuasive techniques are being used. Media texts, such as advertisements, reviews, articles, posters, and leaflets, often employ persuasive techniques to influence the reader's opinions or encourage specific actions. These techniques aim to persuade the audience to buy products, support charitable causes, or agree with the writer's perspective.[36]

Logos act as brand identifiers and can create a sense of trust, potentially persuading readers to pay more for a product. Designed to grab attention, headings and headlines feature exciting or crucial information about the product or cause being promoted. Sub-headings introduce specific sections of the text and support the main headline. Visuals, including a main image and supporting secondary images, aim to attract the reader's attention. Short sentences, quotations, or pieces of information strategically placed around the page to convey key points concisely. Anecdotes or brief stories or accounts of real events used to create an emotional or sympathetic response, supporting the persuasive argument. Memorable phrases intended to remind the reader of a key idea or point of view. Triple repetitions or tripartite lists that add emphasis, often with increasing emotional intensity. Comparisons highlighting differences between viewpoints or products, positioning the writer as fair and trustworthy. Mentioning and explaining the downsides of alternative arguments or products to appear knowledgeable and important. Emotive words deliberately chosen to evoke strong positive or negative feelings in the reader. Vivid descriptions or actual images designed to elicit emotional responses, either positive or negative. Intentional overstatements or exaggerations to emphasise the magnitude of an issue. Phrases like 'think about...' or 'forget your previous ideas...' that create a sense of urgency and compel the reader to act. Funny or ridiculous points are used to make the writer's argument more appealing and memorable.

Descriptive techniques like metaphors and similes encourage the reader to visualise specific scenarios, supporting the persuasive argument. Presenting opinions as facts is common, potentially confusing or convincing the reader. Repeating a single word or phrase multiple times helps further emphasise its importance. Rhetorical questions are often posed without expecting an answer, designed to engage the reader and encourage self-reflection. Shock tactics with imagery or statements are used to surprise or horrify the reader into action. Statistics or factual information are used to provide convincing evidence and add credibility to the argument. Quotations and expert opinions or other sources are used to lend authority and appeal to the argument.

These persuasive techniques aim to influence the reader's emotions, thoughts, and actions, making media texts effective tools for persuasion. The impact on public opinion can be huge. The emotional turn in journalism studies is fuelled by new forms of emotion-driven journalistic work, such as immersive journalism and constructive journalism.[37] However, these innovations, developed to reconnect journalists with disenfranchised and fragmented audiences, highlight the need for a more thorough study of audience perceptions.

Emotion-driven journalism, more than other types, is about reconnecting with the audience. Assumptions about the value emotions hold in terms of effectiveness, informativeness, and economic viability are informed by media effects and related literature. However, determining the importance or value of emotions for journalism must be accompanied by new research strategies that directly examine audience perceptions.

The further development of emotion-driven journalism depends on empirical and theoretical evidence of audience perceptions. Academic narratives on the value of journalistic innovation and investment in emotion-driven journalism should be directly informed by empirical observations of audience expectations. This can be achieved through collaborative research projects that combine both newsroom- and audience-centred data collection or increased efforts to communicate evidence-based insights on audience expectations to journalistic practice.

Research has also explored the role of emotions in crisis coverage, such as how UK news media used fear appeals to report on the coronavirus crisis. Fear appeals involve defining the threat component (e.g., the severity and susceptibility of the crisis) and the efficacy component (e.g., recommended actions to mitigate the threat).[38]

Studies have found that fear appeals were prevalent in coronavirus coverage, with both the threat and efficacy components frequently present. However, there were differences between tabloids and quality outlets, with tabloids more likely to rely on fear-inducing content.

While fear-inducing coverage can raise awareness and promote protective behaviours, it also carries risks, such as desensitising audiences or causing excessive anxiety. Striking the right balance between factual reporting and emotional appeals is crucial in crisis communication.

Overall, the impact of emotional appeals on public opinion is complex and multifaceted. While emotions can engage audiences and promote desired behaviours, empirical research is needed to understand audience perceptions and ensure responsible journalism practices.

Freedom and censorship are key considerations. Many users find platforms enjoyable or helpful in their day-to-day lives despite concerns over misinformation and harassment, no matter what they think of the news they might find there.[39] News is rarely what most people are looking for when using these services, and platforms have been increasingly looking to oblige.

Van Raemdonck and Meyer (2024) insist that disinformation is here to stay and that democracies are inherently vulnerable. However, large segments of the population in some of the most influential democracies are no longer receiving unbiased news and information, not because journalists are being imprisoned as in authoritarian settings, but due to more nuanced efforts to throttle media independence.[40] Common methods include government-backed ownership changes, regulatory and financial pressure, and public denunciations of honest journalists.[41] Governments have also offered proactive support to friendly outlets through measures like lucrative state contracts, favourable regulatory decisions, and preferential access to state information, aiming to make the press serve those in power rather than the public.

Populist leaders present themselves as defenders of an aggrieved majority against liberal elites and ethnic minorities, arguing that the interests of the nation should override democratic principles like press freedom, transparency, and open debate. Viktor Orbán's government in Hungary and Aleksandar Vučić's administration in Serbia have consolidated media ownership in the hands of their cronies, ensuring outlets with the widest reach support the government and smear its perceived opponents. In Hungary, nearly 80% of the media are owned by government allies.

In Israel, Prime Minister Benjamin Netanyahu has repeatedly excoriated investigative reporters and faces corruption charges for allegedly offering regulatory favours to major media firms in exchange for positive coverage. In India, the ruling Bharatiya Janata Party has supported campaigns to discourage speech deemed 'antinational', and government-aligned thugs have raided critical journalists' homes and offices. The media have become widely flattering of Prime Minister Narendra Modi, amid allegations that the government issues directives on how the press should cover his activities and intimidates journalists who push back.

Perhaps the most concerning development is the pressure on press freedom in the USA, the world's leading democratic power, where President Donald Trump's continual vilification of the press has seriously exacerbated an ongoing erosion of public confidence in the mainstream media. Among other steps, the president has repeatedly threatened to strengthen libel laws, revoke the licences of certain broadcasters, and damage media owners' other business interests.

Peñafiel-Saiz et al. (2024) contend the threats to freedom of expression and democracy also come from misinformation and censorship. The COVID-19 pandemic and the ensuing pandemic of misinformation have demonstrated that access to facts and science can be a matter of life and death.[42] With almost 6,000 people around the world hospitalised due to coronavirus misinformation in the first three months of 2020, and at least 800 people may have died due to misinformation related to COVID-19.[43]

Public trust is being eroded. As many as half the respondents in all four countries say they believe journalists try to manipulate audiences to serve the agendas of powerful politicians or care more about getting attention than reporting the facts. Misinformation and harassment are among the leading problems many associate with platforms, and despite positive feelings towards most platforms, large majorities in all four countries agree that false and misleading information, harassment, and platforms using data irresponsibly are 'big problems' in their country for many platforms.

Most studies have found that unofficial and official controls on media significantly affect trust in government. However, the impact of media on trust in government can be negative or positive.[44] Specifically, the media malaise hypothesis indicates that a free press leads to less government trust due to negative news, while the mobilisation hypothesis suggests that mass media enhances citizens' political interest and participation, increasing public trust of the ruling party. Notably, in countries where media is not free, the media is used for shaping political values, propaganda, and mobilising voters or citizens.

To address these hypotheses and follow previous findings, countries can be separated and regressions re-estimated according to their levels of freedom of the press, following datasets like the Freedom House's Freedom of the Press report.

References

1. https://www.act.nato.int/activities/cognitive-warfare/.
2. https://www.bbc.co.uk/bitesize/articles/zwcgn9q.
3. https://www.e-ir.info/2018/10/22/defining-post-truth-structures-agents-and-styles/.
4. https://www.populismstudies.org/Vocabulary/post-truth-politics/.
5. https://en.wikipedia.org/wiki/Post-truth.
6. Cham, T.H., Cheng, B.L., Aw, E.C.X., Tan, G.W.H., Loh, X.M. and Ooi, K.B., 2024. Counteracting the impact of online fake news on brands. *Journal of Computer Information Systems*, *64*(2), pp. 245–264.
7. https://libguides.uvic.ca/fakenews/how-it-spreads.
8. López, A.B., Pastor-Galindo, J. and Ruipérez-Valiente, J.A., 2024. Frameworks, Modeling and Simulations of Misinformation and Disinformation: A Systematic Literature Review. *arXiv preprint arXiv:2406.09343*.
9. Wu, Y., Mustafa, H., Apuke, O.D. and Yu, J., 2024. Exploring how message and situational factors shape people's information processing and belief in fake news on social media: The moderating role of status-seeking motivation. *Psychology of Popular Media*.
10. https://www.ogilvy.com/ideas/5-types-fake-news-why-they-matter.
11. https://library-nd.libguides.com/fakenews/categories.
12. https://guides.lib.uci.edu/Misinfo/bias.
13. https://www.scientificamerican.com/article/biases-make-people-vulnerable-to-misinformation-spread-by-social-media/.
14. https://www.researchgate.net/publication/332064733_This_is_fake_news_Investigating_the_role_of_conformity_to_other_users'_views_when_commenting_on_and_spreading_disinformation_in_social_media.
15. Soetekouw, L. and Angelopoulos, S., 2024. Digital resilience through training protocols: Learning to identify fake news on social media. *Information Systems Frontiers*, *26*(2), pp. 459–475.
16. https://www.bbc.co.uk/teach/articles/zfv7kty.

17. Hammond, S.P., Polizzi, G. and Bartholomew, K.J., 2023. Using a socio-ecological framework to understand how 8–12-year-olds build and show digital resilience: A multi-perspective and multi-method qualitative study. *Education and Information Technologies*, *28*(4), pp. 3681–3709.
18. Vissenberg, J., d'Haenens, L. and Livingstone, S., 2022. Digital literacy and online resilience as facilitators of young people's well-being?. *European Psychologist*.
19. https://royalsociety.org/blog/2022/01/how-to-regulate-misinformation/.
20. https://www.carter-ruck.com/insight/fakes-news-authentic-views/responding-to-fake-news-through-regulation-and-automation/.
21. https://www.brookings.edu/articles/how-to-combat-fake-news-and-disinformation/.
22. https://reutersinstitute.politics.ox.ac.uk/news/how-can-we-combat-fake-news-role-platforms-media-literacy-and-journalism.
23. https://globalnetwork.io/perspectives/2021/05/how-governments-can-take-action-against-fake-news.
24. https://www.brookings.edu/articles/how-to-combat-fake-news-and-disinformation/.
25. https://cognitiveresearchjournal.springeropen.com/articles/10.1186/s41235-020-00252-3.
26. https://www.ncbi.nlm.nih.gov/pmc/articles/PMC7539247/.
27. https://www.ncbi.nlm.nih.gov/pmc/articles/PMC8224890/.
28. https://www.bbc.co.uk/bitesize/articles/zdxj96f.
29. https://butlercc.libguides.com/detecting-misinformation/reliable-sources.
30. https://www.ucumberlands.edu/blog/fact-checking-digital-age.
31. https://www.internetmatters.org/issues/fake-news-and-misinformation-advice-hub/dealing-with-fake-news/.
32. https://hbr.org/2022/02/are-you-aware-of-your-biases.
33. https://niemanreports.org/articles/how-implicit-bias-works-in-journalism/.
34. https://www.researchgate.net/publication/329933676_Professional_versus_Social_Media_News_Credibility_and_Impact.
35. https://journals.sagepub.com/doi/10.1177/17816858231204738.
36. https://www.bbc.co.uk/bitesize/articles/zbsgr2p.

37. https://www.tandfonline.com/doi/full/10.1080/21670811.2019.1708766.
38. https://www.mdpi.com/2673-5172/3/4/42.
39. https://reutersinstitute.politics.ox.ac.uk/trust-gap-how-and-why-news-digital-platforms-viewed-more-sceptically-versus-news-general.
40. Van Raemdonck, N. and Meyer, T., 2024. Why disinformation is here to stay. A socio-technical analysis of disinformation as a hybrid threat. In *Addressing Hybrid Threats* (pp. 57–83). Edward Elgar Publishing.
41. https://freedomhouse.org/report/freedom-and-media/2019/media-freedom-downward-spiral.
42. Peñafiel-Saiz, C., Echegaray-Eizaguirre, L. and Perez-de-Arriluzea-Madariaga, A., 2024. The Impact of Biases on Health Disinformation Research. *Societies*, *14*(5), p. 64.
43. https://www.unesco.org/en/threats-freedom-press-violence-disinformation-censorship.
44. https://www.ncbi.nlm.nih.gov/pmc/articles/PMC7862976/.

CHAPTER 4

Weaponisation of Social Media Linked to Anxiety and Depression

Jamalzadeh et al. (2024) insist that with the number of social media platforms and users increasing daily, it has become easier to create and distribute false information. Mechanisms through which social media can be weaponised can be broadly categorised into two main areas: disinformation campaigns and the spread of hate speech and extreme content.[1]

The weaponisation of social media has triggered many outcomes such as increased societal polarisation and division, erosion of trust in institutions and democratic processes, radicalisation and extremism. Mental health issues like anxiety and depression are being potentially linked to social media weaponisation.[2] Heavy users of social media are potentially linked to risk factors such as poor memory function, increased impulsivity, less empathy, and a higher amount of anxiety.[3]

Fominaya (2024) argues anti-democratic and predominantly far-right-wing movements have mobilised using disinformation including against public health measures, circulating COVID negationist and conspiracy messages. Indeed, the political weaponisation of disinformation has been a notable feature of pandemic mobilisation.[4]

Markariani, L. and Toradze (2024) contend during times of national crisis, any positive information that is apprehensible under these conditions becomes effortlessly shareable and consequently, pseudo-positivity is often utilised as a manipulator to foment a wave of disinfodemy.[5]

T. Singh, *Digital Psychological Warfare*,
https://doi.org/10.1007/978-3-032-15294-7_4

Disinformation campaigns involve coordinated efforts to spread false or misleading information with the intent to disrupt decision-making, erode social cohesion, and delegitimise adversaries.[6] These campaigns typically involve intelligence collection on specific targets. They then move onto development of inciteful and often intentionally false narratives. Then, systematic dissemination occurs across social and traditional media channels.

For instance, the Russian government used such tactics to portray the White Helmets humanitarian organisation operating in Syria as a terrorist group, contributing to violent attacks against the organisation.

Alvisi et al. (2024) argue episodes like the January 6 US Capitol attack and the Rohingya genocide exemplify how disinformation has been weaponised. While attention has been paid to its impact on societal discourse and minority persecution, there remains a gap in analysing its role as a malicious hybrid tool targeting critical infrastructures.[7]

Political manipulation is another form of disinformation campaign aimed at systematically manipulating political discourse within a state. This can involve influencing news reporting, silencing dissent, undermining democratic governance and electoral systems, and strengthening authoritarian regimes. Such campaigns often play out with the development of core narratives, onboarding of influencers and fake account operators, and then the dissemination and amplification on social media occurs.

The former president of the Philippines, Rodrigo Duterte, used Facebook to reinforce positive narratives about his campaign, defame opponents, and silence critics.

Digital hate speech and extreme content is another form of weaponisation. Social media platforms can amplify and disseminate hate speech, particularly in fragile contexts, creating opportunities for individuals and organised groups to prey on existing fears and grievances.[8] This can embolden violent actors and spark violence, either intentionally or unwittingly. The rapid proliferation of mobile phones and internet connectivity magnifies the risks and accelerates the impacts of hate speech.

Myanmar serves as a tragic example, where incendiary digital hate speech targeting the majority Muslim Rohingya people has been linked to riots and communal violence. The same technology that allows social media to galvanise democracy activists can also be used by hate groups seeking to organise and recruit.[9]

Moreover, online platforms' business models depend on maximising user engagement, which often inadvertently promotes extreme content. Users' experiences are mediated by algorithms designed to maximise their engagement, which can drive people towards divisive, misleading, or false content. For instance, YouTube's autoplay function has been criticised for potentially radicalising users by recommending related extreme or conspiracy theory videos.

Social media played a pivotal role in shaping the course of events surrounding the 2016 US presidential election. It facilitated greater voter interaction with the political climate, enabling people to create, comment on, and share election-related content, unlike traditional media.[10] Many candidates extended their campaigning efforts across various social media platforms like YouTube, Facebook, Twitter, Instagram, and Snapchat. They employed diverse techniques to discredit opponents and gain support, leveraging the digital architecture of each platform. Users could further amplify these actions by sharing, liking, or commenting, influencing and changing people's views on specific issues.

Pratelli et al. (2024) analysed the Twitter activity surrounding the 2020 US preelection debate, with a particular focus on the spread of disinformation. They found that 88% of the online traffic was targeting swing states. The sharing of links to unreliable news sources was significantly more prevalent in tweets associated with swing states: in this case, untrustworthy tweets predominantly generated by automated accounts. They concluded that the debate was mostly led by two main communities, one with a predominantly Republican affiliation and the other with accounts of different political orientations. Most of the disinformation came from the former.[11]

Following the election, revelations emerged about widespread personal data misuse by Facebook and Cambridge Analytica for political advertising purposes, as reported by *The Guardian* and *The New York Times*. In response, Facebook's CEO Mark Zuckerberg testified before Congress, and the company was fined $5 billion by the Federal Trade Commission for privacy violations. A separate investigation into Russian interference in the election concluded that Russian intelligence agencies created fake accounts and spread misinformation across multiple social media sites to influence the election in favour of Donald Trump.

The Trump campaign extensively utilised social media platforms, notably Twitter, to reach voters. Unlike other candidates, Trump's Twitter and Facebook posts linked to news media rather than the campaign site, emphasising media appearance over volunteers and donations. Trump's unique social media usage garnered attention as he harnessed Twitter to respond quickly to opponents and tweet about various issues.

In contrast, Hillary Clinton's campaign team re-used established social media strategies and tactics from previous elections. A Pew Research study showed that 80% of Clinton's posts included links to her website or campaign pages, while 78% of Trump's posts linked to news media. On Facebook, Clinton linked to her campaign 60% of the time and the news media a quarter of the time.

Social media also became a primary news source for some demographics. A Pew Research Centre study discovered that 35% of voters aged 18–29 used social media as their primary news source, making it the most popular source among their generation. Overall, social media was the second most popular news source during the election, with 14% of all voters listing it as their main source.

Throughout the 2016 election, the Internet Research Agency attempted to influence the electoral outcome in favour of Donald Trump by creating numerous social media accounts to like, share, and repost positive information about Trump and negative information about Clinton.[12] Russian computer hacks also infiltrated the information systems of the Democratic National Committee and the Democratic Congressional Campaign Committee, and posted the obtained files on websites like DCLeaks, Guccifer 2.0, and WikiLeaks.

Russia's full-scale invasion of Ukraine has set new precedents and pushed existing boundaries in all realms, being called the first commercial space war, the first full-scale drone war, and the first AI war.[13] The invasion is unfolding amidst a status quo where a large majority of people receive breaking news through passive scrolling on social media.[14]

Actors in both Russia and Ukraine have found ways to sway public opinion as the battle to shape the war's historical narrative continues. While the basis of traditional battle remains the same in the twenty-first century, many principal components of war now have a digital foundation. For example, intelligence on Russian troops' border movements and military plans was leaked and trending on social media before Russian President Vladimir Putin declared the full-scale invasion.

Ukrainian civilians resisting occupation can inform their army about Russian movements through social media and specially designed apps. Geo and chrono-located smartphone footage of military aggression under occupation can spread through social media and even serve as evidence in international tribunals.

However, the digital battlespace is most prevalent in the war of information. Both Russia and Ukraine have employed every available tool and distinct tactics to shape public perceptions as the war continues. The speed of online updates and the scale of Russian aggression have pushed mainstream media outlets to rush and break stories before they have finished developing, inadvertently helping propagate misinformation that ultimately aids the Kremlin.

As other pressing conflicts unfold and ordinary citizens face their own problems, attention is bound to be diverted elsewhere, manifesting as 'Ukraine Fatigue', where users become weary of the Ukrainian struggle for freedom on social media. It is under these conditions that Russian capabilities in the information war thrive.

Russia has benefited from pointing out fraught Western history and ongoing political blunders, inciting anti-Western sympathy and gaining ground through social media, particularly in countries that suffered from Western colonisation. By reminding citizens of this painful history and stoking renewed anger against Western responses to current events, Russia continues to fuel mistrust of Western narratives on social media.

As the world becomes more polarised and the Russian invasion continues, anger towards Western governments can play a pivotal role in shaping the narrative of this conflict. Arguments surrounding double standards and hypocrisy have inflamed Ukraine fatigue, distracting from the Ukrainian plight and further shifting how social media users engage with this conflict.

Russia has increasingly incorporated deepfakes and AI into its traditional disinformation campaigns against Ukraine. Fabricated recordings of Ukrainian President Volodymyr Zelensky surrendering, as well as Russian troops celebrating and talking about their victory plans, have been published on Telegram, spreading panic and damaging morale. Doctored images with fascist symbolism directed towards Ukrainians have also been used to dehumanise the enemy and justify aggression.

Russia relies on wearing the enemy out in every form of combat. Their strategies, intent on lowering morale for Ukraine and spreading apathy towards the conflict, will likely aid in calls for political solutions that would freeze the present conflict, something that has consistently favoured Russian strategic aims.

As the world becomes more polarised, the contemporary shaping of the Russia-Ukraine narrative on social media will set the tone for future grounds of information warfare. Policy should focus on combating disinformation by collaborating with digital platforms, hosting transparent discussions surrounding information warfare, promoting digital literacy across social media, and verifying online sources.

ISIS has demonstrated remarkable adaptability and flexibility in its recruitment strategies, continuously evolving and modernising its methods to expand its ideology and reach more people.[15] Their recruitment system is based on three pillars: recruiting followers at an early age, radicalisation in prisons, and exploitation of social networks. The latter plays a crucial role in propaganda and mobilisation of young terrorists.

Recruiters leverage the internet and social media to establish contact with adolescents they would not otherwise be able to reach. This medium is particularly effective for recruiting minors, who represent a large proportion of social media users. In 2007, the Saudi Interior Ministry claimed that 80% of young Saudis recruited by jihadists in the country were recruited via the internet.

ISIS excels at utilising social media for its radical propaganda. Its internal structure allows it not only to influence but also to possess some control over the media narrative. Their strategy involves developing their own media outlets and exploiting 'earned media'. Multiple platforms like websites, forums, virtual rooms, YouTube, Facebook, Instagram, WhatsApp, Telegram, and Twitter are key networks for recruiting fighters.

This extensive use of cyber media to support jihadist ends has led to the coining of the term 'cybercaliphate' to refer to the network woven by ISIS on the internet. This network is professionally structured, with individual jihadists forming their own multilingual production agencies and digital magazines. On Telegram, there are different groups, each specialising in inciting violence, justifying violence through theological questions, showcasing injustices against Muslims worldwide, and providing military training, including instructions on bomb-making and executing terrorist attacks.

The combination of affordability, strategic reach, and ability to micro-target audiences by demographics has made social media platforms the medium of choice for extremist organisations like ISIS.[16] They have easy access to strategic communication and global recruitment at their fingertips. In most cases, if not all, terrorists and extremist groups have primarily used this avenue to fuel, intensify, and internationalise their fight.

Antonia Ward from the US think tank RAND stated in a comprehensive security study that 'ISIS's strategic use of social media demonstrates the resourcefulness of the terrorist-cum-insurgent organisation, which mobilised an estimated 40,000 foreign nationals from 110 countries to join the group'. Increasing internet access and its open standards structure pose significant challenges to international governance and domestic security, particularly in vulnerable countries.

This medium allows ISIS to target a vastly increased recruiting pool while concurrently identifying extremists and avoiding detection by domestic security authorities. Evidence shows an increased number of people attracted from the Middle East and Africa to join ISIS. Consequently, strategic recruitment has enabled ISIS to regain some lost territories and prolong the conflict. The reach granted by social media, coupled with ISIS' strong narrative focusing on religious, social, and material grounds, has contributed to the organisation's success and foreshadows future conflicts.

Myanmar and Rohingya Crisis: Facebook's dangerous algorithms and reckless pursuit of profit substantially contributed to the atrocities perpetrated by the Myanmar military against the Rohingya people in 2017, according to a report by Amnesty International.[17] In the months and years leading up to the crackdown, Facebook in Myanmar had become an echo chamber of anti-Rohingya content, with actors linked to the military and radical Buddhist nationalist groups flooding the platform with anti-Muslim disinformation, portraying the Rohingya as 'invaders' and claiming an impending Muslim takeover.

Content inciting violence and discrimination reached the highest levels of Myanmar's military and civilian leadership. Senior General Min Aung Hlaing, the leader of Myanmar's military, posted on his Facebook page in 2017: 'We openly declare that absolutely, our country has no Rohingya race'. He later seized power in a coup in February 2021. The UN's Independent International Fact-Finding Mission on Myanmar ultimately concluded that the 'role of social media [was] significant' in the atrocities in a country where 'Facebook is the Internet'.

Internal studies dating back to 2012 indicated that Meta (Facebook's parent company) knew its algorithms could result in serious real-world harms. In 2016, Meta's own research acknowledged that 'our recommendation systems grow the problem' of extremism. Despite repeated warnings from local civil society activists between 2012 and 2017 about the risk of contributing to extreme violence, and even a temporary block by Myanmar authorities in 2014 due to Facebook's role in triggering ethnic violence in Mandalay, Meta consistently failed to heed the warnings and enforce its own policies on hate speech.

In one internal document dated August 2019, a Meta employee wrote: 'We have evidence from a variety of sources that hate speech, divisive political speech, and misinformation on Facebook… are affecting societies around the world. We also have compelling evidence that our core product mechanics, such as virality, recommendations, and optimising for engagement, are a significant part of why these types of speech flourish on the platform'.

Rohingya refugee groups have made direct requests to Meta to provide remedy by funding a $1 million education project in the refugee camp in Cox's Bazar, Bangladesh, representing just 0.002% of Meta's profits of $46.7 billion from 2021. However, in February 2021, Meta rejected the Rohingya community's request, stating: 'Facebook doesn't directly engage in philanthropic activities'.

The impact on Democracy is devastating. Governments around the world are increasingly using social media to manipulate elections and monitor their citizens, tilting the technology towards digital authoritarianism.[18] Domestic election interference marred the online landscape in 26 of the 30 countries studied that held national votes over the past year, with disinformation being the most commonly used tactic.

Democratic processes are being eroded and exploited at pace. Authoritarians and populists around the globe are exploiting both human nature and computer algorithms to conquer the ballot box, running roughshod over rules designed to ensure free and fair elections. Domestic state and partisan actors used propaganda and disinformation to distort the online landscape during elections in at least 24 countries over the past year, making it by far the most popular tactic for digital election interference. Often working in tandem with government-friendly media personalities and business magnates, semi-autonomous online mobs transmitted conspiracy theories, inflammatory views, and misleading memes from marginal echo chambers to the political mainstream.

Governments from across the democratic spectrum are indiscriminately monitoring citizens' online behaviour to identify perceived threats – and in some cases to silence opposition. A review of recent public opinion research shows the severity of the crisis facing democracy in the USA.[19] This where 64% of Americans believe US democracy is in crisis and at risk of failing, with over 70% saying democracy is more at risk now than a year ago. They saw 76% think political instability within the country is a bigger danger than external adversaries, suggesting Americans see themselves as a bigger threat to their own democracy. Over 53% expect political divisions to worsen over their lifetime rather than improve.

The explosion of misinformation deliberately aimed at disrupting the democratic process has been a key driver of decreased confidence in the political system. Throughout the 2020 election cycle, Russia's cyber efforts and online actors influenced public perceptions and sought to amplify mistrust in the electoral process by denigrating mail-in voting, highlighting alleged irregularities, and accusing the Democratic Party of voter fraud. The 'big lie' reinforced by President Trump about the 2020 election results amplified the Russian efforts and has lasting implications on voters' trust in election outcomes.

There was widespread belief in voter fraud claims from the 2020 US presidential election across racial and ethnic groups with 57% of White Americans believe there was voter fraud, including 26% who believe there was definitely fraud. Over 38% of Latinos and 30% of African Americans think there might have been at least some fraud and 51.5% of respondents believe 'Black Americans are targets of fake news'.

As a result, public trust in the US election system declined significantly with only 20% feel 'very confident' in the integrity of the election system, 56% said they have 'little or no confidence' that elections represent the will of the people and 42% of youth poll participants believe their vote did not make a difference.

Decreased confidence leads to lower civic engagement, with 26% of respondents in one survey believing their vote does not count. The persistent re-telling of the 'big lie' appears to be suppressing voter turnout in the 2022 primary elections across multiple states like New Mexico, California, Alabama, Mississippi, and Indiana.

Notably, the New Mexico secretary of state sued a county commission who unanimously refused to certify primary results due to vague, unsubstantiated concerns about voting machines. Although the state Supreme Court intervened to certify the results, the widespread media coverage of the debacle has already damaged voter confidence.

The widespread adoption of social media networks – including YouTube, X (formerly Twitter), Instagram, Snapchat, and Facebook – has enabled modern viral marketing efforts and increased their efficacy.[20] With the help of social networks as a 'force multiplier', viral marketing is quicker than traditional marketing campaigns, as well as less expensive. Since it can receive so much traffic in a short time, it can also lead to mainstream media attention.

However, social media can also cause viral marketing efforts to misfire, as messages are altered, misconstrued, considered spam, or called out for missing the mark. If customers believe the viral campaign will compromise their privacy and security, they will likely not share, causing the company's marketing mission to fail and its reputation to be tarnished. Future viral marketing campaigns may be adversely affected by previous unsuccessful attempts.

Organic viral marketing campaigns help businesses grow their customer base and increase brand awareness.[21] The essence of organic viral marketing sets it apart from conventional marketing campaigns. Organic viral marketing uses user-generated content and word-of-mouth promotion to captivate a larger and more engaged audience, instead of paid advertisements and brand-created content.

Organic viral marketing is a type of marketing that spreads quickly and naturally through user-generated content and word-of-mouth, with little involvement or control from the brand. Organic viral marketing campaigns are unique because they rely on social media platforms and online communities, rather than being controlled by the brand.

Several key characteristics contribute to the success of organic viral marketing. Ensuring that the content is easily shareable and connects with the target audience, motivating them to share it with others, is crucial. Using humour, surprise, or inspiration increases the chances of the campaign being remembered and shared. Authenticity is also crucial, as consumers are more likely to engage with content that feels genuine.

The benefits of organic viral marketing are vast. Word-of-mouth marketing helps build brand credibility and trust, as people trust recommendations from friends and peers more than traditional marketing messages. Furthermore, organic viral marketing allows for direct and meaningful interaction with consumers, fostering a deeper level of engagement and connection.

Overall, organic viral marketing campaigns have the potential to reach a wider audience with little to no investment, as the message spreads exponentially through consumer interactions. By creating highly shareable content and leveraging the power of social media networks, brands can take advantage of organic viral marketing to build a loyal customer base and achieve massive success.

In response to the information disorder on social media platforms, governments around the world are imposing transparency requirements in the hopes that they will improve content moderation practices.[22] However, transparency initiatives, the critics say, just distract from the hard work of developing and implementing more effective methods of control.

Transparency is not a single policy tool. It has different dimensions in providing disclosures to users, public reporting, and access to data for researchers.

Disclosure to users includes revealing information about the content moderation standards a social media company has in place, its enforcement processes, and explanations of take downs and other content moderation actions, descriptions of complaint procedures, among other things.

The second dimension of transparency is transparency reporting. This includes reports and internal audits of platform content moderation activity, the risks created through social media company activities, the role of algorithms in distributing harmful speech, assessments of what the companies do about hate speech, disinformation, material harmful to teens, and other problematic content.

The third element of transparency, access to data for researchers, is a very powerful tool, perhaps the most important one of all. It requires social media companies to provide qualified researchers with access to the internal company data that researchers need to conduct independent evaluations.

Seeing all that is involved in implementing transparency measures brings us back to one question: Why do this at all? What good does transparency do? In general, the answer is that it provides public accountability. Mandated public reports on moderation practices are likely to improve content moderation, just as accounting reporting requirements encourage good corporate financial conduct.

Researcher access to internal company data allows independent outside assessments of company conduct and can indicate areas for improvement that the companies themselves might have missed or tried to cover up in their public reports. The difference, of course, is that content moderation has to do with speech. There are good policy reasons to be careful about mandating speech controls – they constantly risk throwing out the baby with the bathwater, the good speech with the bad.

Transparency provides the input that can reveal further steps that policymakers can take to improve social media content moderation.

The world witnessed the worst example of the impact digital platforms can have on society with the debacle at the US Capitol on 6 January 2021.[23] Not only did supporters of Donald Trump try to disrupt the certification of the Electoral College votes, but this deplorable incident was, in large part, fomented over social media.

Digital platforms can be highly profitable businesses that connect users and other market actors in ways not possible before the internet. When they are successful, they generate powerful feedback loops called network effects and then monetise them by selling advertisements. But what happened at the US Capitol illustrates how digital platforms can be double-edged swords. Yes, they have generated trillions of dollars in wealth, but they have also enabled the distribution of fake news and fake products, manipulation of digital content for political purposes, and promotion of dangerous misinformation on elections, vaccines, and other public health matters.

The social dilemma is clear: Digital platforms can be used for evil as well as good. What's the solution? Should platform companies wait for governments to impose potentially intrusive controls and respond defensively? Or should they act pre-emptively?

Governments will inevitably get more engaged in oversight. However, platforms should become more aggressive at self-regulation now. Companies have often risked creating a 'tragedy of the commons' when they put their short-term, individual self-interests ahead of the good of the consuming public or the industry overall, and, in the long term, destroy the environment that made them successful in the first place.

For many decades, companies in the business of producing movies, video games, and television shows and commercials all have faced issues around the appropriateness of 'content' in a way that resembles today's social media platforms. To keep regulators at bay, the movie and video games industries resorted to a self-imposed and self-monitored rating system, still in operation today. The broadcasting and advertisement sectors in the 1950s and 1960s faced pushback on the appropriateness of advertisements, with issues resembling what we see today in online advertising.

First, leading technology companies need to anticipate when government regulation is likely to become a key factor in their businesses. In movies, radio and television broadcasting, airline reservations via computers, and other new industries, there often occurs a vacuum in regulation in the early years, followed by a 'wild west' environment before governments step in to regulate or pressure firms to curb abuses. To avoid problematic government regulation, platform companies need to introduce their own controls on behaviour and usage before the government revokes all Sect. 230 protections, which is currently under debate in Congress.

Second, firms in new industries tend to eschew self-regulation when the perceived costs imply a significant reduction in revenues or profits. Managers rarely like industry regulations that appear 'bad for business'. However, this strategy can be self-defeating. If bad behaviour undermines consumer trust, then digital platforms will not continue to thrive. Section 230 states that 'no provider or user of an interactive computer service shall be treated as the publisher or speaker of any information provided by another information content provider'. This act gave online intermediaries broad immunity from liability for user-generated content posted on their sites. Executives and company lawyers should have felt comfortable making reasonable curation decisions under Sect. 230, but they generally resisted and argued that their legal and political positions would be more secure if they avoided potentially controversial curation.

Third, proactive self-regulation was often more successful when coalitions of firms in the same sector worked together. This coalition-type of activity was seen in movie and video-game rating systems limiting violent, profane, or sexual content; television advertisements rules curbing unhealthy products like alcohol and tobacco; and computerised online airline reservations giving equal treatment to airlines, without favouring the system owners. Similarly, social media companies implemented codes of conduct on terrorist activity. Since individual firms may hesitate to enact self-regulation if they incur added costs that their competitors do not, industry coalitions have the benefit of reducing free-riding. Now is the ideal time for more 'coopetition', where platforms compete as well as cooperate with rivals.

Fourth, firms or industry coalitions get serious about self-regulation primarily when they see a credible threat of government regulation, even if it may hurt short-term sales and profits. This pattern occurred with tobacco and cigarette ads, airline reservations, social media ads for terrorist group recruitment, and pornographic material. That threat should be clear and obvious to digital platforms in 2021.

Prevention efforts aim to reduce the incidence of social media weaponisation through activities that influence policies and regulations.[24] The European Union has developed the General Data Protection Regulation (GDPR), a set of data protection rules outlining regulations for businesses and organisations on processing, collecting, and storing individuals' data while establishing rights for citizens and means for redress.

Civil society-led advocacy activities also contribute to prevention by influencing regulations or technology company practices.[25] Many of these prevention efforts and the required relationships are relatively novel for international humanitarian, development, and peacebuilding organisations.

Monitoring, detection, and threat assessment activities bring together stakeholders from intelligence organisations to civil society groups to identify threats and their potential impact. In Kenya's Tana Delta, the Sentinel Project''s Una Hakika programme counters rumours contributing to inter-ethnic violence by creating a platform for community members to report, verify, and develop strategies to address misinformation.

Building resilience involves helping fragile populations resist the worst impacts of social media weaponisation through digital media literacy training, online and offline awareness-building, education, and strategies to build social cohesion. For example, the Digital Storytelling initiative in Sri Lanka seeks to build skills in citizen storytelling to balance polarising online rhetoric while helping individuals become more responsible consumers of online information.

Mitigation activities aim to minimise harm once weaponised information has already spread, particularly during crises. These might include integrating referral or warning and response components into monitoring systems, establishing crisis and response plans, and addressing and countering online hate speech and radical or violent extremist narratives. The Dangerous Speech Project's Nipe Uwell in Kenya provided public information on dangerous speech and mechanisms to report and remove such speech online during electoral tensions.

Prevention also involves the policies and technical initiatives of tech companies that impact the prevalence of weaponisation on social media platforms, such as developing company community standards, product updates that promote feedback mechanisms, or improving practices to remove inauthentic accounts.

Activities under monitoring, detection, and threat assessment include information and threat mapping, developing open-source rumour monitoring and management systems, identifying and analysing online hate speech, and social network monitoring, analysis, and reporting. PeaceTech Lab's Hate Speech Lexicon workstream seeks to identify and analyse online hate speech in specific contexts, like developing monitoring reports outlining hateful speech and providing predictions for future conflict based on online hate speech in South Sudan.

Social media regulation resembles finding the right balance between allowing individuals to express themselves openly and ensuring everyone stays safe.[26] It involves making rules to stop threats like misinformation from spreading online while covering aspects like data privacy, content moderation, online safety, and protecting democratic processes.

Content moderation is an important part of social media regulation, involving rules to monitor what people share online and stop harmful content like hate speech, fake news, or violent material from being shared. Social media platforms use computer programs and human moderators to check and take down anything that breaks the rules while trying to avoid censoring legitimate expression.

Data privacy regulations ensure that social media platforms are transparent about how they use individuals' data, obtain consent before collecting or using it, and prevent unauthorised access or misuse. The rules aim to ensure data is stored and transferred securely, with companies following high standards to protect user privacy.

Online safety regulations, particularly for children and teenagers, may include age limits, parental controls, and measures to combat cyberbullying, helping create a safer and more friendly online environment. Balancing safety and freedom of expression is crucial when developing these rules.

Regulations also aim to protect the integrity of elections and democratic decision-making processes by mandating transparency around political advertising, preventing fake accounts, and fact-checking information to combat misinformation. The goal is to facilitate honest and open discourse on important issues without deception or manipulation.

Enforcement of social media regulations is critical, with governments potentially establishing dedicated agencies or groups to ensure compliance and impose penalties like restrictions or fines for violations. International cooperation is necessary since online platforms operate globally.

Regulatory frameworks involve consulting various stakeholders, including social media companies, civil society, and the general public, to develop fair and balanced rules through public discussions and feedback. Citizen input helps governments understand diverse perspectives and create regulations that align with societal values.

Hate speech online has been linked to a global increase in violence towards minorities, including mass shootings, lynchings, and ethnic cleansing.[27] Incidents have been reported on nearly every continent. With nearly a third of the world's population active on Facebook alone, individuals inclined towards racism, misogyny, or homophobia have found niches that can reinforce their views and goad them to violence. Social media platforms also offer violent actors the opportunity to publicise their acts.

In Germany, a correlation was found between anti-refugee Facebook posts by the far-right Alternative for Germany party and attacks on refugees. Scholars Karsten Muller and Carlo Schwarz observed that upticks in attacks, such as arson and assault, followed spikes in hatemongering posts.

In the USA, perpetrators of recent White supremacist attacks have circulated among racist communities online and embraced social media to publicise their acts. Prosecutors said the Charleston church shooter, who killed nine Black clergy and worshippers in June 2015, engaged in a 'self-learning process' online that led him to believe that the goal of White supremacy required violent action.

The 2018 Pittsburgh synagogue shooter was a participant in the social media network Gab, whose lax rules have attracted extremists banned by larger platform. There, he espoused the conspiracy that Jews sought to bring immigrants into the USA and render Whites a minority, before killing eleven worshippers at a refugee-themed Shabbat service. This 'great replacement' trope, which was heard at the White supremacist rally in Charlottesville, Virginia, a year prior and originates with the French far right, expresses demographic anxieties about non-White immigration and birth rates.

The 'great replacement' trope was in turn espoused by the perpetrator of the 2019 New Zealand mosque shootings, who killed forty-nine Muslims at prayer and sought to broadcast the attack on YouTube.

In Myanmar, military leaders and Buddhist nationalists used social media to slur and demonise the Rohingya Muslim minority ahead of and during a campaign of ethnic cleansing. Though Rohingya comprised perhaps two per cent of the population, ethnonationalists claimed that Rohingya would soon supplant the Buddhist majority. The UN fact-finding mission said, ‘Facebook has been a useful instrument for those seeking to spread hate, in a context where, for most users, Facebook is the Internet’.

In India, lynch mobs and other types of communal violence, in many cases originating with rumours on WhatsApp groups, have been on the rise since the Hindu nationalist Bharatiya Janata Party (BJP) came to power in 2014.

Sri Lanka has similarly seen vigilantism inspired by rumours spread online, targeting the Tamil Muslim minority. During a spate of violence in March 2018, the government blocked access to Facebook and WhatsApp, as well as the messaging app Viber, for a week, saying that Facebook had not been sufficiently responsive during the emergency.

Amazeen et al. (2024) examine how misinformation-susceptible individuals from historically excluded and marginalised communities engage with science topics (e.g., climate change, vaccines, and health/wellness) and interpret misinformation and corrective intervention strategies. Two focus groups reveal that most participants are highly distrustful of authority figures, celebrity endorsements, and fact-checking strategies to combat misinformation. Research with underrepresented community members’ experiences with science misinformation reveal structural and institutional power dynamics that impede access to accurate information and indicate how missing voices must be included in the efforts at media and information literacy initiatives.[28]

Soetekouw and Angelopoulos (2024) argue digital literacy and training social media users to recognise fake news is vital. They contend that training protocols are vital to counter the effects of fake news, as a scalable solution that empowers users and addresses concerns about the time-consuming nature of fact-checking.[29]

Building resilience involves empowering individuals and communities to identify and respond effectively to misinformation, disinformation, and hate speech online. Digital literacy programmes that teach critical thinking and media analysis skills play a crucial role in this endeavour.[30] These programmes equip people with the ability to analyse online content critically, verify information before sharing it, and become more discerning consumers of digital media. By providing digital literacy skills, individuals become less susceptible to manipulation tactics and divisive rhetoric propagated through weaponised social media.[31]

Hammond et al. (2023) contend that building digital resilience in youngsters is a vital but collective endeavour involving children, parents, youth workers, civil society, teachers, schools, governments, policymakers, Big Tech platforms and internet corporations.[32] Vissenberg et al. (2022) caution against relying on digital literacy as a reliable facilitator in young people's well-being.[33]

Fostering social cohesion and trust within communities is another key strategy for building resilience against the harmful impacts of weaponised social media.[34] When communities have strong social bonds and high levels of trust, they become less vulnerable to the divisive tactics employed by disinformation campaigns and the influence of hateful rhetoric or calls to violence. Community engagement initiatives can take various forms, such as facilitating dialogue and joint problem-solving among diverse community members, supporting local media and civil society organisations, or establishing community-based early warning and response mechanisms.

Initiatives like Mercy Corps' peacebuilding work in Nigeria's Middle Belt region have successfully increased trust and perceptions of security across farmer and pastoralist groups. These initiatives have also included specific efforts to support religious and traditional leaders in analysing and leading discussions aimed at reducing the impacts of hate speech on social media.

The Digital Storytelling initiative in Sri Lanka is another example of a community engagement programme that seeks to build skills in citizen storytelling as a means to counter polarising online rhetoric. By empowering individuals to become responsible consumers and creators of online content, such initiatives can help balance the narrative landscape and promote social cohesion.

In response to the information disorder on social media platforms, governments around the world are imposing transparency requirements in the hopes that they will improve content moderation practices.[35] In the USA, for instance, a new California law would impose a range of disclosure and openness requirements.

Transparency is not a single policy tool; it has different dimensions such as providing disclosures to users. This includes revealing information about the content moderation standards a social media company has in place, its enforcement processes, explanations of takedowns and other content moderation actions, and descriptions of complaint procedures. Each of these outputs provides users with opportunities to complain about problematic content and receive due process when social media companies take action against them.

Public reporting includes reports and internal audits of platform content moderation activity, the risks created through social media company activities, the role of algorithms in distributing harmful speech, assessments of what the companies do about hate speech, disinformation, material harmful to teens, and other problematic content. Transparency reporting could also include a company's assessment of whether its activities are politically discriminatory, a favourite topic of political conservatives.

Access to data for researchers is perhaps the most powerful tool, requiring social media companies to provide qualified researchers with access to internal company data needed to conduct independent evaluations. These outside evaluations would not be under company control and would assess company performance on content moderation and the prevalence of harmful material.

The European Union has developed the Digital Services Act (DSA), a groundbreaking law that will apply to any digital operation serving the EU, forcing them to be legally accountable for everything from fake news to manipulation of shoppers, Russian propaganda, and criminal activity, including child abuse.[36]

The DSA regulates online intermediaries and platforms such as marketplaces, social networks, content-sharing platforms, app stores, and online travel and accommodation platforms.[37] Its main goal is to prevent illegal and harmful activities online and the spread of disinformation, ensuring user safety, protecting fundamental rights, and creating a fair and open online platform environment.

The obligations of different online players match their role, size, and impact in the online ecosystem. Very large online platforms and search engines reaching more than 10% of 450 million consumers in Europe face specific rules, as they pose particular risks in the dissemination of illegal content and societal harms.

Key aspects of the DSA include illegal products. Platforms will be obliged to combat the sale of illegal products and services, affecting platforms like Amazon and Facebook Marketplace. Illegal content is another key area as new measures are designed to crack down on illegal content, including Russian propaganda, interference with elections, hate crimes, online harms like harassment and child abuse, and ensure fundamental rights like freedom of expression and data protection are safeguarded. Platforms will be prohibited from targeting children with advertising based on their personal data or cookies. Big social media firms must redesign their systems to ensure a high level of privacy, security, and safety for minors and prove compliance to the European Commission. They must also redesign content 'recommender systems' to reduce risks to children and assess negative effects on children's mental health. Social media companies will not be able to use sensitive personal data like race, gender, and religion to target users with ads. Platforms will be banned from using manipulative practices like fake countdown timers, hiding important information, or making it difficult to uninstall pre-loaded software and apps.

Consumers will be able to report transgressions and expect changes, while tech companies will be banned from ranking their own services more favourably than others.

The Commission will enforce the DSA together with national authorities, primarily responsible for monitoring and enforcing additional obligations applying to very large online platforms and search engines, such as measures to mitigate systemic risks.

Firms that do not comply could face a complete ban in Europe or fines running up to 6% of their global revenue.

Tech giants like Facebook (now Meta), Twitter (now X), and others have implemented various corporate policies to govern the use of their platforms and address issues related to content moderation, data privacy, and ethical concerns. These policies aim to strike a balance between promoting free speech and preventing the spread of harmful or illegal content.[38]

Many companies have established community standards or acceptable use policies that outline the types of content and behaviour that are permitted on their platforms. These policies typically prohibit hate speech, harassment, incitement to violence, and the dissemination of misinformation or illegal activities.[39] However, the enforcement of these policies has often been criticised as inconsistent or inadequate, leading to calls for greater transparency and accountability.[40]

Tech companies have also implemented measures to protect user privacy and data security. This includes obtaining consent for data collection, implementing secure data storage and transfer protocols, and limiting the use of personal data for targeted advertising or other purposes without explicit user consent. However, concerns have been raised about the extent to which personal data is being collected and used by these companies, as well as the potential for data breaches or misuse.

The rapid growth and influence of social media platforms have raised numerous ethical concerns regarding their impact on society, democracy, and individual well-being. One of the primary ethical dilemmas revolves around the use of personal information and the balance between personalisation and privacy.

As businesses collect and analyse user data to improve their services and target advertisements, there are concerns about the extent to which this practice infringes on individual privacy rights. There are also questions about the ethical implications of using algorithms to curate and recommend content, as these algorithms can potentially reinforce biases, spread misinformation, or promote divisive or extreme content.

Another ethical concern is the potential for social media platforms to be used for manipulation, whether for political, commercial, or other purposes. The ability to microtarget specific groups with tailored messaging and the spread of disinformation or hate speech can undermine democratic processes, fuel social divisions, and enable the radicalisation of individuals.

Tech companies have faced criticism for their role in enabling or amplifying these harmful behaviours, as well as for their perceived lack of transparency and accountability. There have been calls for greater regulation and oversight to ensure that these platforms are operating in an ethical and socially responsible manner.

Raad (2024) concludes that the internet and ad-supported business models facilitate the targeting, dissemination and amplification of false information online. Algorithmic designs, cognitive biases, and platform structures enable false information to spread faster than truth on the internet and are synergistically exploited in influence operations, compromising freedom of thought. Frameworks like DISARM and RICHDATA provide insights into disinformation campaigns' stages and tactics, emphasise the importance of countering harmful content amplification, and recommend strategic measures to increase cost and complexity for influence operators. The USA and other nations need to enact national data collection laws, data brokerage industry regulation, social media company oversight, regulation of third-party players facilitating disinformation, and other measures to enhance media literacy and protect the information ecosystem.[41]

The big tech firms will have us believe that their algorithms are perfect and that there are no technological solutions that could help resolve the social harms caused by their platforms. That is why regulation is needed. There are plenty of technological solutions available.

Algorithms could easily solve this problem if the willingness was there from big tech firms. Algorithms play a crucial role in the operation of social media platforms, governing how content is filtered, ranked, selected, and recommended to users.[42] These algorithms collect various user signals, such as engagement metrics (likes, shares, comments), keywords, hashtags, timing, recency, and user interactions, to determine the relevance and quality of content. By adapting and learning from user interactions, algorithms aim to refine content suggestions and ensure their relevance.

Different social media platforms employ distinct algorithms to curate content based on user preferences and behaviour. For instance, Twitter's algorithm is designed to surface relevant tweets from the daily stream of 500 million tweets, considering factors like user interests, preferences, and past interactions. Facebook's algorithm prioritises content based on timing, user demographics, account credibility, content type, relevance, engagement levels, and connections. Instagram's algorithm tailors content recommendations across various sections (Feed, Stories, Explore, Reels, Search) based on signals such as post recency, user activity, content type, post information, and interaction history.

TikTok's recommendation system curates the 'For You' feed by considering user interactions, location, video details, device settings, and watch time. YouTube's algorithm ranks videos based on performance metrics (likes, shares, comments), click-through rates, watch time, recency, user history, search history, demographics, and location. LinkedIn's algorithm filters posts into categories (spam, low-quality, high-quality) and considers relevance, engagement probability, personal connections, consistency, credibility, recency, and content type.

These algorithms play a vital role in determining the visibility and reach of content on social media platforms, potentially influencing user choices and shaping the information landscape.

Counter-narrative technologies can be developed. The concept of creating counter-narratives to push back against extremist recruitment and propaganda has gained traction in recent years.[43] Organisations like the

Against Violent Extremism network and Jigsaw (an Alphabet incubator) have collaborated with social media companies like Facebook and Twitter to develop and deploy counter-narrative campaigns. These campaigns aim to spark deradicalisation by presenting alternative narratives and perspectives.

Tech and social media companies have committed to supporting counter-narrative efforts by offering pro bono or discounted access to advertising tools, analytical tools for measuring campaign impact, and training for practitioners.[44]

Meta, Twitter/X, and Google are setting up systems to remove fake news and hate speech. However, we must be honest and ask can they ever be relied upon to do so? Why would they do away with their proprietary targeting algorithms when these are their rice bowls? These tech platforms will likely just continue to provide lip service. That is unless regulators step in.

However, there is a need for more long-term cooperation and investment in developing partnerships with credible voices and civil society organisations to support their counter-narrative campaigns.

Advertising and film production companies can also contribute by providing pro bono support to civil society organisations and practitioners in designing effective messages as part of their corporate social responsibilities. They can assist practitioners in understanding how to measure campaign impact and conduct market testing with target audiences.

While counter-narrative technologies and campaigns show promise in combating extremist propaganda and recruitment, sustained collaboration between tech companies, civil society organisations, and government agencies is crucial for their success.

Traberg et al. (2024) argue the persistent influence of social cues, even in the presence of pre-emptive technological response and inoculation, emphasising the need for nuanced interventions to address the complex interplay between emotions, misinformation, and social influence in the digital age.[45]

Social media platforms can inadvertently aid the spread of misinformation to thousands or even millions of people simultaneously.[46] Unfortunately, social media algorithms prioritise engagement, meaning any interaction, even negative ones like angry reactions or comments refuting false information, can inadvertently help the content reach a wider audience.

The phenomenon of 'echo chambers' further exacerbates this issue. When users engage with specific types of content, algorithms tend to show them more similar content, creating a self-reinforcing cycle that limits exposure to diverse perspectives and reinforces existing beliefs or biases. This can lead to increased defensiveness and the potential spread of harmful content or hate speech.

The Spanish startup AyGLOO, in collaboration with the news agency Europa Press, is working on a project to detect fake news using Explainable Artificial Intelligence (XAI).[47] The goal is to design a simple and effective tool for journalists, researchers, and disseminators to verify information circulating on the internet, social media, and forums.[48] The tool is based on XAI, which involves using AI and machine learning methods to help users understand AI results and potential biases, while improving the fairness and transparency of the resulting algorithms. This approach enables journalists to comprehend the reasons why the system considers information to be false or true.

Mukherjee (2024) argues that use of Generative AI is so widespread for disinformation that now the only option to tackling it is to also use AI in disinformation detection and response.[49]

With AI and natural language understanding capabilities, current verification processes can be streamlined by analysing the text of news stories and alerting journalists to potential falsehoods. AI can identify the core elements of a story, such as named entities, events, occasions, and timelines, and find other variations in the consolidated pool of content from different sources and languages.[50] AI agents can also discover cross-posts, newer versions of the same story, references, user discussion threads, and complaints.

A 'Fact-Checking Orchestrator' synthesises lists of stories that need evaluation by a global network of reviewers. This component simplifies the assessment process by making intelligent suggestions and recommendations to reviewers, such as which stories must be checked and what aspects need verification within each story. The global community of professionals and active 'digital citizens' can then discover, evaluate, and vote for/against certain aspects of the story, providing justifications, references, and annotations.

Immutable content store means once a story gains enough confidence through votes and factual checks, AI generalises the findings to all known variations and coverage types, quantifying the reliability of both the core story and its variants. AI components continuously monitor each story for new facts and events that require verification, storing all labelled content, assessments, publisher scores, and metadata permanently as part of global history, preventing the deletion or 'phantom' existence of fake news.

To combat the spread of hoaxes and fake news, various fact-checking tools have emerged, including TinEye, a reverse image search engine that searches the internet for matches based on an image, helping identify unauthorised image usage. Whois is a platform that allows users to look up the registration data of a domain, facilitating the review of a website's veracity, duration, and updates. Google offers a fact-check scanner with a check markup based on the Fact Check Explorer and Fact Check Markup Tool, enabling users to verify information.

These tools provide users, especially those involved in communication, with specialised verification websites to limit the effects of hoaxes and fake news.

Moderating misinformation across social platforms is a delicate balance, and new AI-powered technologies are tipping the scale.[51] First, for any piece of misinformation, platforms must identify and verify it is indeed false. Though this may seem easy, rapidly changing narratives about an event can make determining the truth in real-time difficult. Even major news outlets can mischaracterise crucial details about breaking stories.

Second, once the lie is caught, there are downsides to each way platforms can address it. Misinformation tends to get the most algorithmic attention in the first few hours after it is posted, but if platforms remove it immediately across all sites, they could face accusations of censorship and violations of free speech. If they preserve the post, however, this would allow it to spread further. Oftentimes, the ability to decide comes too late, as there is typically a substantial delay between when information surfaces and the fact-check lands.

New AI moderation approaches include working with AI-driven fact-check tools such as Factinsect to compare claims against proven data. AI is also being tested to spot unique patterns in how misinformation spreads. Meanwhile, leading AI tools such as AI or Not and Sentinel can determine whether an image or video has been altered but are still unable to catch every fake.

For the most impactful response using AI, platforms could offer real-time corrections for highly cited yet mundane misinformation such as the false tweets around the switching of election dates seen in the 2020 election. These insidious alterations can surprisingly cause the most harm and impact the most people.

While effective in some cases, however, AI tools cannot interpret grey areas or analyse nuanced points of view. So, platforms must employ humans to interpret what AI cannot. Third-party fact-checkers will be essential to provide unbiased, expert assessments of new narratives and alert platforms to rising threats. Human content reviewers can also work together with AI tools, using them to flag more complex cases for their final decision.

Algorithms enable content to be moderated at a speed and scale that would not be possible for human moderators operating alone.[52] The onset of COVID-19 and resulting lockdown led to a reduction in the moderation workforce, just as the volume of misinformation was rising. Platforms responded by relying on automated content decisions to a greater extent, without significant human oversight.

Increased reliance on algorithms led to substantially more content being incorrectly identified as misinformation. Participants noted that algorithms still fall far short of the capabilities of human moderators in distinguishing between harmful and benign content. One reason is that misinformation is often subtle and context dependent, making it difficult for automated systems to analyse. This is particularly true for misinformation that relates to new phenomena (such as COVID-19).[53]

Platforms have issued reassurances that the increased reliance on algorithms is only temporary, and that human moderators will continue to be at the core of their processes.

Social media content moderation and filtering are essential for maintaining a safe and enjoyable online experience for users of all ages.[54] These mechanisms help in mitigating various issues, such as cyberbullying, hate speech, misinformation, and the proliferation of harmful content.

Content filtering, with the help of tools like text annotation service, helps identify and remove harmful or inappropriate content, ensuring that users are not exposed to offensive or potentially dangerous material.

Content filtering algorithms are the backbone of social media content moderation. These algorithms are designed to analyse and categorise user-generated content, making decisions on whether to allow, restrict, or remove it based on predefined criteria.

Algorithms often begin by scanning text content for specific keywords or phrases that may indicate hate speech, harassment, or other violations of platform policies. Advanced algorithms incorporate image recognition technology to detect and filter out inappropriate or graphic images and videos.

Machine learning models, often trained with the help of tools like text annotation service, are increasingly being used to improve the accuracy of content filtering. These models can adapt and learn from new data, making them more effective in identifying evolving threats.

Content filtering algorithms also consider the behaviour of users, such as patterns of engagement with content or the frequency of reports against a particular user or piece of content. Understanding the context in which content is posted is vital. Algorithms may take into account the user's history, the content's intent, and the potential impact it may have on the community.

Efforts have been consistently made to develop machine learning-based systems and natural language processing (NLP) algorithms for disinformation detection.[55] However, thus far, there have been no flawless solutions. NLP, a subfield of AI, enables machines to comprehend, interpret, and replicate human language.

One challenge associated with utilising AI and machine learning for disinformation detection constitutes ethical concerns. Biases and prejudices can infiltrate these systems, leading to erroneous outcomes.

Automated fact-checking can include text analysis performed by AI, which is useful in classifying news as true or false. In these cases, in addition to resources based on word occurrences and word relationships (both semantic and syntactic), it is also necessary to have resources based on how humans perform fact-checking. That is, the automated classification of information examines human behaviour in the process of manually detecting disinformation.

Despite significant advancements in NLP techniques for automated text analysis, challenges remain in understanding fundamental human concepts, such as sarcasm or irony. AI-based systems currently struggle to address disinformation that relies on subtler forms of expression beyond explicit content.

A common approach to managing these challenges is to involve humans in the text analysis process, especially when regarding machine learning algorithm training. For example, in a fake news classification project, humans can flag a news story as false or true in the first phase. Then, the programme can learn from these indications to assign characteristics and make classification decisions based on patterns identified in the news.

This approach, referred to as semi-supervised learning, offers the potential to enhance the accuracy of automated text analysis by combining the human ability to comprehend language nuances with the efficiency and scalability of automated text processing.

Fake news and disinformation (FNaD) are increasingly being circulated through various online and social networking platforms, causing widespread disruptions and influencing decision-making perceptions.[56] Despite the growing importance of detecting fake news in politics, relatively limited research efforts have been made to develop artificial intelligence (AI) and machine learning (ML) oriented FNaD detection models suited to minimise supply chain disruptions (SCDs).[57]

Using a combination of AI and ML, and case studies based on data collected from Indonesia, Malaysia, and Pakistan, researchers developed an FNaD detection model aimed at preventing SCDs. This model based on multiple data sources has shown evidence of its effectiveness in managerial decision-making.

Blockchain is a reliable, cheap, and simple mechanism that could help to ensure information is accurate.

Blockchain technology offers a secure and transparent way to verify the origin, authenticity, and integrity of any product or service through immutable digital records that can be accessed and independently verified from anywhere.[58] Solutions like Modulus Blockchain and Kalima Blockchain Proof of Origin (Po0) utilise AI to analyse images, videos, audio, and data, storing the encrypted outputs in a secure, immutable blockchain.[59] This allows for the proof of origin, existence, and authenticity of any product, service, or data to be independently audited and verified at any time.

Kalima's solutions, such as DataLake and DataSafe, enable digital safe storage, archiving, and data authentication thanks to the blockchain mechanism.[60] Data can be shared with trust through a permissioned blockchain to authorised persons, with end-to-end encryption enforcing security and data replication protecting against data loss. Kalima also guarantees that the correct and most up-to-date version of documents will be available to teams, staff, and stakeholders, while allowing access to previous versions and the full history.

By enabling the creation of immutable records, blockchain ensures that once content is recorded, it cannot be altered without detection. This feature is crucial for maintaining the integrity of information. Each piece of content can be timestamped and digitally signed by verified publishers, providing a clear and traceable path back to the source. This means consumers can trust the origin and authenticity of the content they consume, knowing it has not been tampered with.

Furthermore, a decentralised identity management system can be established for publishers, ensuring that only verified entities can publish content. This reduces the risk of false information being disseminated by unverified or malicious sources. By creating a secure and tamper-proof digital identity, blockchain helps maintain the credibility of content publishers.

Additionally, blockchain systems can integrate with AI algorithms to provide real-time verification of content. This allows devices to check the blockchain ledger instantly, ensuring the authenticity of the content being accessed. AI can also help flag unverified or suspicious content, further enhancing the trustworthiness of digital media.

Records stored in a blockchain are immutable and can be relied upon as the truth. Using blockchain, any number of parties may collaborate, negotiate, or transact business without reliance on a potentially untrustworthy arbitrator. The decentralised and immutable nature of blockchain systems allows for product tracking to its origin (traceability) and through every step of the supply chain (authenticity).[61]

Using Cybersecurity methodology can help protect information, authenticate the source of that information, and encrypt information at rest and in transit.

The Advanced Encryption Standard (AES) is a symmetric block cipher algorithm that plays a vital role in enhancing cybersecurity and protecting sensitive data.[62] It is implemented in software and hardware worldwide to encrypt information, making it essential for government computer security, cybersecurity, and electronic data protection.[63]

AES uses multiple cryptographic keys, each undergoing multiple rounds of encryption to better safeguard data confidentiality and integrity. It offers stronger security compared to older algorithms like the Data Encryption Standard (DES) due to its incorporation of multiple encryption rounds, making it harder for threat actors to intercept or steal encrypted information through brute-force attacks.

AES provides robust security by incorporating multiple rounds of encryption, making it harder to break and more resistant to brute-force attacks. As an open-source and widely available solution, AES is cost-effective to adopt and implement. AES is a flexible and simple algorithm, suitable for both hardware and software implementation.

AES encryption is widely used across various applications, including data storage, electronic communication, programming libraries, internet browsers, file and disk compression, wireless networks, databases, login credentials, and virtual private networking (VPN).

While research has explored potential attacks on AES encryption, such as related-key attacks, known-key attacks, and side-channel attacks, implementing proper security measures like strong passwords, multifactor authentication, firewalls, and antimalware software can help mitigate these risks.

Cybersecurity and disinformation attacks often employ similar tactics, techniques, and procedures, making it crucial to integrate security protocols from both domains.[64] Historically, these threats have been treated separately, but a defence-in-depth strategy, borrowed from cybersecurity, can be effective in combating disinformation.

This approach involves a chain of human and AI monitors verifying authenticity and fact-checking, intervening before fake news is posted or removing it after the fact. Education is also a prominent method for reducing risk, with efforts made to enhance public awareness of threats like disinformation, similar to cybersecurity awareness training for phishing emails and malware.

Just as businesses have well-defined strategies for dealing with cybercrime, they need to develop rulebooks for responding to disinformation, harnessing tried-and-tested methods from cybersecurity to minimise damage.

Furthermore, cybersecurity has invested heavily in security best practices, developed rigorous frameworks, guidelines, and standards, and focused on private–public collaboration, including threat modelling and global knowledge databases of vulnerabilities and known bugs. Similar efforts are required in the context of disinformation, promoting transparency, cooperation among fact-checkers and researchers, and empowering individuals to critically assess the information they consume online.[65]

Social media platforms employ algorithms to curate and filter content for users.[66] These algorithms are a series of instructions designed to solve specific problems, perform tasks, or make decisions. In the context of social media, algorithms govern the platform's operation, determining how content is filtered, ranked, selected, and recommended to users. Algorithms influence the choices and information users see on social media platforms.

Algorithmic-driven content curation systems, such as the Facebook News Feed and Instagram Feed, monitor user behaviour, interests, and actions to recommend relevant content. For instance, if a user engages with basketball-related content, they are likely to see more of it. These algorithms aim to refine content suggestions by adapting and learning from user interactions, ensuring that the content remains relevant.

Algorithms collect user signals to match them with relevant content. Key signals include those on user engagement. Likes, shares, and comments indicate that users find the content interesting and relevant. Keywords and hashtags provide context and improve content visibility. Posting consistently and at the right time when the audience is active can boost visibility. Newer posts are prioritised over older ones. Accounts followed, interactions, and click-through rates on links signal relevance and content quality. Follower count, consistency, and engagement impact organic reach. Algorithms consider users' locations and demographics when curating content, potentially promoting content to users in similar locations. Different content types, such as videos, images, and text, are treated based on user interaction, with many platforms favouring more engaging formats like videos. Content gaining popularity and shares signals relevance to the algorithm. The duration users spend watching videos (e.g., Instagram Reels, YouTube Shorts).

Without AI, social media would not exist in its current form. AI has played a significant role in developing and curating algorithms to learn about users and make deliberate decisions based on the collected data.

Social media platforms use AI to detect fake news and filter out offensive, harmful, and disrespectful content. For instance, Twitter uses machine learning models, AI-driven algorithms, user reporting, and human moderation teams to identify and flag misinformation. The algorithm analyses the tweet content and account history to fact-check the accuracy of the information shared.

To maintain quality discussions, platforms employ content moderation tools to identify suspicious posts and comments. For example, Reddit uses machine learning models to spot suspicious comments, which are further reviewed by human moderators. Likewise, Facebook uses an AI tool to detect abuse and fraud in posts, images, and videos, with human reviewers stepping in when needed.

The contemporary technological landscape has witnessed unprecedented advancements that have revolutionised the way information is created, consumed, and manipulated.[67] Emerging technologies have paved the way for sophisticated disinformation campaigns, where AI-generated content can blur the lines between fact and fabrication, leaving unsuspecting audiences vulnerable to deception.

However, while technology has fuelled the rise of disinformation, it also holds the key to potential solutions. AI and NLP, once harnessed by disinformation creators, can now be wielded as powerful tools for detection. Machine learning and data analytics empower researchers and fact-checkers with the ability to sift through vast amounts of information, uncovering patterns that reveal traces of disinformation.

The transformative potential of blockchain technology, for example, also presents a promising path towards tamper-resistant information dissemination, safeguarding content from unauthorised alterations and ensuring its provenance. The tamper-proof nature of blockchain ensures that the data presented is authentic, helping to counter misinformation and enhance trust in online information sources.

By analysing networks and user behaviour, researchers can reverse-engineer orchestrated disinformation campaigns and the role of automated bot accounts, enabling the development of targeted counter-strategies. Fortunately, artificial intelligence (AI) engineers and researchers are working towards solutions to combat these issues.[68] For example, significant headway has been made in algorithmic detection of disinformation across social media.

While AI and emerging technologies have made it easier to promote disinformation, these same technologies can actually help detect disinformation and secure identities. Another excellent example is how Twitter is incorporating misinformation guidance into its user experience design. In May, Twitter announced feature enhancements that would help to combat this issue in response to the mass misinformation that was circulating about the pandemic.

Protecting an individual's digital identity is another area of heightened awareness when it comes to thwarting bad actors and rogue governments – and it's another area where technology is helping. Indeed, decentralised ledger technologies (DLTs), including blockchains, can do a lot more than enable the crypto-economy. In fact, some of the most promising impacts these technologies could have is to enable better government infrastructure, for example, by increasing security and interoperability.

Some governments are considering the use of blockchain as a basis of their digital identity frameworks; and at least one country, Estonia, is completely blockchain-enabled. In fact, Estonia has been leading the way in digital government transformation for some time now; and last year Catalonia, Spain, reportedly substantiated plans to create decentralised identity infrastructure, seemingly to facilitate independence.

The author conducted a short interview with a person who had experienced digital hate speech. This emphasised the impact and underscores the importance of ensuring platforms are not exploited to target marginalised people.

Author: Thank you for agreeing to speak with me today. I understand this has been an incredibly challenging experience for you. Can you share how you became a target of digital hate speech and the context surrounding it?

Victim: As a democracy activist in Myanmar, I have been vocal about human rights issues, particularly the plight of the Muslim Rohingya people. Unfortunately, this made me a target for a hate group that aims to incite communal violence and suppress democratic voices. They orchestrated a coordinated campaign of digital hate speech against me, using social media platforms to spread false and malicious accusations.

Author: It's heartbreaking to hear that. Can you describe the nature of the digital hate speech and how it affected you personally?

Victim: The hate speech was relentless and deeply personal. They used fabricated stories, doctored images, and slurs to discredit me and paint me as an enemy of the state. They accused me of being a traitor and incited violence against me. The sheer volume of hate was overwhelming. It felt like a never-ending wave of vitriol, designed to break my spirit and silence my voice.

Author: How did this targeted abuse impact your mental health and daily life?

Victim: The psychological toll was immense. I experienced severe anxiety, depression, and constant fear for my safety. I couldn't sleep, and every notification on my phone sent a jolt of panic through me. I also became paranoid, worried that people I interacted with might be part of the hate group. It was isolating and exhausting. The stress affected my physical health as well; I lost weight and felt constantly drained.

Author: It's clear that the impact was profound. How did you cope with the situation and what steps did you take to protect yourself?

Victim: Initially, I tried to ignore it, hoping it would fade away. But it only intensified. I decided to take a stand. I reported the hate speech to social media platforms, but the response was inadequate. I also reached out to human rights organisations for support and legal advice. They helped me navigate the process and provided resources to enhance my digital security. Additionally, I sought therapy to address the mental health impacts. Having a professional to talk to made a significant difference.

Author: It's clear that the hate group targeted you specifically because of your activism. How do these groups prey on democracy activists?

Victim: These groups are very strategic in their approach. They monitor social media and other platforms to identify activists who are vocal about democracy and human rights. They then use targeted hate speech and misinformation to discredit these activists and create a sense of division and distrust within the community. By spreading false narratives and propaganda, they aim to isolate activists and make them appear as enemies of the state or threats to societal harmony. This isolation makes activists more vulnerable to attacks and harassment.

In terms of recruitment, they capitalise on fear and anger. They exploit existing societal tensions and grievances to rally support for their cause. For instance, they might use inflammatory language and sensationalist content to provoke communal sentiments. They also recruit individuals who are already predisposed to violence or who feel marginalised, offering them a sense of belonging and purpose within the group. The more chaos they can create, the easier it is for them to recruit new members who are drawn to the promise of power and influence.

Author: That sounds incredibly manipulative and dangerous. Did you experience any fears related to communal violence or riots as a result of the hate group's actions?

Victim: The fear of being a target of communal violence was a constant source of anxiety. The hate group didn't just stop at online harassment; they incited others to take violent actions against me and those like me. There were threats of physical harm, and I had to be very cautious about my whereabouts and interactions. The possibility of riots breaking out was always on my mind, especially since the group was skilled at stirring up emotions and causing unrest. I worried not only for my own safety but also for the safety of my family and fellow activists.

Author: It's distressing to hear how far-reaching the impact of such groups can be. How did you and your fellow activists manage to continue your work in the face of these threats?

Victim: It was incredibly challenging, but we were determined to continue our fight for democracy and human rights. We took several measures to protect ourselves. We improved our digital security by using encrypted communication tools and being more cautious about the information we shared online. We also organised ourselves better, creating networks of support where we could quickly alert each other to potential threats and provide assistance.

Community support was crucial. We reached out to international organisations and media to bring attention to the harassment and threats we were facing. This external pressure helped to some extent in holding the hate group accountable and reducing their influence. Additionally, we held peaceful demonstrations and engaged in community dialogues to counteract the hate group's narrative and promote unity and understanding.

Author: It's inspiring to see such resilience in the face of adversity. What message would you like to share with other activists who might be facing similar challenges?

Victim: I would say, first and foremost, stay strong and stay united. Know that you are not alone, and there are many who stand with you in the fight for justice. Take proactive steps to protect your digital and physical security. Reach out to supportive organisations and use their resources. Most importantly, continue to speak out against hate and violence. Your voice is powerful, and every effort you make contributes to a larger movement for change. Together, we can overcome these challenges and work towards a more just and equitable society.

Author: How did the community and your fellow activists respond to your situation?

Victim: The support from my fellow activists and the community was a lifeline. Many reached out with messages of solidarity and support. We organised online campaigns to raise awareness about the issue and counter the false narratives. It was empowering to see people stand with me and condemn the hate speech. It reinforced the importance of unity and collective action in the face of such adversity.

Author: It's inspiring to hear about the solidarity you received. What do you think social media platforms and governments can do to better address the issue of digital hate speech?

Victim: Social media platforms need to take a more proactive and robust approach to moderating content. They should improve their algorithms to detect hate speech and misinformation quickly. Additionally, there should be stronger legal frameworks to hold perpetrators accountable. Governments need to prioritise the protection of human rights and ensure that laws are in place to combat digital hate speech effectively. Education is also crucial. Raising awareness about the impact of hate speech and promoting digital literacy can help prevent such attacks.

Author: What advice would you give to other activists who might be facing similar challenges?

Author: Thank you for sharing your story with such courage and insight. Your resilience is truly commendable, and I believe your experience will help many others who might be going through similar situations.

References

1. Jamalzadeh, S., Mettenbrink, L., Barker, K., González, A.D., Radhakrishnan, S., Johansson, J. and Bessarabova, E., 2024. Weaponized disinformation spread and its impact on multi-commodity critical infrastructure networks. *Reliability Engineering & System Safety*, *243*, p. 109819.
2. https://pmc.ncbi.nlm.nih.gov/articles/PMC7366944/.
3. Arnd-Caddigan, M. (2015). Sherry Turkle: Alone Together: Why We Expect More from Technology and Less from Each Other: Basic Books, New York, 2011, 348 pp, ISBN 978–0465031467 (pbk).
4. Fominaya, C.F., 2024. Mobilizing during the Covid-19 pandemic: From democratic innovation to the political weaponization of disinformation. *American Behavioral Scientist*, *68*(6), pp. 829–852.
5. Markariani, L. and Toradze, M., 2024. Pseudo-positive Information and COVID-19: Reasons behind Sharing Fake News (Georgian Social Media Analysis). *Athens Journal of Mass Media & Communications*, *10*(2).
6. https://www.mercycorps.org/sites/default/files/2020-01/Weaponisation_Social_Media_Brief_Nov2019.pdf.
7. Alvisi, L., Bianchi, J., Tibidò, S. and Zucca, M.V., 2024. Weaponizing Disinformation Against Critical Infrastructures. *arXiv preprint arXiv:2406.08963*.
8. https://www.wbs.ac.uk/news/how-social-media-platforms-fuel-extreme-opinions-and-hate-speech/.
9. https://www.cfr.org/backgrounder/hate-speech-social-media-global-comparisons.
10. https://en.wikipedia.org/wiki/Social_media_in_the_2016_United_States_presidential_election.

11. Pratelli, M., Petrocchi, M., Saracco, F. and De Nicola, R., 2024. Online disinformation in the 2020 US election: swing vs. safe states. *EPJ Data Science*, *13*(1), p. 25.
12. https://cepr.org/voxeu/columns/how-twitter-affected-2016-presidential-election.
13. https://gjia.georgetown.edu/2024/02/02/russia-ukraine-through-the-eyes-of-social-media/.
14. https://www.npr.org/2023/02/28/1159712623/how-russia-is-losing-and-winning-the-information-war-in-ukraine.
15. https://en.unav.edu/web/global-affairs/como-recluta-el-isis-a-sus-miembros.
16. https://www.cfc.forces.gc.ca/259/290/22/305/AlSarayreh.pdf.
17. https://www.amnesty.org/en/latest/news/2022/09/myanmar-facebooks-systems-promoted-violence-against-rohingya-meta-owes-reparations-new-report/.
18. https://freedomhouse.org/article/social-media-are-growing-conduit-electoral-manipulation-and-mass-surveillance.
19. https://www.brookings.edu/articles/misinformation-is-eroding-the-publics-confidence-in-democracy/.
20. https://www.investopedia.com/terms/v/viral-marketing.asp.
21. https://pcsocial.medium.com/the-10-most-successful-organic-viral-marketing-campaigns-f5983e1ed01c.
22. https://www.brookings.edu/articles/transparency-is-essential-for-effective-social-media-regulation/.
23. https://hbr.org/2021/01/social-media-companies-should-self-regulate-now.
24. https://www.mercycorps.org/sites/default/files/2020-01/Weaponisation_Social_Media_Brief_Nov2019.pdf.
25. https://adaptpeacebuilding.org/2019-12-20-the-weaponisation-of-social-media/.
26. https://mogulpress.com/what-is-social-media-regulation-why-do-we-need-regulatory-frameworks/.
27. https://www.cfr.org/backgrounder/hate-speech-social-media-global-comparisons.
28. Amazeen, M.A., Vasquez, R.A., Krishna, A., Ji, Y.G., Su, C.C. and Cummings, J.J., 2024. Missing voices: examining how misinformation-susceptible individuals from underrepresented communities engage, perceive, and combat science misinformation. *Science Communication*, *46*(1), pp. 3–35.

29. Soetekouw, L. and Angelopoulos, S., 2024. Digital resilience through training protocols: Learning to identify fake news on social media. *Information Systems Frontiers*, *26*(2), pp. 459–475.
30. https://adaptpeacebuilding.org/2019-12-20-the-weaponisation-of-social-media/.
31. Schmid, S., Hartwig, K., Cieslinski, R. and Reuter, C., 2024. Digital resilience in dealing with misinformation on social media during COVID-19: A web application to assist users in crises. *Information Systems Frontiers*, *26*(2), pp. 477–499.
32. Hammond, S.P., Polizzi, G. and Bartholomew, K.J., 2023. Using a socio-ecological framework to understand how 8–12-year-olds build and show digital resilience: A multi-perspective and multi-method qualitative study. *Education and Information Technologies*, *28*(4), pp. 3681–3709.
33. Vissenberg, J., d'Haenens, L. and Livingstone, S., 2022. Digital literacy and online resilience as facilitators of young people's well-being?. *European Psychologist*.
34. https://www.mercycorps.org/sites/default/files/2020-01/Weaponisation_Social_Media_Brief_Nov2019.pdf.
35. https://www.brookings.edu/articles/transparency-is-essential-for-effective-social-media-regulation/.
36. https://www.theguardian.com/world/2023/aug/25/how-the-eu-digital-services-act-affects-facebook-google-and-others.
37. https://commission.europa.eu/strategy-and-policy/priorities-2019-2024/europe-fit-digital-age/digital-services-act_en.
38. https://connect.comptia.org/blog/ethical-issues-in-technology.
39. https://ico.org.uk/media/about-the-ico/policies-and-procedures/4021371/social-media-use-policy.pdf.
40. https://www.gov.uk/government/publications/social-media-acceptable-use-policy/slc-social-media-acceptable-use-policy.
41. Raad, A., 2024. Protecting freedom of thought: mitigating technological enablers of disinformation.
42. https://sproutsocial.com/insights/social-media-algorithms/.
43. https://www.isdglobal.org/isd-publications/the-impact-of-counter-narratives/.
44. https://home-affairs.ec.europa.eu/system/files_en?file=2020-09/issue_paper_cn_oct2015_en.pdf.

45. Traberg, C., Morton, T. and van der Linden, S., 2024. Counteracting socially endorsed misinformation through an emotion-fallacy inoculation. *advances. in/psychology*, *2*, p. e765332.
46. https://www.internetmatters.org/issues/fake-news-and-misinformation-advice-hub/learn-about-fake-news-to-support-children/.
47. https://digital-strategy.ec.europa.eu/en/policies/online-disinformation.
48. https://www.telefonica.com/en/communication-room/blog/technology-to-combat-fake-news/.
49. Mukherjee, A., 2024. Safeguarding Marketing Research: The Generation, Identification, and Mitigation of AI-Fabricated Disinformation. *arXiv preprint arXiv:2403.14706.*
50. https://www.theinnovationmode.com/the-innovation-blog/misinformation-online-a-solution-powered-by-state-of-the-art-tech.
51. https://www.forbes.com/sites/forbestechcouncil/2024/02/12/the-role-of-humans-and-ai-in-social-medias-battle-against-misinformation/.
52. https://www.gov.uk/government/publications/the-role-of-ai-in-addressing-misinformation-on-social-media-platforms.
53. Herman, B.C., Poor, S., Clough, M.P., Rao, A., Kidd, A., De Jesús, D. and Varghese, D., 2024. It's not just a science thing: Educating future STEM professionals through mis/disinformation responsive instruction. *Journal of Research in Science Teaching*.
54. https://annotationbox.com/social-media-content-filtering/.
55. https://www.mdpi.com/2673-5172/4/2/43.
56. https://link.springer.com/article/10.1007/s10479-022-05015-5.
57. https://www.ncbi.nlm.nih.gov/pmc/articles/PMC9628472/.
58. https://medium.com/@konradgulla/embracing-blockchain-for-authenticity-ensuring-the-truth-in-digital-content-19584f6dc025.
59. https://modulusglobal.com/solutions/blockchain/.
60. https://medium.com/@Kalima_KLX/embrace-the-proof-of-origin-poo-of-your-data-and-documents-thanks-to-kalima-blockchain-fff90dfe68c3.
61. https://www.ibm.com/blog/enterprise-blockchain-for-verifying-product-authenticity/.
62. https://www.simplilearn.com/tutorials/cryptography-tutorial/aes-encryption.

63. https://www.techtarget.com/searchsecurity/definition/Advanced-Encryption-Standard.
64. https://istari-global.com/insights/spotlight/disinformation-is-a-cybersecurity-threat/.
65. https://data.europa.eu/en/publications/datastories/leveraging-open-data-tackle-cyber-disinformation.
66. https://sproutsocial.com/insights/social-media-algorithms/.
67. https://edam.org.tr/en/cyber-governance-digital-democracy/the-role-of-technology-new-methods-of-information-manipulation-and-disinformation.
68. https://www.thomsonreuters.com/en-us/posts/legal/ai-battling-disinformation/.

CHAPTER 5

ISIS Radicalisation: A Digital Strategy of Weaponising Grievance

ISIS, the Islamic State of Iraq and Syria, emerged as a formidable force, leveraging digital disinformation tactics to spread its radical ideology and facilitate radicalisation of vulnerable individuals across the globe.[1] This terrorist organisation has adeptly harnessed the power of social media and online platforms, employing sophisticated techniques to disseminate propaganda, recruit followers, and amplify its influence.[2]

Ralstin (2024) contends ISIS has inflicted terror onto civilians through ransoms, kidnapping, beheadings, mass shootings, and bombings. These acts of terror are directly funded through the internet. They use this tool as a mechanism to spread online propaganda and radicalise people, in addition to terrorising civilians with cyberterrorism to collect money.[3]

Rakhma et al. (2024) argue ISIS emphasises the importance of *winning hearts and minds* in their operational strategy. Their objective is to draw sympathisers, propagate their objectives and ideology, and allocate substantial resources. They have utilised TikTok as a platform to garner attention and disseminate propaganda, with the aim of promoting their organisation and recruiting new terrorists. ISIS propaganda on TikTok poses a significant threat to national security. It has the potential to sway the younger generation towards supporting extremist and terrorist ideologies. The aim of their message is to incite hatred, division, and social mistrust towards the state, government, and legitimate leaders.[4]

T. Singh, *Digital Psychological Warfare*,
https://doi.org/10.1007/978-3-032-15294-7_5

The evolution of ISIS' digital disinformation strategy and its psychological impact on target audiences[5] have become crucial areas of examination. We can consider the key figures involved in these online operations, the technological tools and techniques employed, and notable disinformation campaigns that have shaped the global narrative. Additionally, we can explore strategies for detection and prevention, while assessing the broader impact on society and politics, and future trends in this realm.

The psychological impact of ISIS propaganda on target audiences is significant. Propaganda disseminated by ISIS aims to instil fear and panic within target audiences. By introducing generative AI in their propaganda efforts, ISIS can generate a false reality, allowing them to sow chaos and disorder through misinformation and disinformation. Uploading AI-generated content on social media platforms may increase the reach of their disinformation campaigns, as the content can be rapidly shared by millions of followers.[6]

ISIS propaganda often exploits emotionally resonant narratives and manipulates people's attitudes and emotions. For instance, they may use synthetic (fake) images or videos depicting wounded victims or children to evoke an emotional response and impact the audience's perceptions. Having this worldwide effect, social media could be identified as a powerful weapon in today's disinformation wars, whereby people can no longer rely on what they read or hear due to the potential for AI-generated misinformation.[7]

Generative AI presents new avenues for ISIS to amplify their radicalisation and recruitment efforts. Connected with the recruitment process is the possibility of exploiting social media, where AI could be used to amplify propaganda content on various digital platforms, facilitating the spread of extremist ideologies and recruitment of new followers. This could involve encrypted communication channels or other innovative methods enabled by AI technologies.

ISIS adapts conventional recruiting techniques to the digital information environment, allowing for more targeted campaigning, emotionally resonant messaging, and personalised exchanges between operatives and potential recruits. Their tactics include targeting isolated or disenfranchised individuals, highlighting themes of inclusion and participation, and gradually exposing them to more radical ideas.

The Islamic State (ISIS) has evolved its digital disinformation tactics over time, adapting to counter measures taken by social media platforms and leveraging new technologies to spread its propaganda.

In its early days, ISIS employed relatively simple techniques to disseminate disinformation online. They hijacked trending hashtags during major events like the 2014 World Cup to gain visibility and reach a broader audience for their propaganda videos.[8] They also created accounts with strong privacy settings, which would then disseminate content through numerous smaller, unofficial accounts using hashtags, evading detection by Twitter's algorithms.

ISIS developed apps like 'The Dawn of Glad Tidings' to keep its followers updated on the group's activities, allowing them to post tweets, links, hashtags, and images in a way that avoided triggering spam detection. They also used shock tactics, such as the beheading videos of journalists like James Foley, to garner international media coverage and introduce the group to a wider audience.[9]

As social media platforms improved their content moderation efforts, ISIS adapted by employing more sophisticated tactics. They created fake videos mimicking the look and feel of mainstream news outlets like CNN and Al Jazeera, complete with logos, tickers, and professional-quality footage. These videos were disseminated through channels falsely branded as those news organisations, attempting to build a 'fake ecosystem of news'.

ISIS has also leveraged emerging technologies like emojis to bypass content filters, using them in place of words like 'weapon' or 'explosion' to champion their attacks. They have experimented with AI-generated news anchors and graphics to create more realistic-looking propaganda.

Moreover, ISIS has rebranded its messaging to appeal to wider audiences, projecting an image of inclusiveness and belonging rather than solely targeting extremist demographics. Their use of social media allows for targeted campaigning, emotionally resonant narratives, and personalised exchanges with potential recruits.

The Islamic State (ISIS) has had several prominent leaders who have played crucial roles in shaping and executing its digital operations and propaganda strategies. One of the most notable figures is Abu Bakr al-Baghdadi, who became the leader of the Islamic State of Iraq (ISI) in April 2010 after the deaths of its previous leaders.[10] In June 2014, al-Baghdadi announced the establishment of a caliphate stretching from Aleppo in Syria to Diyala in Iraq, renaming the group the Islamic State.

Another influential leader in ISIS' digital operations was Abu Muhammad al-Adnani, who served as the group's spokesman and one of its longest-serving leaders until his death in a US airstrike in August

2016. Al-Adnani played a vital role in disseminating ISIS' propaganda and recruiting efforts through various online channels.

In addition to its top leadership, ISIS has relied on several influential propagandists to amplify its message and attract new recruits through digital platforms. One such figure is Aqsa Mahmood, a British woman who played a leading role among the women of ISIS. Mahmood herself was slowly radicalised as a teenager by articles and posts she read online, and her online presence showed several hundred posts about life in the group, suspected of playing a major role in the recruitment of many young girls from the West.[11]

The Halane sisters, Zahra and Salma, also drew attention through their activity on social media. Originally from Manchester, the sisters, who were 16 when they left their homes, married ISIS jihadists in Raqqa, Syria. After their husbands were killed, the young widows continued to live in Raqqa, posting pictures of their daily lives, including practising target shooting while wearing traditional Islamic attire. Their online presence and portrayal of life within ISIS made them inspiring role models for others seeking to join the group.

ISIS has leveraged various technological tools and techniques to amplify its digital disinformation campaigns. ISIS has experimented with deepfake technology, which involves using artificial intelligence (AI) algorithms to generate synthetic media content like photos, videos, and audio clips that can convincingly depict events or individuals in a misleading manner.[12] Deepfake photos can create realistic profile pictures for inauthentic social media accounts, while deepfake videos use AI to map one person's face onto another's body. Audio deepfakes, or 'voice clones', can produce new sentences as part of video deepfakes using just a few hours of reference audio. ISIS has also explored AI-generated text to create realistic-looking propaganda content with relative ease.

ISIS employs bot networks and troll farms to amplify its disinformation campaigns through tactics like astroturfing and flooding. Chan (2024) suggests *Astroturfing* involves posting overwhelming amounts of content with similar messaging from numerous inauthentic accounts, created by automated bots or professional troll groups, to create the impression of widespread grassroots support for a narrative while concealing its true origin.[13] Flooding, also known as 'firehosing', involves spamming social media posts and comments with the intention of shaping narratives or drowning out opposing viewpoints using fake and automated accounts. These tactics, enabled by AI and advanced technologies, allow ISIS to manipulate the information environment and influence public opinion at speed and scale.

ISIS has also used emojis to bypass content filters on social media platforms, substituting emojis for words like 'weapon', 'explosion', and 'rocket' to champion its terrorist attacks across the Middle East and beyond. This tactic has allowed ISIS to spread hate speech and violent content on Facebook pages posing as mainstream media outlets, accumulating hundreds of thousands of likes, shares, and comments.

ISIS has proven particularly effective in its use of Twitter to disseminate disinformation campaigns. Despite Twitter's efforts to remove ISIS' official accounts in 2014, the group has developed coping mechanisms to maintain control over information flows on the platform. ISIS established accounts with strong privacy settings, whose content was then disseminated through numerous smaller, unofficial accounts using hashtags. The group also utilised the app 'The Dawn of Glad Tidings' to keep followers updated on its activities, allowing ISIS social media operators to post tweets, links, hashtags, and images in a way that avoided triggering Twitter's spam-detection algorithms. During the March on Mosul, this tactic led to the emanation of approximately 44,000 tweets. ISIS also hijacked trending hashtags during the 2014 World Cup, such as #Brazil2014, to appear in related Twitter searches and gain access to a broader audience for disseminating propaganda videos.

ISIS has leveraged disinformation campaigns to promote false narratives and conspiracy theories, such as the 'Pizzagate' conspiracy.[14] This conspiracy falsely alleged that Hillary Clinton was involved in a child sex ring operating out of a Washington, D.C. pizza parlour. Despite its fictitious nature, the story gained significant traction on social media, with one individual even travelling to the pizza parlour with an assault weapon to investigate the claims. Such disinformation campaigns can enable discriminatory and inflammatory ideas to enter public discourse, normalise prejudices, and potentially catalyse violence.

ISIS has employed bot networks and troll farms to amplify its disinformation campaigns through tactics like astroturfing and flooding. Astroturfing involves posting overwhelming amounts of content with similar messaging from numerous inauthentic accounts, created by automated bots or professional troll groups, to create the impression of widespread grassroots support for a narrative while concealing its true origin. Flooding, also known as 'firehosing', involves spamming social media posts and comments with the intention of shaping narratives or drowning out opposing viewpoints using fake and automated accounts. These tactics, enabled by AI and advanced technologies, allow ISIS to manipulate the information environment and influence public opinion at speed and scale.

ISIS propaganda aims to polarise public opinion by portraying the world in stark black-and-white terms, with ISIS as the sole defender of the true faith against a corrupt and decadent West.[15] Their messaging seeks to create division and erode social cohesion by disseminating incendiary rhetoric and distorting facts on the ground. The goal is to obfuscate accountability, undermine community acceptance, and incite panic and violence.

ISIS propaganda also aims to influence elections by stoking fear and division, portraying democratic governments as weak and ineffectual in the face of the ISIS threat. The proliferation of ISIS disinformation through social media platforms allows for the rapid dissemination of false narratives and conspiracy theories, which can normalise prejudices and potentially catalyse violence. For instance, the 'Pizzagate' conspiracy falsely alleged Hillary Clinton's involvement in a child sex ring, gaining significant traction on social media despite its fictitious nature.

Moreover, ISIS leverages bot networks and troll farms to amplify its disinformation campaigns through tactics like astroturfing and flooding. Astroturfing involves posting overwhelming amounts of content from numerous inauthentic accounts to create the impression of widespread grassroots support for a narrative. Flooding involves spamming social media posts and comments to shape narratives or drown out opposing viewpoints using fake and automated accounts. These tactics, enabled by AI and advanced technologies, allow ISIS to manipulate the information environment and influence public opinion at speed and scale.

The ultimate goal of ISIS propaganda is to destabilise societies and undermine confidence in democratic institutions, paving the way for the establishment of an ISIS caliphate. Their innovative use of digitally enabled tools and methods distorts facts and spreads incendiary rhetoric, eroding social cohesion and potentially inciting violence.

Saleh et al. (2024) conclude that active *psychological inoculation* boosts attitudinal resistance against extremist persuasion techniques used by violent extremists like ISIS. They developed and tested a novel online game, Radicalise, which aims to combat the effectiveness of online recruitment strategies used by extremist organisations, based on the principles of active psychological inoculation. The game 'inoculates' players by exposing them to severely weakened doses of the key techniques and methods used to recruit and radicalise individuals via social media platforms: identifying vulnerable individuals, gaining their trust, isolating them from their community and pressuring them into committing a criminal act in the name of the extremist organisation. They conducted a randomised controlled experiment to measure participants' ability and confidence in assessing the manipulativeness of fictitious WhatsApp messages making use of an extremist manipulation technique before and after playing. The second measured participants' ability to identify what factors make an individual vulnerable to extremist recruitment before and after playing. They found that playing Radicalise significantly improved participants' ability and confidence in spotting manipulative messages and the characteristics associated with vulnerability.[16]

Artificial intelligence (AI) and machine learning (ML) techniques have emerged as powerful tools in the fight against digital disinformation and terrorist content online. These technologies can process vast quantities of data and identify patterns and correlations that may be imperceptible to human analysts.[17] They are being leveraged by law enforcement and counter-terrorism agencies to counter the terrorist use of the internet and social media.

One key application of AI and ML is automated content moderation and takedown. Major internet service providers like Google, Facebook, and Twitter rely on machine learning algorithms to detect and remove illegal, dubious, and undesirable content, including terrorist propaganda.[18] These algorithms are also effective in screening for and identifying fake bot accounts used to amplify disinformation campaigns through techniques like astroturfing and flooding.

However, while AI and ML offer significant advantages in terms of speed and scale, their accuracy in detecting disinformation still lags behind human capabilities. Fully automated fact-checking remains a distant goal, and social media platforms continue to employ hybrid models that combine AI for repetitive tasks with human review for more nuanced cases.

Human oversight and intervention are crucial components of any strategy to counter digital disinformation and terrorist content online. While AI and ML can automate many tasks, they are not infallible and can make errors or exhibit biases that require human intervention to correct.

Human moderators play a vital role in reviewing user content, particularly in cases where judgement calls impact freedom of expression. They can scrutinise the design, development, deployment, and use of AI applications and apply corrective measures when necessary. In 2018, Facebook employed 7,500 human moderators to review user content alongside its AI systems.

Moreover, a comprehensive strategy to counter digital disinformation and terrorist content online must involve a wide range of stakeholders, from intelligence organisations to civil society organisations. These stakeholders can collaborate to identify threats, assess their potential impact, and develop mitigation strategies. Mitigation efforts may include integrating referral or warning systems, establishing crisis response plans, and addressing online hate speech and extremist narratives.

By combining the speed and scale of AI and ML with human oversight and a multi-stakeholder approach, governments, private sector companies, and aid organisations can respond to the threat of weaponised information on social media with actions and programmes that match the sophistication of the challenge.

Generative AI models capable of creating unique content from simple prompts are already being deployed for political purposes, taking disinformation campaigns into strange new realms.[19] Campaigns have circulated fake images and audio targeting candidates, including AI-generated campaign ads and deepfake videos mimicking real-life news footage. The rise of tools like ChatGPT, which generates text, has made these technologies accessible to a mass market, demonstrating how easy it is to leverage them.

Text and images generated by AI have the potential for higher actual impact in election scenarios because they can be more subtle and longer-lasting. While humans have always been able to create propaganda, the scale enabled by AI is unprecedented. The same applies to images, where AI can automate and amplify their creation at an unparalleled level.

Terrorist groups could use generative AI to create hallucinations through diverse strategies like psychological warfare, false flag operations, or propaganda to influence people's behaviour. Hallucinations refer to situations where the AI system generates unexpected, unusual, or nonsensical outputs that seem coherent at first glance but contain contradictions or improbable combinations upon closer inspection.

One major concern is the potential for intensive propaganda and disinformation campaigns with the click of a button. When combined with advancements in targeted advertising and other effective propaganda measures, generative AI forecasts a transformation in the speed, scale, and credibility of terrorism influence operations. This could lead to a higher capability to influence people's behaviours and a gap in distinguishing between real and fake online content, allowing terrorist groups to share their ideologies worldwide.

Generative AI could also enable more efficient and tailored propaganda by producing synthetic images, videos, or audio aligned with terrorist organisations' values. This could increase the breadth of propaganda, intensify messages, and affect people's attitudes and emotions, such as using fake pictures of wounded victims or children to have an emotional impact. Uploading such AI-generated content on social media platforms could rapidly spread disinformation as it is shared by millions of followers.

Recent examples include the Islamic State publishing a guide on securely using generative AI tools, a pro-al-Qaeda outlet creating posters likely made with AI, and far-right figures advising others on using AI-generated images to create extremist memes. Pro-Islamic State affiliates have also used generative AI to translate Arabic propaganda into other languages.

Moreover, generative AI could enable ISIS to produce tailored propaganda aligned with their values, such as synthetic images, videos, or audio designed to resonate with specific target audiences. Children, who may be more susceptible to such content, could potentially be exploited, as there have been reported situations of children seeking support through AI chatbots, presenting opportunities for terrorist groups to intervene.

By leveraging generative AI, ISIS could reproduce an individual's likeness, producing illegal content that could be used for propaganda and recruitment purposes. This could further amplify the spread of terrorist materials and potentially influence individuals, particularly those who may be vulnerable or lack critical consumption skills.

A discussion was held with a person who had experienced extreme content and radicalisation online. This was helpful in preparing this chapter and empahasising the point that this content is accessible and this could happen to anyone. More needs to be done to prevent access to extreme content and provide support mechanisms for those who do encounter it.

Author: Thank you for agreeing to share your story today. I know it must be difficult, but your experience can provide valuable insights. Can you start by telling us how you first encountered extremist content online?

Victim: It all started quite innocently. I lost my job and was spending more time than usual online. I was feeling isolated and searching for a sense of purpose and community. I stumbled upon some forums and social media groups that discussed various ideological issues. At first, it seemed like a place where I could express my frustrations and find like-minded people. But gradually, the content became more extreme and started promoting violent ideologies.

Author: It's alarming how quickly that can happen. How did you find yourself becoming more conditioned to these views?

Victim: It was a gradual process. The content was very engaging and persuasive. They used emotional and psychological tactics to draw me in – highlighting injustices, playing on my fears, and offering seemingly clear solutions. Over time, I started to consume more and more of this content, and my views became increasingly radical. I found myself agreeing with extreme ideologies that I would have previously found hateful. I also began to isolate myself from friends and family who didn't share these views, which only deepened my immersion in the radical community.

Author: I'd like to delve a bit deeper into why the extremist content and ideology of ISIS was so appealing to you at that time. Can you describe what aspects of their propaganda drew you in?

Victim: The propaganda was very sophisticated and well-crafted. The slickly produced videos were especially captivating. They used high-quality production techniques, dramatic music, and powerful imagery to create an emotional and compelling narrative. The content was appealing and designed to evoke strong feelings of anger, injustice, and a desire for change. The 'us vs. them' narrative was particularly persuasive. It framed the world in a very black-and-white way, making it easy to identify with the believers and see the non-believers as the enemy.

Author: It's fascinating how they used media to manipulate emotions. How did this narrative influence your perspective?

Victim: The jihadi narrative made it easy to blame the West for everything wrong in my life and the world. It provided a clear and simple explanation for complex issues, which was very appealing. The narrative painted the West as the source of all evil and oppression, and it positioned ISIS as the righteous force fighting against this perceived injustice. This mindset made me feel like I was part of a larger struggle, a mission to challenge a more powerful adversary. It gave me a sense of purpose and belonging that I was missing in my life.

Author: That sense of purpose can be very powerful. What other elements of the extremist content appealed to you and contributed to your radicalisation?

Victim: The content often included stories of heroism and martyrdom, portraying those who fought for the cause as heroes and martyrs. This glorification of violence and sacrifice resonated with me, making me feel like I could be part of something greater than myself. The music and chants used in the videos also had a hypnotic effect, reinforcing the emotional impact of the message. Additionally, the online community was very active and supportive. They created an environment where I felt accepted and valued, which was something I desperately needed at the time.

Author: How did you end up being reported to the Prevent deradicalisation programme, and what was your experience like?

Victim: My behaviour had changed noticeably, and I think it worried the people around me. I was more aggressive, withdrawn, and focused on these radical ideas. A concerned friend reported me to the authorities, and I was referred to the Prevent programme. At first, I was resistant and didn't think I needed help. But through the programme, I was able to talk to counsellors who helped me see the manipulation and brainwashing tactics that had been used on me. They guided me to critically evaluate my beliefs and understand the underlying psychological manipulation I had been subjected to.

Author: How did you begin to step away from these extremist views, and what role did the Prevent programme play in that process?

Victim: The Prevent programme played a crucial role in my deradicalisation. It provided me with the tools and support to question and dismantle the extremist beliefs I had adopted. The counsellors helped me reconnect with my family and friends, which was vital in rebuilding my sense of community and belonging. I also engaged in activities that promoted critical thinking and empathy, which helped me develop a more balanced perspective. Over time, I began to distance myself from the extremist content and focus on positive, constructive ways to address my concerns.

Author: How did you begin to recognise the manipulation and start to question these beliefs?

Victim: The counsellors helped me see how my emotions had been exploited and how the content was designed to manipulate my thoughts and feelings. They encouraged me to evaluate the information I was consuming and question the motives behind it. Engaging in discussions and activities that promoted critical thinking and empathy helped me see the world in a more nuanced way. Reconnecting with my family and friends also provided a different perspective and support system that helped me step away from the extremist views.

Author: It's inspiring to see how far you've come. Now that you're an advocate against extremism, what message would you like to share with others who might be vulnerable to online radicalisation?

Victim: My message is simple: seek support and stay connected with those who care about you. It's easy to fall into the trap of online radicalisation, especially when you're feeling isolated or searching for meaning. But there are positive communities and resources out there that can help you find purpose without resorting to extremism. Stay critical and question everything you see online. Extremist content is designed to exploit your emotions and provide simple answers to complex problems. Seek out multiple perspectives and engage with positive, constructive communities. If you find yourself being drawn into extremist ideologies, don't hesitate to reach out for help. There are resources and people who can support you and guide you back to a healthier path. Remember, you don't have to face this alone, and there is always a way out. If you or someone you know is starting to engage with extremist content, don't hesitate to reach out for help. Programmes like Prevent are there to support you and guide you back to a healthier path. And remember, questioning and evaluating what you see online is crucial – don't accept things at face value.

Author: Thank you for sharing your story with such openness and honesty.

References

1. https://www.rand.org/topics/the-islamic-state-terrorist-organisation.html.
2. https://www.sciencespo.fr/kuwait-program/wp-content/uploads/2018/05/KSP_Paper_Award_Spring_2016_PELLERIN_Clara.pdf.
3. Ralstin, G., 2024. The Rise of ISIS: A Growing Threat to the World. *Pepperdine Policy Review*, *16*(1), p. 8.
4. Rakhma, S., Widodo, P. and Reksoprodjo, A.H.S., 2024. TikTok and Islamic State of Iraq and Syiria (ISIS) Propaganda. *International Journal Of Humanities Education and Social Sciences*, *3*(6).
5. https://www.jstor.org/stable/26343748.
6. https://www.mercycorps.org/sites/default/files/2020-01/Weaponisation_Social_Media_FINAL_Nov2019.pdf.
7. https://www.icct.nl/publication/exploitation-generative-ai-terrorist-groups.

8. https://www.politico.eu/article/islamic-state-disinformation-social-media/.
9. https://www.wired.com/story/isis-created-fake-cnn-and-al-jazeera-broadcasts/.
10. https://www.wilsoncenter.org/article/timeline-the-rise-spread-and-fall-the-islamic-state.
11. https://reutersinstitute.politics.ox.ac.uk/sites/default/files/research/files/Isis%2520and%2520Propaganda-%2520How%2520Isis%2520Exploits%2520Women.pdf.
12. https://www.cisa.gov/sites/default/files/publications/tactics-of-disinformation_508.pdf.
13. Chan, J., 2024. Online astroturfing: A problem beyond disinformation. *Philosophy & Social Criticism*, *50*(3), pp. 507–528.
14. https://www.brookings.edu/articles/how-to-combat-fake-news-and-disinformation/.
15. https://academic.oup.com/book/35146/chapter/299345489.
16. Saleh, N.F., Roozenbeek, J.O.N., Makki, F.A., McClanahan, W.P. and Van Der Linden, S., 2024. Active inoculation boosts attitudinal resistance against extremist persuasion techniques: A novel approach towards the prevention of violent extremism. *Behavioural Public Policy*, *8*(3), pp. 548–571.
17. https://www.un.org/counterterrorism/sites/www.un.org.counterterrorism/files/countering-terrorism-online-with-ai-uncct-unicri-report-web.pdf.
18. https://brill.com/view/journals/shrs/29/1-4/article-p55_55.xml?language=en.
19. https://www.theguardian.com/us-news/2023/jul/20/artificial-intelligence-us-elections.

CHAPTER 6

Artificial Intelligence: Invasion of Privacy, Identity Theft, and Manipulation

The rise of artificial intelligence (AI) and deepfake technologies has brought new complexities to the issue of digital disinformation. In recent years, disinformation on social media has reached an unprecedented scale, fuelled by malicious actors exploiting AI capabilities to create and amplify false or manipulated content for political, ideological, or financial gains.[1] This phenomenon poses significant challenges to society, impacting everything from public discourse to democratic processes.[2]

Husana et al. (2024) argues the case for more effective regulations to limit the use of AI to prevent digital crimes. They argue the Facebook-Cambridge Analytics Scandal raises concerns about the security of personal information on digital platforms.[3]

While defining the boundaries of disinformation remains contentious, it is clear that AI plays a pivotal role in both enabling and combating this insidious problem. We must consider the intricate relationship between AI and digital disinformation and its implications. We can consider this relationship through real-world case studies, and consider potential solutions for safeguarding truth in the digital age.

AI-powered disinformation campaigns have been a reality for many years. The age of information enabled the age of disinformation. Powered by the speed and volume of the internet, disinformation has emerged as an instrument of strategic competition and domestic political warfare. It is used by both state and non-state actors to shape public opinion,

T. Singh, *Digital Psychological Warfare*,
https://doi.org/10.1007/978-3-032-15294-7_6

sow chaos, and erode societal trust. Artificial intelligence (AI), specifically machine learning (ML), is poised to amplify disinformation campaigns – influence operations that involve covert efforts to intentionally spread false or misleading information.

Silva and Vaz (2024) claim these AI-powered disinformation campaigns are hugely damaging and affect public decisions, adherence to policies, prestige of institutions, perception of reality, consumption, and public health. They insist this form of insidious AI-enabled disinformation should be treated as a public problem and incorporated into the public policy research agenda, contributing to the development of strategies to mitigate its effects on government actions.[4]

Truong et al. (2024) argue malicious actors use AI to amplify disinformation targeting specific vulnerable communities. The consequences of such operations are difficult to evaluate due to the challenges posed by collecting data and carrying out ethical experiments that would influence online communities. They find that the presence of hub accounts, a hallmark of social media, exacerbates the vulnerabilities of communities to manipulation.[5]

A wide array of media can now be generated or altered with artificial intelligence, sometimes mimicking real people, often very convincingly. These kinds of deepfakes are cropping up on the internet, particularly on social media. AI-generated fake intimate images of pop star Taylor Swift recently led to X temporarily blocking all searches of the singer. And it's not just celebrities whose likeness is faked: deepfakes of news presenters and politicians are also making the rounds.

Creating AI-generated images has never been easier. With popular and easily accessible tools such as Midjourney, OpenAI's DALL-E, and Microsoft's Copilot Designer, users can obtain images for their prompts in a matter of seconds. DALL-E doesn't allow users to create images of real people and Microsoft's option prohibits 'deceptive impersonation'. Midjourney only mentions 'offensive or inflammatory images of celebrities or public figures' as examples of content that would breach its community guidelines. Violent and pornographic images are also barred from all of these platforms.

Other tools do allow for a wider range of creation and some people are using them. Spanish collective United Unknown describes itself as a group of 'visual guerrilla, video and image creators'. They use deepfakes to create satirical images. Stable Diffusion is so far the only one among the main AI image generators that is open-source, meaning its models can be downloaded and modified, allowing users more freedom in what and who they can depict.

AI-generated images and videos represent a potential danger in the context of elections. But some, including the BBC's disinformation reporter Marianna Spring, are more concerned about audio and its role in disinformation. AI fake audios and videos emerged in India ahead of the 2024 general election, with an example being videos of Manoj Tiwari, a member of parliament for the ruling BJP, addressing audiences in three languages: Hindi, Haryanvi, and English.

Deepfakes have emerged as a prominent form of AI-generated disinformation. Deepfakes involve manipulating or altering visual or auditory information to create convincing fake content, such as videos that replace one person's face with another's.[6] These fabricated videos can be created with malicious intent to deceive viewers and are becoming increasingly realistic and difficult to distinguish from genuine recordings or images. Common forms of deepfakes include face re-enactment, where advanced software manipulates the features of a real person's face. Face generation is prevalent, where software creates entirely new images of faces using data from many real faces, but which do not reflect a real person. Speech synthesis is common, where software models someone's voice to generate fabricated audio.[7]

Deepfakes have already been used to create realistic 'revenge pornography' involving celebrities and members of the public. They are also being used to discredit politicians and business leaders or defraud companies, posing threats ranging from identity theft and privacy concerns to reputational damage and eroding trust in media.

One prominent example involved Venezuelan state media outlets disseminating pro-government messages through AI-generated videos of news anchors from a non-existent international English-language channel.[8] These deepfake videos were produced using Synthesia, a company that specialises in custom deepfakes.

With major elections in the UK, USA, and EU in 2024 alone, deepfakes are increasingly relied upon spread as malicious actors seek to exploit their capabilities to sway public opinion, erode trust in democratic institutions, and spread misinformation about politicians.

Large language models (LLMs) have the ability to create high-volume, human-like texts, which can be leveraged to generate persuasive misinformation.[9] As AI-generated content becomes increasingly indistinguishable from human-written information, and in some cases even perceived as more credible, the risks of synthetic text generation for disinformation remain under-explored.

Once LLMs are used for generating misinformation, the ease and speed of producing high-volume text can significantly magnify views that are otherwise fringe or outright misleading, creating an illusion of a majority perspective.

It has been shown that AI tools are capable of creating deepfakes of political leaders by adapting their actual video, audio, and pictures. For example, a deepfake video surfaced in which Barack Obama was seen calling Donald Trump 'a total and complete dipshit', highlighting the dangers of deepfakes in sowing discord in society and creating chaos in public discourse.

The use of AI in disinformation campaigns is not only plausible but already underway. Powered by computing, ML algorithms excel at harnessing data and finding patterns that are difficult for humans to observe. The data-rich environment of modern online existence creates a terrain ideally suited for ML techniques to precisely target individuals. Language generation capabilities and the tools that enable deepfakes are already capable of manufacturing viral disinformation at scale and empowering digital impersonation.

The same technologies, paired with human operators, can enable social bots to mimic human online behaviour and to troll humans with precisely tailored messages.

These risks may be exacerbated by several trends: the blurring lines between foreign and domestic influence operations, the outsourcing of these operations to private companies that provide influence as a service, and the conflict over distinguishing harmful disinformation and protected speech.

Part of the risk in Mexico is the high percentage of people without formal education, which often leads to problems in identifying mis- and disinformation. A similar issue exists in India. The disparity between India's internet penetration and the population's literacy rate could lead to more people not having the tools to understand these nuances. AI might also convince Indian women to shy away from speaking openly about their political views. Many women have seen that AI has been used to generate photographs of them in sexual positions, which is very objectionable in a patriarchal society like India. Some women may choose to step back from being in the public eye in the face of this threat.

At its best, technology fosters connection, creativity, and activism. But whether it's a single deepfake, a major influence operation deployed with generative AI, or social media feeds made even more addictive through machine learning, the rollout of AI will challenge regulators, captivate the public, and shape lasting narratives ahead of our policymakers' ability to catch up.

Generative artificial intelligence (GAI) adds a new dimension to the problem of disinformation. Freely available and largely unregulated tools make it possible for anyone to generate false information and fake content in vast quantities. These include imitating the voices of real people and creating photos and videos that are indistinguishable from real ones.

We are seeing a whole range of different disinformation created by GAI, from fully AI-generated fake news websites to fake Joe Biden robocalls telling Democrats not to vote. With GAI, the volume of disinformation potentially becomes infinite rendering fact-checking an insufficient tool. As the marginal costs of the production of disinformation fall towards zero, the costs of dissemination are also nearly zero thanks to social media.

Generative AI is the first technology to enter an area that was previously reserved for humans: the autonomous production of content in any form, and the understanding and creation of language and meaning. And this is precisely what links generative AI to the topic of disinformation – the fact that, today, it is often impossible to tell if content originates from a human or a machine, and if we can trust what we read, see, or hear.

Media users are beginning to understand that something is broken in their relationship with media and are confused. 'Some of the indicators that we have historically used to decide we should trust a piece of information have become distorted', Vinton G. Cerf, known as one of the 'fathers of the internet', said in a 2024 video podcast by the international law firm Freshfields Bruckhaus Deringer.

Trust in democratic processes and institutions is eroding. The more polluted our information ecosystem becomes with synthetic text, the harder it will be to find trustworthy sources of information, and the harder it will be to trust them when we've found them. UN Secretary General Antonio Guterres sees this as an 'existential risk to humanity'.

Elections and generative AI have a special connection. This is because the actors involved in elections always pursue specific goals: to either win power for their allies or themselves or to influence a foreign country's political landscape. GAI enables such actors to create 'unreality', and it's becoming a weapon in information warfare and influence operations. Such campaigns are mostly coordinated, concerted, evaluated, measured, and funded by political or foreign actors.

Artificial intelligence (AI) has turbocharged the generation and spread of disinformation in recent years.[10] Governments, political actors, and malicious entities around the world are leveraging AI to manipulate public opinion by generating texts, images, and videos containing false or misleading information.

One prominent example involved Venezuelan state media outlets disseminating pro-government messages through AI-generated videos of news anchors from a non-existent international English-language channel. These deepfake videos were produced using Synthesia, a company that specialises in custom deepfakes. Similarly, in the USA, AI-manipulated videos and images of political leaders, such as a video depicting President Biden making transphobic comments and an image of Donald Trump hugging Anthony Fauci, have circulated on social media.

AI-powered tools include Midjourney, OpenAI's DALL-E, and Microsoft's Copilot Designer. These have made it easier than ever to generate fake images.[11] While these platforms have implemented measures to prevent the creation of violent, pornographic, or deceptive content, their guidelines are not foolproof. For instance, Midjourney only prohibits 'offensive or inflammatory images of celebrities or public figures', leaving room for exploitation. Moreover, open-source tools like Stable Diffusion offer even fewer restrictions, allowing users greater freedom in generating deepfakes.

In addition to content generation, AI is also being leveraged to enhance the *targeting* and *distribution* of disinformation campaigns. Authoritarian regimes, in particular, are employing AI to make online censorship more widespread and effective. Freedom House researchers have documented 22 countries that have passed laws requiring or incentivising internet platforms to use machine learning algorithms to remove unfavourable online speech.

AI-powered bots and algorithms are being used to automatically censor content and manipulate online discussions. For example, chatbots in China have been programmed not to answer questions about the Tiananmen Square protests, while authorities in India have ordered YouTube and Twitter to restrict access to a documentary about violence during Prime Minister Narendra Modi's tenure as chief minister of Gujarat.

AI is enabling the precise targeting of individuals with tailored disinformation campaigns. The data-rich environment of modern online existence creates an ideal terrain for machine learning techniques to identify patterns and target specific demographics or individuals with false or misleading information. AI-generated deepfakes and language models can be used to create highly convincing and personalised content, amplifying the impact of disinformation campaigns.

Political campaigns are increasingly relying on AI. AI-generated content has been increasingly used in political campaigns and elections across various countries, raising concerns about the potential manipulation of public opinion and erosion of trust in democratic processes.[12]

In Moldova, an Eastern European country bordering Ukraine, pro-Western President Maia Sandu has been targeted by AI deepfakes depicting her endorsing a Russian-friendly party and announcing plans to resign. Moldovan officials believe these deepfakes, circulated shortly before local elections, aimed to 'erode trust in our electoral process, candidates and institutions'.

Taiwan has also witnessed the spread of AI deepfakes during its political campaigns. A fake clip on TikTok showed a US congressman promising stronger military support for Taiwan if the incumbent party's candidates were elected, stirring concerns about foreign interference.

Similarly, in Slovakia, audio clips resembling the voice of the liberal party chief were shared widely on social media just days before parliamentary elections, purportedly capturing him discussing plans to rig the vote.

In the USA, robocalls impersonating President Joe Biden urged voters in New Hampshire to abstain from voting in the state's primary election, later traced to a political consultant attempting to highlight the dangers of AI deepfakes.

Public health information is being undermined. Concerns have been raised about the potential impact of AI-powered chatbots, such as ChatGPT, on the dissemination of inaccurate health information and the exacerbation of existing health inequalities.[13]

While ChatGPT is perceived as an advanced search engine capable of generating detailed answers, it lacks the ability to distinguish between factually correct and incorrect information, leading to the provision of imprecise or incorrect information, known as 'hallucinations'.

There is a risk that groups of users may influence ChatGPT and similar AI technologies to propagate false health-related information, a phenomenon already widespread through social media. AI-generated health misinformation could be more challenging to detect due to its perceived credibility and level of detail.

Moreover, chatbots could potentially exacerbate existing health inequalities between the Global North and Global South, as vulnerable populations in the latter may be more susceptible to inaccurate health information disseminated by AI.

To address these concerns, a multifaceted approach has been proposed, including enhancing content validation through partnerships with advisory boards and fact-checking entities, promoting user education initiatives, continuous investment in refining AI algorithms to reduce factual errors, establishing transparency standards in AI model development, and enforcing legal frameworks to hold companies accountable for potential harm caused by their AI products. Additionally, promoting AI technologies that benefit all communities, regardless of their geographical or economic status, and addressing the unique challenges faced by vulnerable populations in the Global South, has been emphasised.

Psychological impact through disinformation cannot be overstated. Disinformation can have a significant impact on public perception, leading to confusion and distrust in institutions, norms, and factual information.[14] Efforts to exploit technical, social, economic, and institutional configurations of media can catalyse social change, sow dissent, and challenge the stability of social institutions. Data & Society's Media Manipulation & Disinformation research examines how different groups use the participatory culture of the internet to turn the strengths of a free society into vulnerabilities, ultimately threatening expressive freedoms and civil rights.

Disinformation has been identified as a major contributor to shaping public perception on various contentious contemporary events, ranging from elections and referenda to the response to the COVID-19 pandemic.[15] Not only can belief in misinformation lead to poor judgements and decision-making, but it also exerts a lingering influence on people's reasoning after it has been corrected – an effect known as the continued influence effect.

Misinformation can confuse and manipulate citizens, creating distrust in international norms, institutions, or democratically agreed strategies.[16] It can disrupt elections and feed disbelief in key challenges such as climate change. The more this phenomenon expands globally and becomes multifaceted, the more necessary it is to address not only the content dimension of disinformation but simultaneously the tactics of manipulative influence that accompany it.

Psychological manipulation is a technique that causes lasting consequences. Efforts to exploit technical, social, economic, and institutional configurations of media can catalyse social change, sow dissent, and challenge the stability of social institutions. This approach takes a sociotechnical approach to understanding the social, political, and economic incentives to game information systems, websites, platforms, and search engines – especially in cases where the attackers intend to destabilise democratic, social, and economic institutions.

Media manipulation tactics include planting and amplifying misinformation and disinformation using humans (troll armies, doxing, and bounties) or digital tools (bots), targeting journalists or public figures for social engineering (psychological manipulation), gaming trending and ranking algorithms, and coordinating action across multiple user accounts to force topics, keywords, or questions into the public conversation.

Among the emerging technologies and tools available to spread disinformation are Manufactured amplification (artificially boosting the reach of information by manipulating search engine results, promoting hashtags or links on social media), *Bots* (social media accounts operated by computer programmes, designed to generate posts or engage with social platforms' content), *Astroturf campaigns* (masking the real sponsor of a message, giving the false impression that it comes from genuine grassroots activism), *Impersonation of authoritative media*, people or governments (through false websites and/or social media accounts), *Micro-targeting* (using consumer data, especially on social media, to send different information to different groups), *Deepfakes* (digitally altered or fabricated videos or audio).

When we can no longer believe what we see, truth and trust are at risk. Even before entering the political scene, deepfake technology had already been used to fabricate pornographic content for criminal purposes, thereby violating the right to privacy and human dignity.

Like all emerging technologies, Generative AI (GAI) presents both opportunities and challenges in the fight against disinformation. While freely available and largely unregulated tools enable anyone to generate false information and fake content on a massive scale, GAI can also provide a greater number of content consumers with trustworthy information, thereby counteracting disinformation.

Schmitt et al. (2024) contend that to combat the increasing amount of disinformation online, humans need to be supported by AI-based tools to increase the effectiveness of detecting false content. The utilisation of LGAIMs for disinformation detection falls in the high-risk category (defined in the EU's AI Act) leading to several obligations that need to be followed after the enforcement of the AI Act. The obligations include risk management, transparency, and human oversight which pose the challenge of finding adequate technical interpretations, balancing technological advancement with ethical and legal imperatives, advocating for a collaborative approach to utilising LGAIMs in safeguarding information integrity and fostering trust in digital ecosystems.[17]

Organisations are exploring ways to leverage GAI to combat misinformation and disinformation. For instance, reputable media houses could potentially use GAI to generate factual content more efficiently, ensuring a wider dissemination of accurate information. However, this approach requires robust safeguards to prevent biases or inaccuracies in the generated content.

The proliferation of GAI tools poses significant threats to the integrity of information ecosystems. These tools enable the creation of '*unreality*', making GAI a potent weapon in information warfare and influence operations. Malicious actors can leverage GAI to generate vast quantities of false narratives, country-specific misinformation, and manipulative content aimed at swaying public opinion or harming individuals or organisations.

Moreover, GAI can 'hallucinate', producing content not based on factual data or examples provided during training, leading to the dissemination of inaccurate information. This phenomenon has already been observed, such as when Google's Bard chatbot incorrectly claimed that the James Webb Space Telescope had captured the first images of an exoplanet.

Addressing these threats requires a multi-pronged approach.

Governments and NGOs must come together to ensure technology platforms are appropriate regulated to ensure ethical behaviour.

Companies developing GAI models should establish transparency standards and be held accountable for potential harm caused by their AI products.

Partnerships with advisory boards and fact-checking entities can enhance content validation and reduce factual errors in GAI outputs.

Initiatives to educate users on identifying and evaluating AI-generated content are crucial for building public resilience against disinformation.

Implementing legal frameworks to regulate the use of GAI and hold companies responsible for harmful outputs can help mitigate misuse.

The AI research community should develop a publication risk framework and ethical principles to guard against the misuse of their research by disinformation operators.

Online platforms should formalise mechanisms for cross-platform collaboration and sharing threat information to enable coordinated responses against disinformation campaigns.

Platforms should increase transparency and access to vetted researchers to audit and improve recommendation algorithms, countering the creation of information bubbles that contribute to polarisation.

Generative AI's impact on disinformation is a complex issue requiring a whole-of-society effort involving governments, technology companies, researchers, media organisations, and individual users. Proactive measures are necessary to harness GAI's potential for good while mitigating its risks and safeguarding the integrity of information ecosystems.

Olivieri and Guadagno (2024) conclude it is possible to combat information warfare if there is a proactive strategy for countering disinformation. The development of Early Warning and Control Systems (EWACS) leverage AI-assisted narrative discovery to monitor the digital information landscape continuously. By identifying emerging threats and inauthentic activity, strategic communicators gain valuable insights for crafting counter-narratives and pre-emptive communication strategies. Key components of the proposed approach include deterrence by denial and resilience-building measures.[18]

There are many approaches that can be used in the fight against these negative tactics and techniques. Automated fact-checking can include text analysis performed by AI, which is useful in classifying news as true or false.[19] In these cases, in addition to resources based on word occurrences and word relationships (both semantic and syntactic), it is also necessary to have resources based on how humans perform fact-checking. That is, the automated classification of information examines human behaviour in the process of manually detecting disinformation.

In fact-checking conducted by humans, contextual factors are considered, including the historical background, individuals involved, locations, and other relevant specifics related to the event. Thus, when automated detection of disinformation includes these characteristics, it is closer to human accuracy.

Automated technologies have limitations in evaluating individual statements. Current AI systems excel at identifying simple statements and assertions, but they struggle with more complex ones. The same limitation applies to expressions, in which context and culture are necessary. Despite significant advancements in NLP techniques for automated text analysis, challenges remain in understanding fundamental human concepts, such as sarcasm or irony. AI-based systems currently struggle to address disinformation that relies on subtler forms of expression beyond explicit content. Additionally, linguistic barriers and specific cultural/political environments in each country pose even greater challenges.

A common approach to managing these challenges is to involve humans in the text analysis process, especially when regarding machine learning algorithm training. For example, in a fake news classification project, humans can flag a news story as false or true in the first phase. Then, the programme can learn from these indications to assign characteristics and make classification decisions based on patterns identified in the news. This approach, referred to as semi-supervised learning, offers the potential to enhance the accuracy of automated text analysis by combining the human ability to comprehend language nuances with the efficiency and scalability of automated text processing.

While AI is viewed as a game-changer and as being able to facilitate both the 'abilities to self learn and a race to improve decision quality', human moderators still play a crucial role in content moderation and detecting disinformation.[20]

By using AI for detection of disinformation and enable response measures, we can shift the cost-gain calculation of adversaries and enhance societal resilience. The aim is to create an environment where propagandists face increased challenges in achieving their objectives.

However, distinguishing information from misinformation requires identifying the veracity of the content, and distinguishing disinformation from content that is not intended to mislead requires understanding the author's intentions.[21] Determining the veracity of a statement is difficult due to limited access to the reported events, and fact-checkers must verify the claim correctly, which involves checking verifiable claims and verifying the claim accurately.

While practical problems like the need to travel or gain specialised training can limit what a fact-checker can accomplish, there are also harder problems. Distinguishing factual claims from non-factual claims is not always straightforward, especially when evaluating questionable news items. There are also disagreements regarding morally or ethically thick concepts, where whether a claim counts as verifiable fact or opinion involves whether the individual agrees with the values expressed in the article.

Another challenge is disagreement among experts, as there are people, including scientists and other experts, who are critical of current research, and it is important that their voices not be discounted on the basis of their dissent alone. Determining an author's intentions is also a challenge, as deceptive authors frequently exploit their target audiences' trust networks in such a way that accusations of intentional deception fall on deaf ears.

Given the difference in stakes and time to prepare, the linguistic cues that detect deception in other areas may not generalise to fake news. Even narrowing the scope of deceivers from criminals or experiment participants to journalists does not guarantee that various authors find themselves in similar situations such that their writing will exhibit the same deceptive features.

While AI can assist in content moderation and detecting disinformation, human moderators play a vital role in addressing the nuances and complexities involved in distinguishing information from misinformation, understanding author intentions, and verifying the veracity of claims. A combination of AI-based techniques and human expertise is necessary to effectively combat the spread of disinformation.

The impact on Democracy cannot be overstated. Realising the possibilities of AI requires a clear and sustained focus on maintaining the public's trust.[22] People need to be confident that AI is being developed and used in a responsible and trustworthy manner. Trust and acceptance depend on the AI application, with people being most confident in universities and defence organisations to develop, use, and govern AI, and least confident in government and commercial organisations.

There is strong global endorsement for principles that define trustworthy AI, as trust is contingent on assuring such principles are in place. People expect AI to be regulated with external, independent oversight – and they view current regulations and safeguards as inadequate. Independent media will play a crucial role in charting and demystifying AI's civic disruptions in real time, holding tech companies accountable for the harms caused by their products.

AI may not single-handedly sway an election, but what's at stake is our shared reality. By partnering with media outlets like POLITICO in Europe, the EU is taking leadership in advancing responsible tech regulation.[23] The EU's large market size means that changes to meet its standards can have global repercussions, as companies adjust their products and policies worldwide. However, Europe struggles to rein in the tech industry due to misaligned incentives, underfunded regulators, and regulatory bottlenecks in certain countries. Elevating the political importance of tech regulation is needed to prevent ambitions from becoming mired in bureaucracies. The threats posed by AI-driven disinformation are daunting but not insurmountable through rigorous journalism, robust regulation, and a renewed commitment to democratic oversight of technology and corporations.

We emphasise the importance of collaboration between diverse stakeholders, including governmental organisations, academia, NGOs, and journalists. By harnessing the collective expertise from multiple fields, more effective strategies can be developed to safeguard information integrity and restore public trust.

Public trust in AI is shifting in a direction contrary to what major tech companies are hoping for, as suggested by a recent survey based on Edelman data.[24] The study suggests that trust in companies building and selling AI tools dropped to 53%, compared to 61% five years ago, with an even more pronounced decline in the USA from 50% to just 35%.

When it comes to AI, 'trust' encompasses not only trusting AI to give the right answers but also the broader trust that society puts in AI. This includes whether we trust those who create and use AI systems to do it ethically and with our best interests at heart. Trust is fundamental to achieving the widespread support needed to integrate AI across world-changing use cases.

The danger is that a lack of trust in AI could stall progress, hindering AI's potential to solve real-world problems. For people to trust AI, it has to be implemented ethically, with consideration of how it will affect our lives and society. Being transparent about AI is crucial, as transparent AI means building tools, processes, and algorithms that are understandable to non-experts.

If AI needs the public's trust, then the public needs to be involved in AI governance. This means actively seeking their input and feedback on how AI is used (and when it shouldn't be used) at both a democratic level, via elected representatives, and at a grassroots level.

References

1. https://akademie.dw.com/en/disinformation-current-definitions-and-examples/a-67786912.
2. https://www.unhcr.org/innovation/wp-content/uploads/2022/02/Factsheet-4.pdf.
3. Husana, S.M., Hibatullah, F. and Romdoni, M., 2024. Limiting the Use of AI By Creating Regulations that Can Prevent the Occurring of Digital Crime. *International Journal of Law Society Services*, *4*(1), pp. 1–14.
4. Silva, E.C.D.M. and Vaz, J.C., 2024. How disinformation and fake news impact public policies?: A review of international literature. *arXiv preprint arXiv:2406.00951.*
5. Truong, B.T., Lou, X., Flammini, A. and Menczer, F., 2024. Quantifying the vulnerabilities of the online public square to adversarial manipulation tactics. *PNAS Nexus*, p. pgae258.
6. https://akademie.dw.com/en/generative-ai-is-the-ultimate-disinformation-amplifier/a-68593890.
7. Singh, T. (2024). *Artificial Intelligence and Ethics: A Field Guide for Stakeholders* (1st ed.). CRC Press. https://doi.org/10.1201/9781003502708.
8. https://www.nytimes.com/2023/02/07/technology/artificial-intelligence-training-deepfake.html.
9. https://dl.acm.org/doi/fullHtml/10.1145/3544548.3581318.
10. https://www.technologyreview.com/2023/10/04/1080801/generative-ai-boosting-disinformation-and-propaganda-freedom-house/.
11. https://reutersinstitute.politics.ox.ac.uk/news/how-ai-generated-disinformation-might-impact-years-elections-and-how-journalists-should-report.
12. https://apnews.com/article/artificial-intelligence-elections-disinformation-chatgpt-bc283e7426402f0b4baa7df280a4c3fd.
13. https://www.ncbi.nlm.nih.gov/pmc/articles/PMC10644115/.
14. https://datasociety.net/research/media-manipulation/.
15. https://www.nature.com/articles/s44159-021-00006-y.
16. https://www.europarl.europa.eu/RegData/etudes/STUD/2021/653635/EXPO_STU(2021)653635_EN.pdf.
17. Schmitt, V., Tesch, J., Lopez, E., Polzehl, T., Burchardt, A., Neumann, K., Mohtaj, S. and Möller, S., 2024, May. Implications

of Regulations on Large Generative AI Models in the Super-Election Year and the Impact on Disinformation. In *Proceedings of the Workshop on Legal and Ethical Issues in Human Language Technologies@ LREC-COLING 2024* (pp. 28–38).
18. Olivieri, A. and Guadagno, R., 2024, June. Strategies for Combating Adversarial Information Operations: Theory and Practical Applications. In *European Conference on Cyber Warfare and Security* (Vol. 23, No. 1, pp. 341–347).
19. https://www.mdpi.com/2673-5172/4/2/43.
20. https://link.springer.com/article/10.1007/s10479-022-05015-5.
21. https://www.ncbi.nlm.nih.gov/pmc/articles/PMC7875590/.
22. https://kpmg.com/xx/en/home/insights/2023/09/trust-in-artificial-intelligence.html.
23. https://www.politico.eu/sponsored-content/the-impact-of-ai-on-disinformation-and-democracy/.
24. https://www.forbes.com/sites/bernardmarr/2024/03/19/is-the-public-losing-trust-in-ai/.

CHAPTER 7

Cambridge Analytica: Psychographic Profiling and Micro-targeting

Reis et al. (2024) argue the Facebook-Cambridge Analytica scandal marked a watershed moment, revealing the expansive misuse of personal data for political purposes, enabling mass disinformation campaigns designed to rig elections. This had huge implications that to continue to this day with emerging issues such as the use of artificial intelligence, biometrics, and surveillance technologies, which pose unique challenges to existing privacy paradigms. It poses questions regarding safeguarding individuals' privacy rights in an era of rapid technological innovation.[1]

Mauk and Grömping (2024) contend that electoral disinformation undermines democratic trust by inflaming incorrect negative beliefs about the fairness of elections or to shore up dictators by creating falsely positive ones. Free and fair democratic elections are one of the cornerstones of liberty. Their research suggests disinformation campaigns are associated with less accurate and more polarised beliefs about election fairness.[2]

Cambridge Analytica Ltd. (CA), previously known as SCL USA, was a British political consulting firm that came to prominence through the Facebook–Cambridge Analytica data scandal.[3] It was established in 2013 as a subsidiary of the private intelligence company SCL Group, which was active in military and political arenas. The men who ran Cambridge Analytica and its parent SCL were described as having close ties to the Conservative Party, royalty, and the British military.

T. Singh, *Digital Psychological Warfare*,
https://doi.org/10.1007/978-3-032-15294-7_7

Cambridge Analytica was founded by long-time SCL executives Nigel Oakes, Alexander Nix, and Alexander Oakes, with Nix as CEO. Nigel Oakes had founded the predecessor SCL Group in the 1990s, and in 2005, he established SCL Group together with his brother Alexander Oakes and Alexander Nix. The company's owners included several of the Conservative Party's largest donors, such as billionaire Vincent Tchenguiz, former British Conservative minister Jonathan Marland, Baron Marland, and the family of American hedge fund manager Robert Mercer.

Cambridge Analytica (SCL USA) was incorporated in January 2013 with its registered office in Westferry Circus, London, and just one staff member, its director and CEO Alexander James Ashburner Nix. Nix was also the director of nine similar companies sharing the same registered offices in London, including Firecrest technologies, Emerdata, and six SCL Group companies, including 'SCL elections limited'.

Cambridge Analytica's ability to psychographic microtarget traces back to a 2010 Facebook rollout of open graph that included a new version of its API, which allowed developers to access social connections between people and their interests and likes. Aleksander Kogan, an academic at the University of Cambridge, used this tool to research Facebook users and determine what might influence their behaviour.[4] He eventually gave this data to Cambridge Analytica, a company that provided data-driven services to political campaigns. Cambridge Analytica claimed to be able to use Facebook data for its clients to better target political messages to people that could be influenced, also known as 'psychographic micro-targeting'.[5]

Facebook shut down access for new apps to this API in 2014, and the API access was fully shut down in 2015. However, in 2018, it was revealed that Cambridge Analytica had purchased data from Kogan concerning the personal psychological profiles of roughly 270,000 Facebook users.[6] Due to the terms and conditions of the Facebook platform at that time, the company was able to indirectly access data from the Facebook friends of those users, allowing Cambridge Analytica to access a far larger pool of data concerning 87 million users – without the knowledge or consent of almost any of them.

Denemark (2024) argues that Cambridge Analytica Scandal is the best example of use of psychographic profiling and micro-targeting was provided by Cambridge Analytica during the US 2016 presidential elections and during the Brexit campaign. Cambridge Analytica, officially for research purposes, created psychographic personality profiles of 100 million registered voters in the USA and use them to target specific campaign segments of Donald Trump. During Brexit campaign, Cambridge Analytica was the leading consulter of Leave.EU, where Cambridge Analytica used algorithmic tools to profile potential voter for 'leave'. During the Brexit 'leave' campaign, Cambridge Analytica primarily focused on 'Left Behind' group of people who felt 'increasingly left behind by society and globalization', were 'unhappy with the economy and the NHS, but immigration is most important issue', were 'suspicious of the establishment including politicians banks and corporations' and were 'worried about their economic security, deterioration of public order and the future generally'. Data about those potential voters were illegally sourced by Cambridge Analytica from UKIP database, Facebook, insurance companies, and other personal data processors. Based on all this data, Leave.EU could target disinformation on immigration, NHS and EU on each individual based on his profile in order to convince him to vote for leaving the EU.[7]

Documents leaked from Cambridge Analytica revealed the company's involvement in manipulating elections and exploiting ethnic tensions in various countries around the world. The BBC obtained documents boasting about the company's interference in foreign elections, such as organising rallies in Nigeria to weaken support for the opposition in 2007.[8] The documents also claim that Cambridge Analytica deliberately exploited ethnic tensions in Latvia during the 2006 national elections to help their client. In Trinidad and Tobago's 2010 elections, the company claims to have orchestrated an 'ambitious campaign of political graffiti' that 'ostensibly came from the youth' to allow their client party to 'claim credit for listening to a "united youth"'.

Whistleblowers like Christopher Wylie and Brittany Kaiser played a crucial role in exposing Cambridge Analytica's unethical practices. Wylie, the company's former director of research, testified before the United States Senate Judiciary Committee, claiming that 'anything goes' at Cambridge Analytica and describing it as 'a corrupting force in the world'.[9] He revealed how the company used Facebook's data to categorise people based on political ideology.

Kaiser, another former employee turned whistleblower, decided to release over 100,000 documents related to Cambridge Analytica's work in 68 countries, aiming to expose the 'industrial scale' of voter manipulation.[10] The leaked documents confirm the firm's involvement in the Brexit campaign, contradicting their previous denials.[11]

The impact on international elections was far wider than envisaged. The leaked documents and whistleblower revelations shed light on Cambridge Analytica's far-reaching influence on elections worldwide. In Kenya, the company allegedly helped the Jubilee administration craft its political campaign, with the government providing terabytes of critical personal data. Wylie claimed that with this data, he could remotely access individuals' private computers and monitor their online activities from London.

Norman (2024) argues the role of Cambridge Analytica in election interference in Kenya and Nigeria was instrumental and poses a serious threat to democracy, national self-determination, and the autonomy of the people. This threat to de-democratise elections continues to present day.[12] Threats to democratic processes are made even worse in some African countries with open vote-buying by politicians and vote-rigging by incumbent political leaders.

The firm's alleged involvement in the Brexit campaign in the United Kingdom raised concerns about foreign interference and the erosion of democratic institutions. Lord Hain, a former Labour minister, described the SCL case as 'lifting the lid on a potential horror story' of companies using data to manipulate voters.

In the United States, Cambridge Analytica's connections with Russian oil company Lukoil and its involvement in Trump's 2016 presidential campaign sparked investigations into potential Russian ties and interference. Democratic officials emphasised the need for improved scrutiny over concerns about the company's data being used to target American voters.

The leaks and revelations highlighted the increasing influence of wealthy actors and corporations in elections, eroding the idea that parties are led by the best people rather than the wealthiest. They also raised concerns about the lack of data privacy laws and the diversion of funds from social programmes to corporate entities, undermining fair electoral contests and accountability.

Cambridge Analytica played a significant role in Kenyan President Uhuru Kenyatta's election campaigns in 2013 and 2017. According to the company's website, they conducted 'the largest political research project ever conducted in East Africa' in 2013, sampling 47,000 people to create voter profiles based on 'key national and local political issues, levels of trust in key politicians, voting behaviours/intentions, and preferred information channels'.[13] They then used this data to 'devise an online social media campaign to generate a hugely active online following'.

Mark Turnbull, the managing director of Cambridge Analytica Political Global, was covertly filmed by Channel 4 boasting about the company's involvement, claiming, 'We have rebranded the entire party twice, written the manifesto, done research, analysis, messaging. I think we wrote all the speeches and we staged the whole thing - so just about every element of this candidate'.[14]

Cambridge Analytica's involvement in Kenya's elections extended to the 2017 presidential race as well. Turnbull stated that the company had conducted 'two rounds of 50,000 (participant) surveys' and played a role in 'just about every element of his [Kenyatta's] campaign'.

The 2017 election was marred by misinformation and disinformation campaigns, with a 'critical mass' of Kenyan voters exposed to the internet and social media for the first time. One notable instance was a video titled 'The Real Raila', which depicted a post-apocalyptic scenario under an imagined presidency of Kenyatta's opponent, Raila Odinga. The video, traced back to a US digital advertising firm linked to President Donald Trump's campaign, was viewed over 141,000 times on YouTube.

There were also reports of misleading videos and photos circulating on social media, portraying past occurrences as ongoing events during the electoral process. Privacy International, a London-based charity, highlighted the need to examine the involvement of Western PR and digital media firms in election campaigns across the world, beyond just Cambridge Analytica's role in Kenya.

Cambridge Analytica's involvement in the Brexit campaign was initially denied by both the Leave.EU campaign and the United Kingdom Independence Party (UKIP), but internal emails and revelations from former employees exposed the firm's work for these groups.

Leave.EU and UKIP repeatedly denied using Cambridge Analytica to target voters during the Brexit referendum. However, Brittany Kaiser, the former head of business development at Cambridge Analytica, stated that Leave.EU used datasets created by the firm to target voters with online political messages aimed at swaying public opinion in 2016.

Internal emails between Cambridge Analytica and the political groups, submitted to the British parliament, contradicted the earlier denials and revealed the company's work for Leave.EU and UKIP ahead of the 2016 referendum.

Cambridge Analytica employed various strategies to influence voters during the Brexit campaign. The firm harvested millions of Facebook profiles of US voters, amounting to one of the tech giant's biggest data breaches. This data was used to build a powerful software programme capable of predicting and influencing choices at the ballot box through targeted political advertisements.[15]

Documents obtained by The Observer showed that by late 2015, Facebook had discovered the unprecedented scale of data harvesting but failed to alert users and took limited steps to recover and secure the private information of over 50 million individuals.

The discovery of this data harvesting and its use in targeting voters raised urgent questions about Facebook's role in the US presidential election and the EU referendum. Both Facebook and Cambridge Analytica's CEO initially denied having or using private Facebook data, but these claims were contradicted by the revelations.[16]

By the end of August 2014, Christopher Wylie had successfully compiled 2.1 million profiled records from 11 target US states, with the plan to use this data to communicate and refine messages in Republican campaigns backed by Robert Mercer and Steve Bannon leading up to the 2016 primaries.

Cambridge Analytica claimed to offer a 'secret sauce' of 253 psychological predictions about individuals based on their Facebook data. Unlike traditional Facebook advertising limited to broad demographics and basic interests, Cambridge Analytica could craft tailored messages targeting specific personality traits. For instance, a neurotic, extroverted, and agreeable Democrat could be targeted with a radically different message than an emotionally stable, introverted, intellectual one, each designed to suppress their voting intention.

The company developed a 120-question survey to probe personality traits and rolled it out to hundreds of thousands of Americans.[17] Responses were scored on the 'big five' personality traits: openness, extroversion, agreeableness, conscientiousness, and neuroticism. This data was combined with polls, voter records, and online activity to create personality models for voters.

During the 2016 Republican primaries, the Cruz campaign embraced data science and political psychology, dividing voters into six psychological profiles and tailoring messaging accordingly. For instance, 'timid traditionalists' received different messaging than 'temperamental' voters, even on the same topics.

In contrast, the Trump campaign initially viewed data as 'overrated' in politics. However, Cambridge Analytica staffers embedded with Trump's digital strategist Brad Parscale played a key role in the campaign's online efforts, including fundraising, outreach to undecided voters, and boosting Election Day turnout.

Alexander Nix, Cambridge Analytica's CEO, claimed the company 'did all the research, all the data, all the analytics, all the targeting, we ran all the digital campaign, the television campaign, and our data informed all the strategy'. However, a source close to the operation stated that psychological profiling never factored into the Trump campaign due to its lack of digital infrastructure.

Despite the differing accounts, the revelations sparked investigations by multiple state attorneys general into Cambridge Analytica's misuse of 50 million Facebook users' personal data, raising concerns about the company's role in potentially influencing American voters.

Digital strategies and psychometrics played a key role. Cambridge Analytica's data collection process involved sophisticated techniques.

They created a 'training set' by gathering data from hundreds of thousands of people through personality quizzes and surveys. This allowed them to collect Facebook likes, personality test results, and other relevant information.[18]

Thereon they identified the 'feature set' – the underlying Facebook data they wanted to use for making predictions, such as likes, text data, and browsing activity.

They established 'target variables' – the traits or characteristics they aimed to predict, such as personality traits or political orientation.

The 'My Personality' app was developed by researchers at Cambridge University's Psychometrics Centre. This app allowed users to take a personality questionnaire based on the 'Big Five' personality traits (openness, conscientiousness, extraversion, agreeableness, and neuroticism).[19]

Collaboration took place with Aleksandr Kogan, a Cambridge University academic, who created a separate app called 'thisisyourdigitallife'. This app harvested data not only from users who took the personality quiz but also from their Facebook friends, amassing a database of 3 million profiles.[20]

Employing machine learning techniques, including ensemble models that combined different approaches, to analyse the massive dataset and develop algorithms for inferring personality traits from Facebook activity.

Cambridge Analytica claimed to offer a 'secret sauce' of 253 psychological predictions about individuals based on their Facebook data. This allowed them to engage in sophisticated micro-targeting techniques.

Unlike traditional Facebook advertising limited to broad demographics and interests, Cambridge Analytica could craft tailored messages targeting specific personality traits.

For instance, a neurotic, extroverted, and agreeable Democrat could be targeted with a radically different message than an emotionally stable, introverted, and intellectual one, each designed to influence their voting intention.

By the end of August 2014, Cambridge Analytica had compiled 2.1 million profiled records from 11 target US states, with plans to use this data for Republican campaigns leading up to the 2016 primaries.

The firm's psychometric model claimed to move beyond broad demographic targeting and into the realm of 'dog-whistle campaigning', tailoring messages based on individuals' psychological profiles.

However, questions remain about the accuracy and effectiveness of Cambridge Analytica's psychometric model in influencing voter behaviour.

Analysis of targeted campaigns reveals Cambridge Analytica was a political consulting company that attempted to use the psychological profiles of roughly 90 million Facebook users to influence their political decisions.[21] The firm was able to use the data points it collected to build models that allowed psychological profiling of the variety of users, including their political affinities, personality traits like extroversion or introversion, and how they would react to certain campaigns. Using these profile-based models, the company managed to run different campaigns suitable for different kinds of users, which allegedly influenced election choices.

Cambridge Analytica claimed to offer a 'secret sauce' of 253 psychological predictions about individuals based on their Facebook data. Unlike traditional Facebook advertising limited to broad demographics and basic interests, Cambridge Analytica could craft tailored messages targeting specific personality traits. For instance, a neurotic, extroverted, and agreeable Democrat could be targeted with a radically different message than an emotionally stable, introverted, intellectual one, each designed to influence their voting intention.

By the end of August 2014, Cambridge Analytica had compiled 2.1 million profiled records from 11 target US states, with plans to use this data for Republican campaigns leading up to the 2016 primaries. The firm's psychometric model claimed to move beyond broad demographic targeting and into the realm of 'dog-whistle campaigning', tailoring messages based on individuals' psychological profiles.

In the United States, Cambridge Analytica was able to influence many campaigns.

In 2016, American senator Ted Cruz hired Cambridge Analytica to aid his presidential campaign.[22] The Federal Election Commission reported that Cruz paid the company $5.8 million in services. This is when Cambridge Analytica started to create individual psychographic profiles, which were then used to create tailored advertisements for each person to sway them into voting for Cruz.

Trump's 2016 presidential campaign used the harvested data to build psychographic profiles, determining users' personality traits based on their Facebook activity.[23] The campaign team used this information as a micro-targeting technique, displaying customised messages about Trump to different US voters on various digital platforms. Ads were segmented into different categories, mainly based on whether individuals were Trump supporters or potential swing votes.

As described by Cambridge Analytica's CEO, the key was to identify those who might be enticed to vote for their client or be discouraged to vote for their opponent.[24] Supporters of Trump received triumphant visuals of him, as well as information regarding polling stations. Swing voters were instead often shown images of Trump's more notable supporters and negative graphics or ideas about his opponent, Hillary Clinton. For example, the collected data was specifically used by 'Make America Number 1 Super PAC' to attack Clinton through constructed advertisements that accused Clinton of corruption as a way of propping up Trump as a better candidate for the presidency.[25]

In the United Kingdom, Cambridge Analytica was allegedly hired as a consultant company for Leave.EU and the UK Independence Party during 2016, as an effort to convince people to support Brexit.[26] These rumours were the result of the leaked internal emails that were shared with the British parliament. Brittany Kaiser declared that the datasets that Leave.EU used to create databases were provided by Cambridge Analytica.[27]

However, the official investigation by the UK Information Commissioner was unable to conclude that Cambridge Analytica was involved 'beyond some initial enquiries' and the regulator did not identify any 'significant breaches' of data protection legislation or privacy or marketing regulations 'which met the threshold for formal regulatory action'.[28,29]

The Facebook data breach was immense in scale. The Facebook–Cambridge Analytica data scandal involved the harvesting of personal data from millions of Facebook users without their consent by the British consulting firm Cambridge Analytica. The data was collected through an app called 'thisisyourdigitallife', developed by Aleksandr Kogan, a researcher at Cambridge University.

The app consisted of a personality quiz that collected not only the data of users who took the quiz but also the data of their Facebook friends, amassing a database of up to 87 million Facebook profiles. This was possible due to Facebook's policies at the time, which allowed third-party apps to access data not just from users who installed the app but also from their friends.

Cambridge Analytica then used this harvested data to build psychological profiles of voters and target them with personalised political advertisements during elections, including the 2016 US presidential election and the UK's Brexit referendum.

While Kogan claimed the data was collected for academic purposes, it was later revealed that he had violated Facebook's policies by passing the data to Cambridge Analytica, a commercial entity. Facebook initially claimed that no systems were infiltrated and no passwords or sensitive information were stolen but later acknowledged the severity of the data misuse.

The revelations about the Facebook data breach and its exploitation for political purposes sparked widespread outrage and investigations into the social media giant's data privacy practices.

In July 2019, Facebook was fined a record $5 billion by the Federal Trade Commission (FTC) for violating users' privacy rights. The UK's Information Commissioner's Office also fined Facebook £500,000 for exposing users' data to a 'serious risk of harm'.

In the aftermath of the scandal, Facebook's stock fell by about 24%, equivalent to $134 billion, though it later recovered its losses. The company also experienced a significant decrease in user activity, with likes, posts, and shares dropping by almost 20% in the first full month after the breach.

Facebook CEO Mark Zuckerberg testified before Congress, acknowledging the company's mistakes and promising to implement stronger data privacy measures. However, the scandal raised broader concerns about the lack of regulation and oversight in the tech industry, as well as the potential for personal data to be exploited for political gain.

The data analytics firm that worked with Donald Trump's election team and the winning Brexit campaign harvested millions of Facebook profiles of US voters, in one of the tech giant's biggest ever data breaches, and used them to build a powerful software programme to predict and influence choices at the ballot box.

The data was collected through an app called thisisyourdigitallife, built by academic Aleksandr Kogan, separately from his work at Cambridge University. Through his company Global Science Research (GSR), in collaboration with Cambridge Analytica, hundreds of thousands of users were paid to take a personality test and agreed to have their data collected for academic use.

In the 2010s, personal data belonging to millions of Facebook users was collected without their consent by British consulting firm Cambridge Analytica, predominantly to be used for political advertising. [...] In July 2019, it was announced that Facebook was to be fined $5 billion by the Federal Trade Commission due to its privacy violations. [...] In October 2019, Facebook agreed to pay a £500,000 fine to the UK Information Commissioner's Office for exposing the data of its users to a 'serious risk of harm'. [...] Since April 2018, the first full month since the breaking of the Cambridge Analytica data breach, the number of likes, posts, and shares on the site had decreased by almost 20% and has decreased ever since, with the aforementioned activity only momentarily increasing during the summer and during the 2018 US midterm elections.

Facebook's PR machine spent much of the first 24 hours after the story broke engaged in a pedantic and self-defeating argument over whether or not what had occurred constituted a 'data breach'. By information security standards, Facebook was correct that what occurred was not a 'data breach' – as representatives wrote, 'no systems were infiltrated, and no passwords or sensitive pieces of information were stolen or hacked'.

In response, Facebook apologised for their role in the data harvesting, and their CEO Mark Zuckerberg testified in front of Congress.

Whistleblowers like Christopher Wylie, a former Cambridge Analytica employee, played a pivotal role in exposing the company's unethical practices. He collaborated with Aleksandr Kogan, a Cambridge University academic, to obtain personal data from millions of Facebook users without their consent. In an interview with The Observer, Wylie revealed, 'We exploited Facebook to harvest millions of people's profiles. And built models to exploit what we knew about them and target their inner demons. That was the basis the entire company was built on'.

Wylie provided a dossier of evidence, including emails, invoices, contracts, and bank transfers, which showed that over 50 million profiles, mostly belonging to registered US voters, were harvested from Facebook in one of the largest data breaches. He shared this information with the National Crime Agency's cybercrime unit and the Information Commissioner's Office.

Another whistleblower, Brittany Kaiser, a former Cambridge Analytica employee, decided to release over 100,000 documents related to the company's work in 68 countries, aiming to expose the 'industrial scale' of voter manipulation. She confirmed that the datasets used by Leave.EU during the Brexit campaign were provided by Cambridge Analytica.

Investigations by various authorities and media outlets uncovered several key findings regarding Cambridge Analytica's operations.

The Times reported that in 2014, Cambridge Analytica acquired private Facebook data of tens of millions of users, the largest known leak or data breach in Facebook's history. This data was used to build psychological profiles of voters and target them with personalised political advertisements.

The Times also reported that people at Cambridge Analytica and its British affiliate, SCL Group, were in contact with executives from Lukoil, the Kremlin-linked oil giant, as Cambridge built its Facebook-derived profiles. This raised concerns about potential Russian interference in elections.

Cambridge Analytica suspended its CEO, Alexander Nix, after a British television channel released an undercover video in which he suggested the company had used seduction and bribery to entrap politicians and influence foreign elections.

Christopher Wylie, the former Cambridge employee, testified to the UK Parliament that the company helped swing the results in favour of Britain's withdrawal from the European Union.

The Times revealed that an employee at Palantir Technologies, founded by Trump backer Peter Thiel, helped Cambridge Analytica harvest Facebook data, and the two companies briefly considered a formal partnership to work on political campaigns.

These revelations sparked investigations into Cambridge Analytica's data misuse, potential foreign interference in elections, and the lack of data privacy regulations in the tech industry.

Christopher Wylie, who worked with a Cambridge University academic to obtain the data, told the Observer: 'We exploited Facebook to harvest millions of people's profiles. And built models to exploit what we knew about them and target their inner demons. That was the basis the entire company was built on'. [...] He has passed it to the National Crime Agency's cybercrime unit and the Information Commissioner's Office. It includes emails, invoices, contracts, and bank transfers that reveal more than 50 million profiles – mostly belonging to registered US voters – were harvested from the site in one of the largest-ever breaches of Facebook data.

Brittany Kaiser, a former Cambridge Analytica employee, decided to release over 100,000 documents related to Cambridge Analytica's work in 68 countries, aiming to expose the 'industrial scale' of voter manipulation.

Brittany Kaiser declared that the datasets that Leave.EU used to create databases were provided by Cambridge Analytica.

The Times reported that in 2014 contractors and employees of Cambridge Analytica, eager to sell psychological profiles of American voters to political campaigns, acquired the private Facebook data of tens of millions of users – the largest known leak in Facebook history. [...] The Times reported that Cambridge suspended its chief executive, Alexander Nix, after a British television channel released an undercover video in which he suggested that the company had used seduction and bribery to entrap politicians and influence foreign elections. [...] Testifying to Parliament a few days later, a former Cambridge employee, Christopher Wylie, contended that the company helped swing the results in favour of Britain's withdrawal from the European Union. [...] The Times showed how an employee at Palantir Technologies – an intelligence contractor founded by the Trump backer and tech investor Peter Thiel – helped Cambridge harvest Facebook data. The article reported that Palantir and Cambridge executives briefly considered a formal partnership to work on political campaigns. Though the deal fell through, a Palantir employee continued working with Cambridge to figure out how to obtain data for psychographic profiles.

The Cambridge Analytica scandal, as described in the leaked documents, 'commenced a categorically new form of political manipulation'. The firm used 'an ambitious campaign of political graffiti' to influence democratic processes, as seen in the 'graffiti' it produced to 'ostensibly' promote its client's interests during elections.

Regarding the Cambridge Analytica scandal, the leaked documents state that 'the firm helped swing the results in favour of Britain's withdrawal from the European Union'. This suggests that Cambridge

Analytica played a role in influencing public institutions, such as through the 'graffiti' it produced to promote its client's interests during elections.

Revelations that digital consultants to the Trump campaign misused the data of millions of Facebook users set off a furore on both sides of the Atlantic. The documents proved that Cambridge Analytica, where former Trump aide Stephen K. Bannon was a board member, used data improperly obtained from Facebook to build voter profiles. This news thrust Facebook into its biggest crisis ever.

In 2014, contractors and employees of Cambridge Analytica acquired the private Facebook data of tens of millions of users – the largest known leak in Facebook's history. Cambridge Analytica received warnings from its own lawyer, Laurence Levy, as it employed European and Canadian citizens on campaigns, potentially violating American election law. The Times also found that tranches of raw data still existed beyond Facebook's control.

The articles drew an instant response in Washington, where lawmakers demanded that Mark Zuckerberg, Facebook's chief executive, testify before Congress. In Washington, the Federal Trade Commission moved to investigate whether Facebook had violated an early agreement to safeguard user data.

After remaining silent for days, spurring the social media hashtag #WheresZuck, Zuckerberg spoke with The Times about steps Facebook was taking to address users' anger. Facebook's chief technology officer, Mike Schroepfer, issued a new estimate that as many as 87 million users, most of them in the United States, were affected by the data harvesting.

Amid the crisis, Facebook users whose data was harvested reacted with anger and resigned annoyance at how tech giants use personal information. The Times reported on a series of assessments of Facebook's privacy programmes, conducted by the consulting firm PwC on behalf of federal regulators.

Zuckerberg made his first appearance before Congress, testifying to Senate and House committees. In April 2018, Facebook decided to implement the EU's General Data Protection Regulation in all areas of operation and not just the EU. Facebook also established Social Science One as a response to the event.

The Cambridge Analytica scandal sparked widespread public outrage and intense media scrutiny of Facebook's data privacy practices. The Times reported on a growing number of Facebook users, including the singer Cher, deleting their accounts in response to the revelations.

The Times also broke news of the departure of Facebook's top security official, who had clashed with other executives on how to handle discontent over the platform's role in spreading disinformation. As Facebook reeled from the crisis, The Times delved into the relationship between Cambridge Analytica and John Bolton, the conservative hawk named national security adviser by President Trump.

The Times and The Observer reported allegations that the 2016 'Brexit' campaign used a Cambridge Analytica contractor to help skirt election spending limits, further fuelling concerns about the firm's influence on democratic processes.

In the aftermath of the scandal, Facebook's stock fell by about 24%, equivalent to $134 billion, though it later recovered its losses. Since April 2018, the first full month after the Cambridge Analytica data breach, the number of likes, posts, and shares on the site had decreased by almost 20%, though user growth eventually increased.

The culmination of Facebook's response was Zuckerberg's 3,000-word treatise on the company's 'privacy-focused' future, which was met with scepticism from privacy experts who saw it as a strategic move to protect market share rather than a genuine commitment to privacy.

Cambridge Analytica's financial dealings and contracts were closely scrutinised during investigations into the company's operations. According to The New York Times, a minimum of $15 million was invested into the company by billionaire Robert Mercer, one of its major investors. Steve Bannon's stake in the company was estimated to be between $1 million and $5 million, though he divested his holdings in April 2017 after becoming White House Chief Strategist.

The Observer obtained a contract dated 4 June, 2014, confirming that SCL, an affiliate of Cambridge Analytica, entered into a commercial arrangement with GSR (Global Science Research), a company founded by Aleksandr Kogan. This arrangement was entirely premised on harvesting and processing Facebook data. Cambridge Analytica spent nearly $1 million on data collection, yielding over 50 million individual profiles that could be matched to electoral rolls.

The Times also reported that Cambridge Analytica provided early versions of its Facebook-derived profiles to John Bolton's 'super PAC' in 2014, marking the technology's first large-scale use in an American election. Additionally, the Times found that tranches of raw data from the Facebook breach still existed beyond Facebook's control.

Economic impact on electoral processes was significant. Cambridge Analytica's data harvesting and profiling activities had significant economic implications for electoral processes. The algorithm and database developed by the company, based on the harvested Facebook data, created a powerful political tool. It allowed campaigns to identify potential swing voters and craft messages more likely to resonate with them, potentially influencing their voting behaviour.

The Times and The Observer reported allegations that the 2016 'Brexit' campaign used a Cambridge Analytica contractor to help skirt election spending limits, further fuelling concerns about the firm's influence on democratic processes. The company's involvement in high-profile political campaigns, such as the 2016 US presidential election and the UK's Brexit referendum, raised questions about the potential economic impact of such data-driven tactics on the outcomes of these elections.

A minimum of 15 million dollars has been invested into the company by Mercer, according to The New York Times. Bannon's stake in the company was estimated at 1 to 5 million dollars, but he divested his holdings in April 2017 as required by his role as White House Chief Strategist.

The Observer has seen a contract dated 4 June, 2014, which confirms SCL, an affiliate of Cambridge Analytica, entered into a commercial arrangement with GSR, entirely premised on harvesting and processing Facebook data. Cambridge Analytica spent nearly $1 m on data collection, which yielded more than 50 million individual profiles that could be matched to electoral rolls. It then used the test results and Facebook data to build an algorithm that could analyse individual Facebook profiles and determine personality traits linked to voting behaviour. The algorithm and database together made a powerful political tool. It allowed a campaign to identify possible swing voters and craft messages more likely to resonate.

The Times delved into the relationship between Cambridge Analytica and John Bolton, the conservative hawk named national security adviser by President Trump. The Times broke the news that in 2014, Cambridge provided Mr. Bolton's 'super PAC' with early versions of its Facebook-derived profiles – the technology's first large-scale use in an American election.

The Times also found that tranches of raw data still existed beyond Facebook's control. The Times and The Observer reported allegations that the 2016 'Brexit' campaign used a Cambridge Analytica contractor to help skirt election spending limits. The story implicated two senior advisers to Prime Minister Theresa May.

References

1. Reis, O., Eneh, N.E., Ehimuan, B., Anyanwu, A., Olorunsogo, T. and Abrahams, T.O., 2024. Privacy law challenges in the digital age: a global review of legislation and enforcement. *International Journal of Applied Research in Social Sciences*, *6*(1), pp. 73–88.
2. Mauk, M. and Grömping, M., 2024. Online Disinformation Predicts Inaccurate Beliefs About Election Fairness Among Both Winners and Losers. *Comparative Political Studies*, *57*(6), pp. 965–998.
3. https://en.wikipedia.org/wiki/Cambridge_Analytica.
4. https://www.theguardian.com/news/2018/mar/17/cambridge-analytica-facebook-influence-us-election.
5. Morphett, K., Carah, N. and Gartner, C., 2024. Ethical and legal issues in conducting tobacco and nicotine research using social media data. *Nicotine and Tobacco Research*, *26*(Supplement_1), pp. S57–S59.
6. https://www.investopedia.com/terms/c/cambridge-analytica.asp.
7. Denemark, J., 2024. The risk of artificial intelligence for democracy and the EU's first efforts to regulate it. *The Lawyer Quarterly*, *14*(1).
8. https://www.bbc.co.uk/news/uk-43528219.
9. https://en.wikipedia.org/wiki/Facebook%E2%80%93Cambridge_Analytica_data_scandal.
10. https://www.theguardian.com/uk-news/2020/jan/04/cambridge-analytica-data-leak-global-election-manipulation.
11. https://www.aljazeera.com/opinions/2020/1/18/cambridge-analytica-and-the-end-of-elections.
12. Norman, I.D., 2024. Foreign Election Interference in Africa's De-Democratization Culture. *European Journal of Law and Political Science*, *3*(3), pp. 23–33.
13. https://www.bbc.co.uk/news/world-africa-43471707.
14. https://www.cnbc.com/2018/03/23/cambridge-analytica-and-its-role-in-kenya-2017-elections.html.
15. https://bipartisanpolicy.org/blog/cambridge-analytica-controversy/.

16. https://www.theguardian.com/news/2018/may/06/cambridge-analytica-how-turn-clicks-into-votes-christopher-wylie.
17. https://www.npr.org/2018/03/20/595338116/what-did-cambridge-analytica-do-during-the-2016-election.
18. https://www.theguardian.com/news/2018/may/06/cambridge-analytica-how-turn-clicks-into-votes-christopher-wylie.
19. https://www.frontiersin.org/journals/psychology/articles/10.3389/fpsyg.2021.581448/full.
20. https://www.gsb.stanford.edu/insights/science-behind-cambridge-analytica-does-psychological-profiling-work.
21. https://www.investopedia.com/terms/c/cambridge-analytica.asp.
22. https://en.wikipedia.org/wiki/Facebook%E2%80%93Cambridge_Analytica_data_scandal.
23. https://www.nytimes.com/2018/04/04/us/politics/cambridge-analytica-scandal-fallout.html.
24. https://www.theguardian.com/news/2018/mar/17/cambridge-analytica-facebook-influence-us-election.
25. https://www.theguardian.com/technology/2019/mar/17/the-cambridge-analytica-scandal-changed-the-world-but-it-didnt-change-facebook.
26. https://www.theguardian.com/books/2019/oct/29/mindfck-christopher-wylie-targeted-brittany-kaiser-cambridge-analytica-review.
27. https://www.theguardian.com/news/2018/mar/17/cambridge-analytica-facebook-influence-us-election.
28. https://www.nytimes.com/2018/04/04/us/politics/cambridge-analytica-scandal-fallout.html.
29. https://bigcloud.global/cambridge-analytica-hijacking-democracy/.

CHAPTER 8

Psychological Manipulation in the Brexit Referendum

Mirza et al. (2024) argue that the Facebook-Cambridge Analytica scandal underscored the pervasive risks of personal data misuse on social media platforms, prompting a clamour for stringent regulations. Cambridge Analytics played a crucial role at the heart of the widespread disinformation campaigns during the Brexit Referendum.[1]

Social proof is the perception of widespread agreement on a topic, even if artificially created through coordinated campaigns, that can influence individuals to adopt the same viewpoint.[2]

Disinformation through the deliberate dissemination of false or misleading information with the intent results in deception or misleading society. It can take various forms, such as fabricated news stories, doctored images or videos, and the manipulation of facts or statistics.[3]

There are several common types of disinformation. Fake news is entirely fictitious stories designed to misinform or manipulate public opinion. Propaganda is information spread to promote a particular political agenda or ideology. Conspiracy theories are unsubstantiated claims that attempt to explain events or circumstances as part of a secret plot. Clickbait are sensationalised headlines or content designed to attract attention and drive web traffic.

The Brexit referendum campaign was marred by numerous instances of disinformation and misleading claims from both sides. One of the most prominent examples was the claim made by the Leave campaign that the

T. Singh, *Digital Psychological Warfare*,
https://doi.org/10.1007/978-3-032-15294-7_8

UK would save £350 million per week by leaving the EU, with the implication that this money could be redirected to the National Health Service (NHS).[4] However, this figure was widely criticised as a 'misuse of official statistics' because it did not account for the rebate the UK received from the EU.[5]

Another claim made during the campaign was that Turkey and four other countries could join the EU within 4 years, leading to an influx of 5.2 million additional immigrants to the UK. This claim was later acknowledged as an exploitation of fears surrounding immigration by Michael Gove, one of the leading figures in the Leave campaign.

Other notable instances of disinformation included claims that the UK would be able to negotiate individual trade deals with EU member states (which is not permitted under EU rules), and that a Brexit vote would lead to Scotland renewing its push for independence (which did not materialise in the 2017 general election despite 62% of Scottish voters supporting Remain).

These examples highlight the prevalence of disinformation during the Brexit campaign and the potential impact it had on public opinion and voter behaviour.

Social media platforms played a significant role in the spread of disinformation during the Brexit referendum campaign. The Leave camp was more effective in leveraging social media, setting the tone of the debate across major platforms like Facebook, Twitter, and Instagram.[6] They had a more powerful and emotionally charged message, which facilitated the viral spread of Leave ideas.

The Leave camp outnumbered the Remain camp on various platforms, with a 7 to 1 advantage on Twitter and twice as many supporters on Instagram. Moreover, Leave supporters were five times more active than Remain activists on Instagram. Their posts received 26% more likes and 20% more comments on average, indicating higher engagement. The top three most frequently used hashtags (#Brexit, #Beleave, and #VoteLeave) were all from the Leave camp, demonstrating their dominance in shaping online conversations.

Disinformation actors employed various tactics, such as creating networks of fake personas and websites to increase the believability of their messages.[7] They generated falsified articles or research papers, which were sometimes unwittingly shared by legitimate organisations and users. Synthetic media content, including doctored images, videos, and audio clips, was also used to mislead viewers.[8]

Astroturfing, or creating the impression of widespread grassroots support, was another common tactic.[9] Disinformation campaigns would post overwhelming amounts of content with the same or similar messaging from several inauthentic accounts, either created by bots or troll farms. Flooding, or spamming social media posts and comment sections with the intention of shaping a narrative or drowning out opposing viewpoints, was also employed.

The Leave camp's dominance on social media created a perception of wide-ranging public support for their cause, acting as a self-fulfilling prophecy and attracting more voters to back Brexit. Their emotional and straightforward message resonated better with social media users than the Remain camp's reliance on rational and economic arguments.

Disinformation actors capitalised on conspiracy theories by generating narratives that aligned with the conspiracy worldview, increasing the likelihood of resonating with the target audience. They also targeted prominent individuals and organisations to amplify their narratives, adding perceived credibility and seeding them at the grassroots level.

The overwhelming Leave sentiment across social networking platforms was consistent and undeniable, yet many Remain supporters chose to ignore the voice of the Internet, believing it had no connection with the real political world. However, the volume of tweets urging Britain to #VoteRemain was quickly dwarfed by the enormous turbulence caused by the trending #IVotedLeave hashtag on the day of the referendum.

The Leave campaign was significantly more effective in leveraging social media platforms during the Brexit referendum. They outnumbered and out-tweeted pro-Europeans on Twitter by a factor of 1.75–2.3. Similar patterns were observed on other platforms like Google, Instagram, and Facebook, where Eurosceptic views were communicated with greater intensity by a larger number of users.[10]

The Leave camp's dominance on Twitter correlated with voting patterns in the referendum, as local authority districts with a higher share of Twitter users supporting Leave tended to vote in favour of exiting the EU. Leave supporters exhibited less openness and primarily engaged with other Leave supporters, indicating the presence of an echo chamber. Their simple slogans like 'vote Leave', 'take control', and 'Brexit' were well-suited for social media messaging, contributing to their online success.

Pro-Brexit pages referred to user-generated content almost twice as much as anti-Brexit pages (23.5% vs. 14.0%), confirming the tendencies of Brexit supporters to focus on alternative sources and appear as grass-roots movements.[11] They also favoured connecting with alternative media platforms (23.5%) compared to anti-Brexit pages (11.2%), masquerading as bottom-up movements while hiding their elite support.

The Leave campaign employed various tactics, such as creating networks of fake personas and websites to increase the believability of their messages. They generated falsified articles or research papers, which were sometimes unwittingly shared by legitimate organisations and users. Synthetic media content, including doctored images, videos, and audio clips, was also used to mislead viewers. Astroturfing and flooding techniques were employed to create the impression of widespread grassroots support and shape narratives or drown out opposing viewpoints.

The Brexit Party, in particular, was highly successful in the online battle leading up to the European elections. They accounted for 51% of all shared content on Facebook and Twitter despite producing only 13% of the content.[12] Their campaign was 'overwhelmingly negative', focused on attacking Labour, and prioritised older Facebook users in England rather than younger demographics or residents of Scotland and Northern Ireland. The analysis identified dozens of pro-Brexit party accounts with a 'high likelihood of being inauthentic'.

In contrast, the Remain campaign's social media presence was significantly less effective. They were outnumbered and less active on various platforms, with a 7 to 1 disadvantage on Twitter and half the number of supporters on Instagram compared to the Leave camp. Remain supporters were also five times less active than Leave activists on Instagram, with their posts receiving 26% fewer likes and 20% fewer comments on average.

The Remain camp's messaging relied more on rational and economic arguments, which resonated less with social media users compared to the Leave camp's emotional and straightforward messaging. Initiatives like #CatsAgainstBrexit trended but had limited impact.[13] The Remain campaign focused more on specific economic issues related to trade and business, with domestic agendas entering the fray closer to the referendum date. This relative lack of diverse policies might have hindered their ability to reach a wider audience on social media.

While the Leave camp's success on social media was partially attributed to potential inauthentic bot activity, a significant factor was the clarity and simplicity of their messaging, which the Remain parties struggled to match. The press coverage leading up to the referendum also favoured leaving the EU, with 82% of newspaper articles weighted for circulation supporting the Leave campaign. This imbalance of Eurosceptic information and views across both online and offline channels likely contributed to the widespread exposure of the Leave campaign's narratives.

The Brexit referendum revealed significant differences in voting patterns across various demographic groups. A study by found that individuals with higher cognitive abilities were more likely to vote Remain. Specifically, only 40% of people in the lowest decile of the cognitive ability distribution voted Remain, whereas approximately 73% of those in the highest decile voted Remain.[14]

The study also highlighted a notable overlap in cognitive abilities between Leave and Remain voters. Approximately 36.3% of Leave voters had higher cognitive abilities than the average Remain voter. This suggests that while cognitive ability played a role, it was not the sole determinant of voting behaviour.

The study by Alabrese et al. (2019) used a nationally representative sample of 6,366 individuals from 3,183 heterosexual couples in the UK Understanding Society panel survey. After controlling for various socioeconomic and sociodemographic characteristics, they found statistically and economically significant evidence that higher cognitive ability (and having a partner with higher cognitive ability) was associated with an increased propensity to vote Remain.

The mean cognitive ability score for Leave voters (−0.245) was lower than that of Remain voters (0.188), with a statistically significant difference of 0.433 standard deviations ($t = 17.5$, $p < 0.001$). A one standard deviation increase in cognitive ability was associated with a 5.5 percentage point increase in the likelihood of voting Remain, representing a 9.7% increase relative to the mean level of voting Remain in the sample.

Furthermore, a one standard deviation increase in a partner's cognitive ability, controlling for the individual's cognitive ability, was associated with a 4.3 percentage point (7.6%) increase in the likelihood of voting Remain. A one standard deviation cognitive ability advantage over one's spouse increased the likelihood of voting Remain by 10.9%.

While these findings suggest a correlation between cognitive ability and voting behaviour, it is important to note that other factors, such as socioeconomic status, education, and personal beliefs, likely played a role in shaping individual voting decisions.

Disinformation poses significant threats to the right to privacy and data security. It can enable the collection and misuse of personal data for targeted manipulation.[15] The sensitivity of political data, including voter preferences, demographic information, and contact details, necessitates implementing stringent security measures. Political parties must adopt industry-standard encryption, secure data storage solutions, and regular security audits to prevent unauthorised access, data breaches, and cyberattacks.[16]

Training staff and volunteers on data security best practices is crucial to prevent accidental data leaks or breaches. For instance, a political campaign could employ end-to-end encryption for all digital communications, including emails and messaging apps, and use a secure, encrypted database to store sensitive supporter information. Regular security training sessions should be held to ensure personnel understand the importance of strong passwords, recognise phishing attempts, and know how to handle data securely.

Legislative and executive bodies have moved to regulate the spread of disinformation by elaborating codes of practice, guidelines, and setting up verification networks to debunk disinformation. Governments are taking positive steps to improve transparency in political advertising, such as verifying the identity of individuals and organisations purchasing advertisements on social media and allowing users to see why they are being targeted by messages.

Other legislation requires social media companies to create a public archive of all advertisements bought and sold, holding political parties accountable for any dark advertisements they purchase during campaigns.[17] However, new regulations that seek to thwart the spread of 'false' or 'fake' content could have a chilling effect on free speech. Instead, governments should look towards mechanisms that would encourage the enforcement of existing laws to deal with harmful forms of content.

Carefully crafted laws and regulations can inhibit political actors from using disinformation and other deceptive online practices for personal and political gain in ways that erode the democratic information environment.[18] At the same time, the adoption of overly broad legislation can have chilling implications for political and electoral rights. Regulation must adapt to the changed reality of how individuals encounter, interact with, and create political and electoral information in the digital age.

While national legislation governing the use of digital media during elections and campaigns has the potential to close loopholes exploited by domestic actors to manipulate the information environment, regulation that would significantly alter the global business practices of social media platforms is an unrealistic goal at the national level. However, regulating the actions of domestic actors during electoral periods or discrete laws that create pressure on the ways platforms operate within a country are viable areas for reform.

The importance of *media literacy* in combating disinformation has become increasingly evident in the digital age. Individuals are constantly exposed to an overwhelming amount of information, some of which may be misleading or inaccurate.[19] This is particularly relevant in the context of substance misuse, where misinformation can have serious consequences for individuals and public health.

In the digital age, individuals are bombarded with information from various sources, including social media, news outlets, and online forums. This information can be biased, inaccurate, or even intentionally misleading, leading to the spread of disinformation. Media literacy is essential in helping individuals critically evaluate the information they encounter and distinguish fact from fiction.[20]

Media literacy education is crucial for adults as well as children. It's not something that is learned once and then completed; rather, it is a life-long process as digital and media environments are constantly evolving. Being media literate opens up opportunities to engage more fully and more creatively with the online (and offline) media world.

Individuals can develop media literacy skills by learning to critically analyse the information they encounter, considering the source, bias, and potential agenda behind the content. This includes questioning the credibility of the information, cross-checking with reliable sources, and being aware of common tactics used to spread disinformation.

Institutions, such as educational systems and healthcare providers, can also play a crucial role in promoting media literacy. By incorporating media literacy education into curricula and providing resources for individuals to develop these skills, institutions can empower people to navigate the digital landscape more effectively and make informed decisions about their health and well-being.

The UK government has recognised the importance of media literacy in combating online harms and disinformation. The Online Harms White Paper set out a commitment to develop an Online Media Literacy Strategy ahead of the implementation of the online harms regulator.[21] The aim of the strategy is to educate and empower internet users across the UK to manage their online safety.

Over 170 organisations are currently involved in delivering media literacy education in the UK. The Media Literacy Strategy sets out the government's multi-year plan to bring coordination to the media literacy landscape and outlines a Media Literacy Framework of best practice principles to inform the content and delivery of media literacy education. The areas covered by the framework include data and privacy, online environment, information consumption, online consequences, and online engagement.

The strategy also identifies six key challenges faced by the media literacy sector: evaluation, funding, hard-to-reach audiences, vulnerable users, building audience resilience to disinformation, and coordination. The government is committed to tackling these challenges and will publish an annual Media Literacy Action Plan outlining the initiatives to be delivered that forthcoming year. These initiatives will take action against the identified challenges and respond to the changing needs of the media literacy sector.

Prior literature suggests that social media data can be used to forecast political election outcomes. Most studies have focused on analysing a single social media platform, while few have explored the potential of leveraging data across multiple platforms for election predictions.[22]

Candidates' personal attributes, such as political experience, have also been identified as critical factors influencing election results. However, there is limited research on the interacting effect of social media presence and candidate attributes in predicting election outcomes.

The findings from existing studies indicate that both the number of Facebook likes and Twitter followers a candidate has are positively associated with their election performance. Furthermore, a candidate's political experience moderates the association between their number of Facebook likes and election outcomes, as well as the association between their number of Twitter followers and election outcomes. This research adds to the discussion on how social media can predict election results by considering different social media platforms and the roles of candidate attributes.

Looking ahead to future general elections, there are signs that digital technology will be used more intensively than in previous campaigns.[23] Following legislative changes, political parties in the UK can now spend £54,010 in each constituency, compared to a previous limit of £30,000. This means the cumulative limit on election spending has increased from around £19 million to £34 million. While this additional funding may be allocated to various causes, one of the quickest and easiest ways for parties to spend it is on online political advertising and digital content.

Therefore, it is likely that there will be even more spending on platforms like Facebook and Google than in the past.

Social media platforms themselves have also introduced new verification processes for those wanting to place political ads. In the UK, advertisers must confirm their identity by providing a passport and proof of address, significantly raising the barrier to entry compared to the past when no verification was required.

Another factor contributing to the changing landscape is the shifting demographics of popular social media platforms. While Facebook is still widely used by 77% of UK adult internet users, its user base tends to skew older. In contrast, platforms like TikTok, although less widely used (42% of UK adult internet users), are more popular among younger voters, with 85% of internet users aged 16–24 having used TikTok in 2022. For campaigners trying to reach specific demographics, Facebook may no longer be the answer. While it remains a viable option for contacting older voters, other platforms may be more effective for reaching younger audiences.

As a result, there is a clear incentive for political parties to create audience-specific content tailored to different platforms. Major parties have begun advertising for roles such as video creators and meme producers. For example, the Conservative Party has reportedly hired digital experts and strategists from New Zealand and Australia, who have successfully used accounts on platforms like TikTok and Twitch in recent political campaigns. For these reasons, campaigners are likely to branch out from established social media networks and develop content and profiles across a range of different digital media platforms.

Alongside this change, there are signs that campaigns may increasingly work with influencers, as has happened in other parts of the world. In the USA, for instance, the Democrats used influencers to spread a 'get out the vote' message during the 2022 mid-term elections. Additionally, super PACs (non-party campaign groups able to raise and spend significant sums on election campaigns) like American Bridge have deliberately used online influencers and podcasters to target diverse groups of women.

While the UK remains Europe's tech powerhouse, with local startups raising $29.9 billion in 2022 (more than French and German rivals combined), the country's digital ambitions face challenges from its politicians.[24] Over 6 years since the UK voted to leave the European Union, London's tech strategy has been a victim of countless government reshuffles, a lack of coordination between lawmakers on priorities, and frustration from industry groups and digital rights campaigners over what the UK is trying to achieve.

As artificial intelligence (AI) and machine learning (ML) technologies advance, they are poised to amplify the impact of disinformation campaigns.[25] These campaigns involve covert efforts to intentionally spread false or misleading information and can be broken down into multiple stages, including reconnaissance, infrastructure development, content creation, amplification, and sustained engagement with unwitting users through trolling.

Convincing the public that the information they perceive is genuinely real, rather than fake or AI-generated, will pose a considerable challenge as AI becomes adept at mimicking reality.[26] Political parties must not only persuade the public of the authenticity of their messages but also enhance public awareness regarding the potential presence of manipulated content – a challenge they did not face to this extent in the past.

Additionally, parties should consider the role of influencers, especially micro-influencers, on political and social media channels. These individuals do not belong to political parties, are not candidates, and are not news journalists, but they possess considerable influence and maintain a significant online presence – a phenomenon that would not have existed before the rise of social media. Typically, micro-influencers have around 100,000 followers or more, and they maintain close relationships with their followers based on authentic engagement. If a political party can connect with these individuals, it can significantly enhance the trustworthiness of its message, as messages delivered by someone followers trust and admire are more likely to resonate than traditional advertising methods.

The next phase of political campaigning is anticipated to be heavily influenced by generative AI, particularly large language models and deep fakes, which are game-changing developments. The potential impact of these new tools on campaigning is wide open, with many uncertainties. Researchers and practitioners must explore whether computers and AI will remain tools to augment and enhance human decision-making in campaigning or whether they will shift to the forefront and drive strategy.

Until now, fake news stories have become increasingly credible and realistic, blurring the line between what's fake and what's genuine. However, a major scandal involving an entirely fabricated, AI-generated campaign story, image, or video going viral and influencing voters to change their votes has not yet occurred. The key question for researchers of digital elections is not if, but when this will happen, and how it will be possible for voters to maintain trust in the political system, leaders, and parties when such convincing content raises doubts about its authenticity. This would mark a new phase in politics beyond the campaign sphere, and with vital elections for the EU, the USA, and the UK coming up in 2024, it may be closer than anticipated.

One of the most prominent claims made by the Leave campaign was that the UK would save £350 million per week by leaving the EU,[27] with the implication that this money could be redirected to the National Health Service (NHS).[28] However, this figure was widely criticised as a 'misuse of official statistics' because it did not account for the rebate the UK received from the EU.[29]

Another claim made during the campaign was that Turkey and four other countries could join the EU within 4 years, leading to an influx of 5.2 million additional immigrants to the UK. This claim was later acknowledged as an exploitation of fears surrounding immigration by Michael Gove, one of the leading figures in the Leave campaign.

The Leave campaign made various claims about immigration statistics, including that the UK could not control its borders while remaining in the EU.[30] However, these claims were often exaggerated or misrepresented the actual situation.[31]

Both sides of the campaign made conflicting claims about the potential economic impact of leaving the EU. The Leave campaign often dismissed or downplayed negative economic forecasts, while the Remain campaign emphasised the potential risks to the UK economy.

The Leave campaign claimed that the UK would regain full sovereignty and control over its laws by leaving the EU. However, this claim was criticised as oversimplifying the complex relationship between EU and national laws.[32]

The Leave campaign claimed that the UK would be able to negotiate individual trade deals with EU member states, which is not permitted under EU rules.[33]

There were claims made by the Leave campaign about the potential creation of an EU army, which was seen as a threat to British sovereignty. However, the validity of these claims was disputed.[34]

There were claims made by the Leave campaign that food prices would decrease after leaving the EU. However, these claims were not supported by evidence and were disputed by experts.

The Leave campaign made claims about the potential positive impact of Brexit on employment and job creation in the UK. However, these claims were often based on speculative assumptions and were challenged by economic experts.

References

1. Mirza, S., Villa, C. and Pöpper, C., 2024. Media talks privacy: Unraveling a Decade of Privacy Discourse around the World. *Proceedings on Privacy Enhancing Technologies*, *4*, pp. 102–122.
2. https://arabcenterdc.org/resource/identity-politics-2-0-cyber-geopolitics-and-the-weaponization-of-social-media/.
3. https://www.city.ac.uk/research/impact/case-studies/social-media-bots-used-to-boost-political-messages-during-brexit-referendum.
4. https://www.independent.co.uk/news/uk/politics/final-say-brexit-referendum-lies-boris-johnson-leave-campaign-remain-a8466751.html.
5. https://www.independent.co.uk/news/uk/politics/final-say-brexit-referendum-lies-boris-johnson-leave-campaign-remain-a8466751.html.
6. https://www.referendumanalysis.uk/eu-referendum-analysis-2016/section-7-social-media/impact-of-social-media-on-the-outcome-of-the-eu-referendum/.
7. https://www.cisa.gov/sites/default/files/publications/tactics-of-disinformation_508.pdf.
8. https://www.city.ac.uk/research/impact/case-studies/social-media-bots-used-to-boost-political-messages-during-brexit-referendum.
9. https://www.ox.ac.uk/news/2021-01-13-social-media-manipulation-political-actors-industrial-scale-problem-oxford-report.
10. https://eprints.lse.ac.uk/84614/1/Hanska-Ahy__tweeting-for-brexit.pdf.
11. https://www.tandfonline.com/doi/full/10.1080/14742837.2021.1928484.
12. https://www.theguardian.com/politics/2019/jun/29/how-brexit-party-won-euro-elections-on-social-media.
13. https://networkconference.netstudies.org/2019Curtin/wp-content/uploads/2019/05/Yan_18842588_A1_FINAL.pdf.

14. https://www.ncbi.nlm.nih.gov/pmc/articles/PMC10664886/.
15. https://www.europarl.europa.eu/RegData/etudes/STUD/2021/653635/EXPO_STU(2021)653635_EN.pdf.
16. https://www.michalsons.com/blog/data-protection-in-political-campaigns/71021.
17. https://www.carter-ruck.com/insight/fakes-news-authentic-views/responding-to-fake-news-through-regulation-and-automation/.
18. https://counteringdisinformation.org/topics/legal/complete-document-legal-and-regulatory-responses.
19. https://www.tandfonline.com/doi/full/10.1080/14659891.2023.2194421.
20. https://edmo.eu/areas-of-activities/media-literacy/the-importance-of-media-literacy-in-countering-disinformation/.
21. https://www.gov.uk/government/publications/online-media-literacy-strategy.
22. https://dl.acm.org/doi/10.1145/3651227.
23. https://ukandeu.ac.uk/all-change-in-digital-election-campaigning/.
24. https://www.politico.eu/article/uk-technology-politics-policy-brexit/.
25. https://cset.georgetown.edu/publication/ai-and-the-future-of-disinformation-campaigns/.
26. https://erc.europa.eu/projects-statistics/science-stories/how-technology-reshaping-political-campaigns.
27. https://conversion-uplift.co.uk/brexit/the-boris-johnson-brexit-bus-lie-of-350m/.
28. https://www.nuffieldtrust.org.uk/news-item/the-brexit-referendum-five-years-on-what-has-it-meant-for-the-nhs.
29. https://www.healthjobs.co.uk/health-care-uk/blog/what-happened-to-brexit-s-350m-nhs-pledge/.
30. https://www.kcl.ac.uk/policy-institute/research-analysis/the-publics-brexit-misperceptions.
31. https://ukandeu.ac.uk/sovereignty-and-brexit-control-of-what-exactly/.
32. https://bylinetimes.com/2024/02/01/four-years-on-kemi-badenochs-sketchy-brexit-benefits/.

33. https://www.independent.co.uk/voices/brexit-trump-fact-check-lies-truth-eu-referendum-campaign-fake-news-online-facebook-a8590231.html.
34. https://ukdefencejournal.org.uk/fact-check-can-the-uk-be-forced-into-an-eu-army/.

CHAPTER 9

Russian Psychological Techniques in the 2016 US Election

During the Cold War, the Soviet Union established a global influence campaign, referred to as aktivnyye meropriyatiya – or 'active measures'.[1] Active measures are secret psychological operations. These covert political operations use psychological and informational warfare to influence world events. They are a key part of Russia's foreign policy and geopolitical strategy.

Active measures would include disinformation including spreading false information through media manipulations, forgery, and other means. Political repression through persecuting political dissidents and infiltrating churches. Supporting underground groups, such as communist, socialist, and opposition parties, as well as revolutionary, criminal, and terrorist groups in other countries. Creating and placing agents of influence to stage insurrections in countries of interest.

Soviet active measures focused primarily on the United States, which it referred to as the 'main enemy' (or glavnyy protivnik), though Moscow also targeted US allies. The Soviets had multiple goals in conducting active measures, such as undermining support in the United States and overseas for policies viewed as threatening to Moscow, discrediting US intelligence and law enforcement agencies, weakening US alliances and US relations with partners, and increasing Soviet power and influence across the globe.

T. Singh, *Digital Psychological Warfare*,
https://doi.org/10.1007/978-3-032-15294-7_9

Well before the election of Ronald Reagan, the KGB and intelligence agencies from countries like Czechoslovakia (now the Czech Republic and Slovakia) in the Warsaw Pact – the Cold War military alliance that included the Soviet Union and countries in Eastern and Central Europe – attempted to influence US politics. In the 1960s, for example, the intelligence service from Czechoslovakia ran a propaganda campaign against US Senator Barry Goldwater, the Republican candidate for US president. Moscow was deeply concerned about Goldwater's anti-Soviet views, and Soviet and Czechoslovak agencies orchestrated a disinformation campaign labelling Goldwater as a racist and a KKK sympathiser.

In the 1968 presidential election, the Soviet leadership and the KGB strongly opposed the anti-Communist Richard Nixon and secretly offered to subsidise the campaign of Hubert Humphrey, the Democratic nominee. In 1976, Service A of the KGB again adopted active measures to disparage Democratic Senator Henry 'Scoop' Jackson, an anti-Soviet hawk, in the presidential election. On 25 February, 1983, KGB headquarters instructed agents in the United States to start planning activities to defeat Reagan in the 1984 presidential election.

The May 2014 Ukrainian presidential election was disrupted by cyberattacks over several days, including the release of hacked emails, attempted alteration of vote tallies, and distributed denial-of-service attacks to delay the final result. They were found to have been launched by pro-Russian hackers.[2] Around the same time as Russia's attempt to hack the 2014 elections, the Obama administration received a report suggesting that the Kremlin was building a disinformation program which could be used to interfere in Western politics.

According to a February 2018 criminal indictment, more than two years before the election, two Russian women obtained visas for what the indictment alleged was a three-week reconnaissance tour of the United States, including battleground states such as Colorado, Michigan, Nevada, and New Mexico, to gather intelligence on American politics. The 2018 indictment alleged that another Russian operative visited Atlanta in November 2014 on a similar mission.

State and non-state actors employed various *digital marketing techniques* to distort the media landscape during elections, making it the most popular tactic.[3] These techniques included propagandistic news, outright fake news, paid commentators, bots (automated accounts), and hijacking real social media accounts.[4]

Populists and far-right leaders have grown adept at creating *viral disinformation* and harnessing networks that disseminate it.[5] Some networks are explicitly directed by state or party officials, while others are semi-autonomous, lending support to their political champions and receiving encouragement in return. These online mobs amplify conspiracy theories, inflammatory views, and misleading memes from small echo chambers to the political mainstream.

Far-right groups may enjoy more success because false, shocking, negative, exaggerated, and emotionally charged content tends to spread faster and wider on social media platforms. Moreover, electoral authorities in most countries lack sufficient oversight mechanisms for identifying and thwarting this type of electoral interference.

The Internet Research Agency (IRA), also known as Glavset or the Trolls from Olgino, was a Russian company engaged in online propaganda and influence operations on behalf of Russian business and political interests.[6] It was linked to Yevgeny Prigozhin, a former Russian oligarch, and based in Saint Petersburg.

The agency employed fake accounts on major social networking sites, discussion boards, online newspaper sites, and video hosting services to promote the Kremlin's interests in domestic and foreign policy, including Ukraine, the Middle East, and the 2016 United States presidential election. More than 1,000 employees reportedly worked at the agency in 2015.

The IRA gained attention after a 2014 BuzzFeed News article expanded on government documents published by hackers, revealing the agency's efforts to influence public opinion using social media. In 2018, a United States grand jury indicted 13 Russian nationals and three Russian entities, including the IRA, on charges of violating criminal laws with the intent to interfere with US elections and political processes.[7]

The IRA's tactics included posting, and influence operation activity increased before and after the 2016 election, exacerbating existing political divisions in the United States.

Vićić and Gartzke (2024) contend that Russia's cyber-enabled influence operations (CEIO) ensured 126 million Americans were exposed to Russia's efforts to influence the 2016 US election on Facebook. They proved far more consequential than other, more flamboyant forms of cyber conflict. CEIOs highlight the human dimension of cyber conflict. Focused on *'hacking human minds'* and affecting individuals behind keyboards, as opposed to hacking networked systems, CEIOs represent an emergent form of state cyber activity. Data for studying CEIOs are often publicly available. They employed semantic network analysis (SNA) to assess the text of actual advertisements from a prominent CEIO. Their analysis showed that African-Americans, not White conservatives, were the target demographic that Russia sought to influence.[8]

Guadagno et al. (2024) conducted research on the US electorate to gauge their experiences as unknowing targets of disinformation. Participants were US citizens naive to the actions of the different entities using social media to target Americans with disinformation in the months leading up to the 2016 US presidential election. Results indicated participants reported notable changes in their interactions on social media with disruptions to relationships. Participants reported they argued with their connections more, observed others disagree more, and reported an increase in the loss of friends and family connections with unfriending or unfollowing. Most participants reported increased psychological distress. Not one participant mentioned Russian election interference or disinformation as the cause of these interpersonal difficulties. Analysis of text responses did not include any mention of disinformation, Cambridge Analytica, or Russia as causes of these disruptions. Results suggest that social media use has implications for individuals' social relationships, and these disruptions may impact their psychological functioning.[9]

Russia utilised various social media platforms in an attempt to influence the 2016 US presidential election through disinformation campaigns.[10]

Facebook has been a problematic platform for the spread of propaganda, with its algorithms and targeted advertising capabilities exploited to microtarget users with divisive and misleading content, often playing on people's emotions and biases.[11]

Twitter has also been a hotbed for the spread of propaganda and misinformation.[12] The platform's real-time nature and lack of effective moderation allowed for the rapid dissemination of false narratives and conspiracy theories.[13]

YouTube, the popular video-sharing platform, was used to host and promote extremist content, including videos that radicalised viewers and spread disinformation.[14]

Instagram, with its visually driven content, became a platform for the spread of propaganda[15] through the use of memes, infographics, and other visual media.[16]

Tumblr and other smaller social media platforms were also utilised to spread propaganda and extremist ideologies, often targeting younger and more impressionable users.

The Internet Research Agency (IRA), a Russian troll farm with ties to the Kremlin, spearheaded a vast campaign across multiple platforms, including Twitter, Facebook, Instagram, YouTube, Google +, Tumblr, and PayPal. The IRA employed various tactics, such as creating coordinated networks of accounts that promoted each other's posts and events, and adapting digital marketing techniques to target audiences across multiple channels.

When one of the IRA's campaigns, Black Matters US, was suspended on Facebook, its Twitter account complained about the move and accused the social network of 'supporting White supremacy'. The researchers criticised the 'belated and uncoordinated response' from companies like Facebook, Twitter, and Google to Russia's disinformation campaign.

The Russian disinformation campaign targeted various demographic groups in the United States, particularly conservative groups and African-American voters.

Conservative Groups: The Internet Research Agency (IRA), based in Saint Petersburg, Russia, created thousands of social media accounts that purported to be Americans supporting radical political groups and planned or promoted events in support of Trump and against Clinton. They reached millions of social media users between 2013 and 2017.

Monitoring 7,000 pro-Trump social media accounts over a 2 + 1/2-year period, researchers J. M. Berger, Andrew Weisburd and Clint Watts found the accounts denigrated critics of Russian activities in Syria and propagated falsehoods about Clinton's health.

A Senate inquiry has concluded that the Russian fake news campaign targeted 'no single group... more than African-Americans'.[17] It says Russian operatives used social media to deter Black people from voting and planted subtly racist content to incite conflict between ethnicities. More than 66% of Facebook adverts posted by the Russian troll farm contained a term related to race.

African-American community voters were discouraged from voting and from supporting Hillary Clinton. Posts with titles like 'Our Votes Don't Matter', 'Don't Vote for Hillary Clinton' and 'A Vote for Jill Stein is Not a Wasted Vote' were specifically targeted at Black voters. Russian ads aimed at African-Americans mimicked social justice movements that were already active in the Black community and tried to create a negative response from other US ethnic groups.

The Black Matters Facebook page, created by Russian operatives, was meant to imitate the Black Lives Matter movement. Almost 100% of its YouTube content involved videos of violence perpetrated against African-American men. Alleged police brutality against African-Americans featured on Blacktivist video and Instagram posts as well as news stories with racial undertones, like the NFL kneeling protests.

Russia's Internet Research Agency borrowed heavily from the Soviet-era strategy of seeking to exploit American racial division to deepen unrest during the civil rights movement and after.[18] Russian operatives portraying themselves as Black Americans were among the most prolific fake accounts used during the 2016 election and in the early months of the Trump administration. All but one of the 50 most widely retweeted posts by the Internet Research Agency were from fake accounts purporting to belong to Black Americans.

Some posts directly urged Black voters to skip the election, such as a Facebook ad on Election Day targeting those with an interest in civil rights, saying, 'Not one represents Black People. Don't go to vote. Only this way we can change the way of things…'

Russian disinformation efforts may have influenced public perceptions of the electoral process and satisfaction with democracy.[19] Research suggests that heightened attention to political news and the perception that misinformation influenced others during the campaign can indirectly reduce satisfaction with democracy, particularly among independents and Democrats.[20]

However, framing the discussion around Russian interference with varying levels of certainty can shape perceptions differently.[21] A study found that framing Russian disinformation with uncertainty reduced perceptions that Republicans had been influenced, indirectly increasing faith in electoral results and satisfaction with democracy. Conversely, framing the discussion with certainty increased perceptions that Democrats had been influenced, indirectly reducing faith in electoral results and satisfaction with democracy.

The findings highlight how the framing of discussions around foreign interference can potentially impact public trust in electoral processes and democratic institutions, even in the absence of direct effects on voting behaviour.

Russia employed various tactics to create fake profiles and accounts on social media platforms to spread disinformation during the 2016 US presidential election. The Internet Research Agency (IRA), a Russian troll farm, spearheaded a vast campaign across multiple platforms, including Twitter, Facebook, Instagram, YouTube, Google +, Tumblr, and PayPal.[22]

The IRA created thousands of social media accounts that purported to be Americans supporting radical political groups. These accounts denigrated critics of Russian activities in Syria and propagated falsehoods about Hillary Clinton's health. Some accounts portrayed themselves as Black Americans, with all but one of the 50 most widely retweeted posts by the IRA being from fake accounts purporting to belong to Black Americans.

Russia adapted digital marketing techniques to distribute false news and propaganda across multiple channels during the election. These techniques included propagandistic news, outright fake news, paid commentators, bots (automated accounts), and hijacking real social media accounts.

One tactic involved creating coordinated networks of accounts that promoted each other's posts and events. For example, when the IRA's campaign 'Black Matters US' was suspended on Facebook, its Twitter account complained about the move and accused the social network of 'supporting White supremacy'.

Russia had a particular focus on targeting conservatives with posts on immigration, race, and gun rights, as well as undermining the voting power of left-leaning African-American citizens by spreading misinformation about the electoral process. The messaging clearly sought to benefit the Republican Party and Donald Trump's campaign.

In January 2022, some US voters in New Hampshire received automated phone messages in which President Joe Biden's voice urged them not to vote in the state's Democratic Party primary election. However, it wasn't actually Biden; the message had been generated by artificial intelligence (AI). Experts warn that deepfakes pose a high risk to US voters by injecting false content into elections and eroding public trust.[23]

Russia utilised various social media platforms in an attempt to influence the 2016 US presidential election through disinformation campaigns.

Facebook has been a problematic platform for the spread of propaganda, with its algorithms and targeted advertising capabilities exploited to microtarget users with divisive and misleading content, often playing on people's emotions and biases. The Internet Research Agency (IRA), a Russian troll farm, created thousands of social media accounts that purported to be Americans supporting radical political groups. These accounts denigrated critics of Russian activities in Syria and propagated falsehoods about Hillary Clinton's health.[24]

Twitter has also been a hotbed for the spread of propaganda and misinformation. The platform's real-time nature and lack of effective moderation allowed for the rapid dissemination of false narratives and conspiracy theories. The IRA accounts portrayed themselves as Black Americans, with all but one of the 50 most widely retweeted posts by the IRA being from fake accounts purporting to belong to Black Americans.

YouTube, the popular video-sharing platform, was used to host and promote extremist content, including videos that radicalised viewers and spread disinformation. Instagram, with its visually driven content, became a platform for the spread of propaganda through the use of memes, infographics, and other visual media.

The IRA spearheaded a vast campaign across multiple platforms, including Twitter, Facebook, Instagram, YouTube, Google +, Tumblr, and PayPal. These various accounts would promote each other's posts and events. For example, when the IRA's campaign 'Black Matters US' was suspended on Facebook, its Twitter account complained about the move and accused the social network of 'supporting White supremacy'.

The Russian disinformation campaign during the 2016 US presidential election heavily targeted African-Americans with race-related content.[25] According to reports prepared for the US Senate intelligence committee, the 'most prolific' efforts were made to target Black Americans. Analysts found that Russians used social media 'troll farms' to 'confuse, distract, and ultimately discourage' Black people from voting for Hillary Clinton.

Much of the material was intended to inflame anger among Black Americans about issues like poverty, incarceration, and the use of force by police, thereby 'diverting their political energy away from established political institutions'. Some Russian propaganda posts falsely assured Black voters they could vote from home on their mobile devices instead of casting ballots in person.

The Internet Research Agency (IRA) engaged with unwitting Americans to further its reach beyond the digital realm and into real-world activities targeting African-Americans. For example, IRA operatives convinced individuals to sign petitions, share personal information, and teach self-defence courses while posing as US political activists.[26]

Russia's disinformation tactics also aimed to polarise conservative audiences by exploiting racial divisions and stoking fears about societal changes.[27] Ego-justifying and group-justifying motives lead individuals to defend their own pre-existing beliefs and those of their in-group, respectively. Presumably, distorting images of the out-group as deviant, hostile, stubborn, extreme, and unreasonable serves to justify treating the out-group unfavourably.

Those who embrace more conservative-rightist attitudes, identities, and leaders are more authoritarian and social-dominance-oriented (supportive of group-based hierarchies) than those with liberal-leftist ideologies. In-group favouritism, out-group derogation, and refusal to compromise seem to be more strongly associated with conservative ideology and Republican identification in the USA than with liberal ideology and Democratic identification.

Russian propaganda likely aimed to scare White citizens into thinking their nation was changing by putting 'Black activist language out on social media', such as falsely showing Black Lives Matter activists with guns and claiming they planned to exercise their second-amendment rights. This could mobilise White voters in support of Trump by playing on fears of societal changes and racial tensions.

The Mueller report, released in April 2019, detailed the findings of the special counsel's investigation into Russian interference in the 2016 US presidential election and potential obstruction of justice by President Trump.[28] The report found that Russia had interfered in the election in a 'sweeping and systematic fashion' through a social media disinformation campaign and the hacking of Democratic Party emails.[29] However, the report did not find sufficient evidence to charge any US person with crimes related to Russian election interference.

The report also examined 10 instances of potential obstruction of justice by the president, but ultimately did not make a determination on whether the president had committed a crime. While the special counsel's investigation did not find that the Trump campaign coordinated with the Russian government, Mueller's indictments have shown that people in Trump's orbit were often happy to accept help from Russians when it was offered.

In addition to the Mueller report, several Senate committees have also investigated Russian interference in the 2016 election. The Senate Intelligence Committee released a series of bipartisan reports detailing Russian interference efforts and vulnerabilities in US election systems.

The reports found that Russia's interference campaign was 'far more widespread' than previously known and included attempts to infiltrate election infrastructure in all 50 states.

The reports also highlighted the need for improved information sharing between federal, state, and local officials, as well as increased funding and security measures to protect election systems. Experts disagree about how to quantify the impact of Russia's social media campaign, but some argue that it's very likely Russia did sway the outcome of the 2016 election.

Russia employed various digital marketing techniques during the 2016 US presidential election to distort the media landscape and sway public opinion.[30] These included cross-device targeting, programmatic advertising, lookalike modelling, geolocation targeting, online video advertising, and psychographic/emotion-based targeting.

Cross-device targeting allowed marketers to identify and reach the same individual across multiple devices like mobile, TV, and computers by creating a persistent 'identity-graph'. Programmatic advertising involved automated ad buying and placement processes to target specific customers in real-time based on their context.

Lookalike modelling used big data analytics to identify and target individuals similar to a campaign's existing supporters without direct consent. Geolocation targeting took advantage of mobile device signals to identify and target people based on their physical location. Online video advertising delivered emotional content effectively across devices.

Psychographic targeting leveraged advances in neuroscience, data analytics, and behavioural tracking to target people based on their psychological traits and emotional responses. These techniques allowed campaigns to reach and influence voters with unprecedented precision and scale.

Russia's disinformation efforts during the election aimed to reduce voter confidence and sow discord by exploiting digital advertising capabilities like micro-targeting and 'dark ads'.[31]

Micro-targeting allowed campaigners to direct tailored messages to specific groups based on personal data like demographics, interests, and location. This raised transparency concerns, as only the voter, campaigner, and platform knew the targeting criteria and ad spend details.[32] Regulators.

'Dark ads' referred to the lack of transparency around micro-targeted political ads only visible to the intended audience. There were concerns about the potential for foreign actors to covertly influence voters through such untraceable targeted messaging.

To address these issues, social media companies like Facebook, Google, and Twitter committed to labelling political ads with sponsor information and creating searchable ad libraries with targeting data and costs. However, meaningful implementation aligning with election laws was deemed necessary for true transparency.

The UK's election rules also required campaigners to report ad spending against the right limits and provide detailed invoices on targeting parameters. Lack of compliance made it difficult to determine if campaigners gained unfair advantages through undisclosed digital ad buys. Overall, while digital marketing expanded outreach abilities, stronger guardrails were needed to maintain electoral integrity. It may be that the EU takes more fundamental action on regulation.[33]

References

1. https://www.csis.org/analysis/russian-meddling-united-states-historical-context-mueller-report.
2. https://en.wikipedia.org/wiki/Russian_interference_in_the_2016_United_States_elections.
3. https://policyreview.info/articles/analysis/role-digital-marketing-political-campaigns.
4. https://freedomhouse.org/report/freedom-on-the-net/2019/the-crisis-of-social-media/digital-election-interference.
5. https://time.com/5565991/russia-influence-2016-election/.
6. https://en.wikipedia.org/wiki/Internet_Research_Agency.
7. https://www.washingtonpost.com/politics/2019/11/18/how-russia-weaponized-social-media-got-caught-escaped-consequences/.
8. Vićić, J. and Gartzke, E., 2024. Cyber-enabled influence operations as a 'center of gravity'in cyberconflict: The example of Russian foreign interference in the 2016 US federal election. *Journal of Peace Research*, *61*(1), pp. 10–27.
9. Guadagno, R., Olivieri, A. and Kimbrough, A., 2024, June. Social Media in the Aftermath of the 2016 US Presidential Election: Disruption at the Cost of Connection. In *European Conference on Cyber Warfare and Security* (Vol. 23, No. 1, pp. 172–180).
10. https://www.bbc.co.uk/news/technology-46590890.

11. https://www.cnn.com/2016/12/26/us/2016-presidential-campaign-hacking-fast-facts/index.html.
12. https://time.com/5565991/russia-influence-2016-election/.
13. https://cepr.org/voxeu/columns/how-twitter-affected-2016-presidential-election.
14. https://www.washingtonpost.com/news/the-switch/wp/2016/03/25/inside-youtubes-explosive-transformation-of-american-politics/.
15. https://www.vox.com/2018/12/17/18144924/instagram-russian-election-interference-social-media-report-new-knowledge-oxford.
16. https://www.bloomberg.com/news/articles/2018-12-17/instagram-was-bigger-russian-election-tool-than-facebook-report.
17. https://www.bbc.com/news/technology-49987657.
18. https://www.washingtonpost.com/technology/2020/08/26/race-divisions-highlighted-disinformation-2016/.
19. https://www.tandfonline.com/doi/full/10.1080/15205436.2022.2119871.
20. https://www.fpri.org/article/2019/05/perceptions-of-russian-interference-in-u-s-elections-matter-as-much-as-the-actual-involvement/.
21. https://www.brennancenter.org/our-work/analysis-opinion/new-evidence-shows-how-russias-election-interference-has-gotten-more.
22. https://www.bbc.com/news/technology-46590890.
23. https://www.aljazeera.com/news/2024/6/19/a-lack-of-trust-how-deepfakes-and-ai-could-rattle-the-us-elections.
24. https://www.theguardian.com/technology/2017/oct/30/facebook-russia-fake-accounts-126-million.
25. https://www.theguardian.com/world/2018/dec/24/race-russian-election-interference-senate-reports.
26. https://www.intelligence.senate.gov/press/senate-intel-committee-releases-bipartisan-report-russia%E2%80%99s-use-social-media.
27. https://www.nature.com/articles/s44159-022-00093-5.
28. https://www.acslaw.org/projects/the-presidential-investigation-education-project/other-resources/key-findings-of-the-mueller-report/.
29. https://www.pbs.org/newshour/show/inside-the-mueller-report-a-sophisticated-russian-interference-campaign.

30. https://policyreview.info/articles/analysis/role-digital-marketing-political-campaigns.
31. https://www.electoralcommission.org.uk/sites/default/files/pdf_file/Digital-campaigning-improving-transparency-for-voters.pdf.
32. https://www.campaignlive.co.uk/article/brands-wary-advertising-tiktok-amid-rising-political-disinformation/1875735.
33. https://digital-strategy.ec.europa.eu/en/policies/code-practice-disinformation.

CHAPTER 10

Russia: Disinformation War

During the Cold War era, the Soviet Union extensively employed propaganda and disinformation tactics, referred to as 'active measures', against Western nations and their populations.[1] In the post-Soviet period, under the leadership of Boris Yeltsin, the first President of Russia, the term 'disinformation' was discussed in relation to the Soviet-era tactics, aiming to differentiate the new Russia from its predecessor.

However, in the post-Yeltsin era, particularly after the 2008 Russian invasion of Georgia, Russian disinformation has been described as a crucial tactic in Russia's military doctrine. This modern form of disinformation propaganda has been characterised as a 'firehose of falsehood' due to its high volume of channels and willingness to disseminate outright falsehoods, even at the cost of inconsistency. Unlike Soviet-era tactics, contemporary Russian disinformation leverages the internet, claimed amateur journalism, and social media.

The Russian government claims that its disinformation efforts are merely a response to the West's attempts to promote democracy in Russia and the post-Soviet states, employing similar instruments and techniques.[2] From the perspective of Russian security policy, the expansion and implementation of non-military warfare and soft power are reactions to Western pressure on Russia and its position in the post-Soviet realm.

Russia's information warfare is an approach born out of weakness, providing more flexibility against challengers with greater economic

T. Singh, *Digital Psychological Warfare*,
https://doi.org/10.1007/978-3-032-15294-7_10

and technological resources. The Russian General Staff has extensively debated non-linear warfare, with Chief of the General Staff Valery Gerasimov's 2013 speech highlighting the use of disinformation, political, economic, humanitarian, and other non-military measures to achieve political goals.

The Russian leadership perceives non-military means of influencing foreign states as threats against which Russia must defend itself. The mass demonstrations in Moscow and St. Petersburg in 2011–2012, before Vladimir Putin's re-election as president, further fuelled the paranoia of the Russian security elite. Russian leaders believe that social groups, including protestors, are manipulated by controlled media and propaganda, lacking independent agency.

Ziemer et al. (2024) conclude that having a Russian identity and being exposed to Russian media is positively correlated with a heightened susceptibility to disinformation. Inoculation improves participants' ability to recognise disinformation correctly and perceive it as less credible, heightens perceptions of Russia's responsibility for the war, and strengthens solidarity with Ukraine. Inoculation effects on disinformation susceptibility were not significantly impaired by identity.[3]

Wenzel et al. (2024) identified Russian disinformation strategies related to the war in Ukraine and established the extent of their penetration in Central European countries. The countries in question were susceptible to Russia-related disinformation efforts to a highly varying degree. Poland was immune to narratives about the Ukraine war imposed by official and unofficial actors connected to the Russian authorities and their supporters. On the other hand, Slovak society was receptive to such sentiments, while Czechs are somewhere between these poles.[4]

The Russian elite perceives the influence and activities of Western governmental and nongovernmental institutions in post-Soviet countries as instruments of war aimed at weakening or toppling the Russian government. Consequently, Russian leaders have concluded the need to protect themselves from outside influence and employ offensive counter measures.

Internet freedoms in Russia are strictly controlled. Russia has significantly expanded laws and regulations tightening control over internet infrastructure, online content, and the privacy of communications.[5] The government has built up an entire arsenal of tools to reign over information, internet users, and communications networks.[6]

New laws and regulations adopted in the past two years expanded the authorities' already significant capacity to filter and block internet content automatically, no longer depending on providers' cooperation to implement the block. The 2019 'sovereign internet' law requires internet service providers (ISPs) to install equipment that allows authorities to circumvent providers and automatically block content the government has banned and reroute internet traffic themselves. A 2018 law introduces fines for search engines providing access to proxy services, such as virtual private networks (VPNs) that allow a user access to banned content or provide instructions for gaining access to such content. Regulations adopted in 2019 require VPNs and search engine operators to promptly block access to the websites on the list maintained by the federal government's informational system, which includes a regularly updated list of officially banned sites.

Amendments to existing counterterrorism legislation entered into force that require telecommunications and internet companies registered with Russian authorities as 'information dissemination organisers', for example, messenger apps and social media, to store and share information about users without a court order. The amendments build on previous data localisation laws, which require companies processing the personal data of Russian citizens to store private data of internet and mobile app users in Russia and hand the information over to security services upon request. In 2019, Russia's Federal Security Service (FSB) required these companies to install special equipment giving the FSB automatic access to their information systems and encryption keys to decrypt user communications without authorisation through any judicial process.

These laws and regulations effectively reinforce a raft of laws adopted in previous years, and described in a 2017 Human Rights Watch report, that enable the authorities to unjustifiably ban a wide range of content.[7] Since 2017, the government has also increased the number of official agencies with powers to order content blocking, and increased the fines for organisations, including internet service providers, proxy services, and search engines, that refuse to take down such content or that provide means to circumvent content blocking.

The 'sovereign internet' law envisages the full transfer of control over online communication networks to a government agency, from shutting down networks within certain areas of Russia, through cutting Russia off from the World Wide Web. If carried out as planned, the sovereign internet law will also enable the government to directly block whatever content it deems undesirable.

The impact on citizens is huge. These internet-related requirements are embedded in an even broader set of laws and regulations aimed at stifling freedom of expression, both online and offline. Some of the recently adopted laws limit space for public debate in general, and especially on topics the government deems divisive or threatening, such as LGBT rights, political freedoms, or, most recently, the COVID-19 pandemic.

Other legislation apparently aims at further undermining privacy and secure communications on the internet, making no digital communication in Russia safe from government interference. Russia clamped down harder on news and free speech than at any time in President Vladimir V. Putin's 22 years in power, blocking access to Facebook and major foreign news outlets and enacting a law to punish anyone spreading 'false information' about its Ukraine invasion with up to 15 years in prison.[8]

The crackdown comes as the Kremlin scrambles to contain discontent over the war and to control the narrative as Russia faces its most severe economic crisis in decades as a result of this week's crushing Western sanctions. For now, popular Russian social networks like VKontakte remain accessible, along with Instagram, Twitter, and YouTube. But analysts expect a further crackdown, heightening the importance of the messaging and social networking app Telegram, which the Kremlin tried and failed to block in 2018.[9]

Until recently, Russia's mostly uncensored internet had provided an outlet for Russians to express dissent and to read news reports outside the Kremlin propaganda bubble that envelops much of the country's traditional news media. But amid the war in Ukraine, which has touched off protests across the country and an outpouring of opposition from Russians online, the Kremlin appears to see the internet as a newfound threat.

Authoritarianism ensures strict control mechanisms are used. Russia has implemented strict government-mandated monitoring and filtering systems to limit the type of information its citizens can access online, in order to maintain control over the population.[10] The Kremlin, which holds anti-Western political views, insists that these steps are necessary to prevent the United States from spying on Russia and to benefit Russian citizens.

Russian authorities require bloggers with more than 3,000 daily readers to register with the state, a move criticised as an attempt by the Kremlin to remove the veil of anonymity common on the internet. The government has also expanded laws and regulations to tighten control over internet infrastructure, online content, and the privacy of communications.[11]

New laws and regulations adopted in recent years have expanded the authorities' capacity to automatically filter and block internet content without relying on providers' cooperation. The 2019 'sovereign internet' law requires internet service providers (ISPs) to install equipment that allows authorities to circumvent providers and automatically block banned content or reroute internet traffic themselves. Regulations adopted in 2019 also require virtual private networks (VPNs) and search engine operators to promptly block access to websites on the government's banned list.

Amendments to existing counterterrorism legislation require telecommunications and internet companies to store and share user information with security services without a court order. The Federal Security Service (FSB) has mandated that these companies install special equipment giving the FSB automatic access to their information systems and encryption keys to decrypt user communications without authorisation.

During the 2014 Sochi Olympics, Russia showcased its complete control over social media by banning international reporters from using personal smart devices, such as smartphones, tablets, or digital cameras, to capture video or take photographs while covering the event. Journalists were required to use only professional video and image capturing equipment.

After the massive Moscow demonstrations in December 2011 protesting Vladimir Putin's election win, the Kremlin intensified its efforts to control the internet, traditional news media outlets, and social media venues. The political legitimacy of the Kremlin and Putin as the newly elected president was openly questioned through these public protests and online discontent.

Russia has become Europe's largest internet market, with 78 million people having access to the internet, and 82 percent of online users having an account on at least one social media network. Russians with online access spend an average of 12.8 hours per month on social media networks, compared to the global average of 5.7 hours per month. Social media has become one of the few remaining venues for disenchanted Russians to voice their views and frustrations with the Kremlin anonymously and without fear of persecution.

Social media bots, also known as social bots, are bot programmes designed to carry out specific tasks on social media platforms.[12] Examples of tasks they can perform include managing social media profiles, sharing pre-written posts across different platforms and profiles, or liking/viewing specific content.

There are different types of bots used for malicious purposes.

Misinformation bots are programmed to repeatedly share misinformation and fake news links on social media. They may find articles or videos and leave false stories or claims to vilify their intended targets or support particular narratives.

Review bombing bots leave negative reviews on sites like Yelp or product listings on retail sites like Amazon. This is done to drive consumers away from a competitor's product or service by burying it with negative reviews.

Amplification bots are used to make it appear as if a fringe opinion or controversial view has widespread support. They create social media groups and repeatedly share content to artificially inflate the perceived popularity of a particular stance.

Poll bots are used to repeatedly fill out polls with specific results, skewing the poll outcomes. This can influence public perception of political climates, voting behaviour, or brand popularity.

Bots are commonly used on social media platforms to spread false information, promote particular stories or viewpoints, and push specific agendas in an organised manner.[13] This can be done by sharing fake news or engaging in behaviours like trying to get something to trend, artificially amplifying conversations through multiple accounts, generating fake engagements, or using hashtags in a spammy way.

Research shows that malicious bots can deceive and manipulate public opinion, influence stock markets, and spread misinformation and fake news on social media dialogues.[14] For example, Twitter has around 23 million social bots, accounting for 8.5% of total users, and over two-thirds of tweets are estimated to come from these bots. This highlights how social bots can be vectors for spreading misinformation and shaping public opinion on social networking sites.

Bots can shape public opinion by triggering actions from human users through various mechanisms, such as repeatedly sharing misinformation, creating an illusion of widespread support for a particular stance, or skewing poll results. This can influence people's perceptions, attract them to fringe political views, or even lead to radicalisation in extreme cases.

Social media has generated a wealth of propaganda and disinformation surrounding the Russia-Ukraine War, becoming a veritable information battleground as both countries use social media to discredit each other and influence global opinion.[15]

On 25 February, 2022, the day after Russia first launched its attack on Ukrainian territory, social media affiliated with the Russian government spread the rumour that Ukrainian President Volodymyr Zelenskyy had fled abroad. After the news spread, President Zelenskyy uploaded a short video to social media showing himself in the Ukrainian capital, Kyiv, countering this propagated disinformation, a key modern-day tool of warfare propaganda.

Another propaganda technique uses emotive footage to foster suspicion. For example, a video viewed more than 1.3 million times in various Facebook posts claimed to depict Russian and Ukrainian soldiers fighting on 26 February, 2022, stating: 'The battle between Ukraine and Russia is heating up'. However, the claim turned out to be false, as the video had been circulating since at least 2019 in posts about French Foreign Legion troops in battle in Mali.

Social media users, including those in the Arab World, are not merely unwitting victims of misleading information. A large number believe false narratives because of their political realities and to meet their own political views, known as Uses and Gratifications Theory (UGT) by media theorists. UGT assumes that audience members are not passive consumers of media but rather have agency and assume an active role in interpreting and integrating media into their lives, seeking out specific media to satisfy specific needs.

Accordingly, people consume certain television channels or social media platforms because these outlets frame information or directly convey messages that support their pre-existing beliefs and views. Over recent decades, people in Arab countries have sought out pro-Putin Russian analysts due to Russian support for Arab causes in international forums.

Most Arabs may have no stance on the Russia-Ukraine conflict due to the geographical distance of the war. Additionally, Arab public opinion might also reflect the perspectives of their respective governments, which view the conflict as European. This type of audience, one which holds no strong opinions, might be more easily influenced by propaganda and disinformation in the media and needs to be trained in dissecting information.

Seeing the daily realities of war has led to a sentiment of guilt on social media that perpetuates mass posting.[16] Many feel pressure to raise awareness and share posts about ongoing conflicts as a salient form of activism. While this may have helped put Western public opinion in Ukraine's court from the outset, mass posting has not always worked in Ukraine's favour.

The speed of online updates born from millions of users and the scale of Russian aggression have pushed mainstream media outlets to rush and break stories that compete with the current pace of social media cycles before they have finished developing. This has undermined the value of legitimate open-source investigations being carried out to debunk Russian claims and unintentionally helped propagate misinformation that ultimately aids the Kremlin.

Moreover, as other pressing conflicts continue to unfold in the world and ordinary citizens are confronted by their own problems, attention is bound to be diverted elsewhere, manifesting in a form of compassion fatigue (dubbed 'Ukraine Fatigue'), where users become weary of the Ukrainian struggle for freedom on social media. It is under these conditions that the Russian capabilities in the information war begin to thrive.

As compassion fatigue sets in, Russian disinformation against Ukraine can permeate social media spaces more effectively. One of Russia's most successful information tactics on global public opinion about the war in Ukraine is a particular brand of misinformation that simply draws attention to Western faults. Despite currently engaging in an active occupation, Russia has incited anti-Western sympathy and used it to gain ground through social media – particularly in countries that suffered from Western colonisation, such as those in Africa and across Latin America. By reminding citizens of this painful history and stoking renewed anger against Western responses to current events, Russia continues to fuel a mistrust of Western narratives on social media.

As the world becomes more polarised and the Russian invasion continues, anger towards Western governments can play a pivotal role in shaping the narrative of this conflict. Arguments surrounding double standards and hypocrisy have inflamed Ukraine fatigue, distract from the Ukrainian plight, and can further shift the way social media users engage with this conflict. Such deflection is not an uncommon tactic for occupying powers, made even more possible now through artificial intelligence (AI).

The disinformation surrounding Russia's large-scale invasion of Ukraine in February 2022 marked an escalation in Russia's longstanding information operations against Ukraine and open democracies.[17] The flow of – and disruption caused by – Russian disinformation has significantly increased since Russia's invasion in February 2022.

In turn, Ukraine's response to the Russian disinformation threat has built upon progress made in strengthening the information and media environment since 2014 and in establishing mechanisms to respond directly to information threats. These include efforts to provide accurate information, ensure that media organisations can continue operations, and policy efforts to combat the threats posed by Russian state-linked media.

Internationally, governments rapidly recognised the disinformation threat in the context of Russia's large-scale aggression against Ukraine. In response, they have highlighted narratives and tools used by the Russian government, sanctioned media and personalities, and supported media environments domestically, as well as in Russia and Ukraine. International organisations similarly executed fact-checking and debunking programmes, as well as provided cross-organisational mechanisms for information sharing and technical support.

Compared to Russia, Ukraine ranks much higher in the World Press Freedom index, and has seen improvement in its score since 2014. Up to the invasion in February 2022, Ukraine's democracy was strengthening: the media landscape was broadening; the country pursued efforts to curtail corruption and promote transparency, including through its membership in the Open Government Partnership; and reforms were undertaken to support media integrity, local democracy, and elections.

Ukraine's efforts to strengthen its media sector since 2014 have been an essential pillar of its resilience to mis- and disinformation during Russia's current war against the country. The establishment of a public broadcaster, UA:PBC (Public Broadcasting Company of Ukraine, rebranded as Suspilne in 2019), in January 2017 was a key element of Ukraine's efforts to meet European standards and practices.

Alongside UA:PBC's formalisation and professionalisation, other major reforms of Ukraine's media environment include privatising state-owned print media, notably via the 2015 Law No. 917-VIII on Reforming State and Communal Print Media, which required state-owned printed media to be privatised by the end of 2018. Reforms have been supported by foreign donors, notably Germany and Sweden, as well as the United

States through the National Endowment for Democracy's (NED) Centre for International Media Assistance.

However, Ukraine's media environment also suffered from several challenges prior to Russia's invasion. Funding in Ukraine's media space, as elsewhere, is a major issue. While UA:PBC can theoretically compete with privately owned media for licences (it is also free), competing on quality is much harder, especially as it received only 60% of its legislated entitlement in 2020 and 82% in 2021. Ukrainian media remains significantly influenced by the financial support and political agendas of oligarchs who may promote their personal economic and political interests at the expense of the public interest.

Since 2014, Ukraine has developed a rich civil society landscape supporting the media sector. For example, civil society organisations (CSOs) focus on responding to mis- and disinformation, conduct monitoring and debunking activities, as well as producing research and indices, such as the Freedom of Speech Baromet'.

Across the globe, citizens are very concerned about false information in their newsfeeds[18] and accusations of disinformation are thriving online. As perceiving that information is false has real consequences, this research note aims to map mis- and disinformation beliefs related to the Russian war in Ukraine in 2022.

Although misinformation beliefs in general may result in the avoidance of established information or support for conspiracy theories, disinformation beliefs may further result in cynical views on politics or even anti-democratic behaviours. The main findings show that people are most likely to associate falsehoods related to the war with intentional manipulation or deception. In a communication context where disinformation, conspiracy theories, and 'fake news' accusations have become omnipresent, citizens may struggle to accept the honesty of information sources.

Considering that beliefs about the threats of false information are not always directly related to the actual prevalence of mis- and disinformation, it is crucial to map perceptions of both misinformation and disinformation in the context of the war in Ukraine. Especially amidst disruptive events and crises, news users are likely to believe that information is inaccurate or deceptive.

Considering that overall trust in the media is generally lowest in Northern and Latin America, and highest in Northern and Western Europe, the variety of included countries covers the diversity of trust in the media across the globe. Considering the presence of biases in domestic coverage of a foreign conflict, people may also be likely to associate the information they receive with mis- and disinformation.

Perceptions related to the unintentional dissemination of falsehoods, for example, due to a lack of expert knowledge, may reflect the critical media literacy skills that citizens need to navigate today's complex information setting. Even though disinformation beliefs associated with Russian propaganda or malign influence campaigns may reflect an accurate assessment of the information war at times, Levels of perceived misinformation are not representative of the prevalence of false information.

Considering that the levels of perceived misinformation are not directly related to the actual prevalence of false information across countries, and likely to be informed by ideological biases, it is important to map the levels of perceived misinformation among citizens. Considering that the strict adherence to traditional journalistic norms of objectivity and neutrality in a war context is thus questionable, people may also be likely to associate the information they receive with mis- and disinformation.

Russia's disinformation campaigns specifically seek to undermine trust in public institutions in OECD countries, which has recovered to 45% after falling to even lower levels following the 2008 global financial crisis.[19] These campaigns often rely heavily on made-up facts and incite conspiracies, which can more easily thrive by exploiting already low levels of confidence among citizens. An Edelman survey of ten countries found that only 48% trusted their governments as sources of information about the COVID-19 virus. The polarisation and distrust that derive from disinformation have long-lasting negative implications for government action, democracy, and inclusive growth.

In the United States, public opinion research shows that democracy is in serious trouble. An NPR survey found that 64% of the American population believes US democracy is in crisis and at risk of failing, with over 70% saying democracy is more at risk now than a year ago. A Quinnipiac University survey reveals that 76% of respondents think political instability within the country is a bigger danger than external adversaries, suggesting Americans recognise they are a bigger threat to their own democracy.[20] Alarmingly, 53% expect political divisions to worsen over their lifetime.

One driver of decreased confidence is the explosion of misinformation aimed at disrupting the democratic process, confusing and overwhelming voters. During the 2020 US election cycle, Russia's cyber efforts and online actors influenced public perceptions and sought to amplify mistrust in the electoral process by denigrating mail-in voting, highlighting alleged irregularities, and accusing the Democratic Party of voter fraud. The 'big lie' reinforced by President Trump about the 2020 election results amplified the Russian efforts and has lasting implications on voters' trust in election outcomes.

A robust 57% of White Americans believe there was voter fraud in the 2020 presidential election, including 26% who believe there was definitely fraud. Racial and ethnic minorities are also susceptible, with 38% of Latinos and 30% of African Americans thinking there might have been fraud. Only 20% feel 'very confident' in the integrity of the US election system, and 56% have 'little or no confidence' that elections represent the will of the people.

Decreased confidence decreases civic engagement, with 26% of respondents in a survey believing their vote does not count. The 2022 primary elections included candidates perpetuating the myth that the 2020 election was stolen, undermining confidence and appearing to suppress voter turnout. Voter turnout was generally low across the country compared to recent midterm elections, with election officials suggesting a lack of trust in the voting system as a factor.

Russia has long engaged in an information campaign of propaganda and disinformation as a major part of its foreign policy, which has intensified since the invasion of Ukraine in February 2022. While Western media outlets have generally condemned the invasion, this has done little to discourage Russia from continuing to actively promote propaganda and disinformation on social media in an attempt to undermine support for Ukraine.[21]

The social media tactics used by the Russian state to create an environment of disinformation have been well-researched, particularly in English and Russian communities, pointing to a well-organised, coordinated community of actors. Such groups include the Internet Research Agency, for which operations have been suggested in German, Italian, Arabic, French, and Spanish, although the focus of the study is the group's US operations. The surprising popularity of the topic discovered in Japanese and, to a lesser extent, Korean, also points to similar mechanisms at play that are worth investigating from a more detailed perspective.

Russian propaganda has been documented in several Western countries during previous conflicts, and the underlying narratives are often recycled from past propaganda campaigns, aiming to destabilise democratic countries by sowing doubt and polarising citizens.[22] With the rise of the internet, propaganda campaigns increasingly make use of social media, giving rise to concerns that social media may be strategically used to increase political division and influence public opinion as a tool of modern warfare.

A particular threat of social media is that propaganda campaigns can reach unprecedented levels of online exposure. While previous campaigns from the Internet Research Agency relied largely upon trolls to spread propaganda, it is likely that current influence operations make increasing use of bots. Bots allow producing high volumes of software-controlled social media profiles at low cost and have previously been deployed to spread disinformation, fake news, and hate speech on social media, aiding in the spread of low-credibility content by amplifying early-stage diffusion.

The Russian government has significantly expanded laws and regulations tightening control over internet infrastructure, online content, and the privacy of communications, building up an entire arsenal of tools to reign over information, internet users, and communications networks. New laws and regulations adopted in recent years have expanded the authorities' capacity to automatically filter and block internet content without relying on providers' cooperation.

The 2019 'sovereign internet' law requires internet service providers (ISPs) to install equipment that allows authorities to circumvent providers and automatically block banned content or reroute internet traffic themselves. Regulations adopted in 2019 also require virtual private networks (VPNs) and search engine operators to promptly block access to websites on the government's banned list.

Amendments to existing counterterrorism legislation require telecommunications and internet companies to store and share user information with security services without a court order. The Federal Security Service (FSB) has mandated that these companies install special equipment giving the FSB automatic access to their information systems and encryption keys to decrypt user communications without authorisation.

These laws and regulations effectively reinforce a raft of laws adopted in previous years, enabling the authorities to unjustifiably ban a wide range of content. Since 2017, the government has also increased the number of official agencies with powers to order content blocking and increased fines for organisations that refuse to take down such content or provide means to circumvent content blocking.

The 'sovereign internet' law envisages the full transfer of control over online communication networks to a government agency, from shutting down networks within certain areas of Russia to cutting Russia off from the World Wide Web. If carried out as planned, the sovereign internet law will also enable the government to directly block whatever content it deems undesirable.

In contrast to China, the Internet in Russia is currently not being systematically filtered, with many considering Russia as a relatively closed regime that pursues an open Internet policy.[23] While Putin was able to implement measures that tightened control over political censorship in traditional mass media, particularly television, the Internet has remained officially uncensored so far.

However, new measures passed since the 2022 invasion of Ukraine show Russia moving away from Western influences and adopting a more authoritarian approach to digital censorship.[24] One notable distinction is Russia's reliance on its courts, which often rubber-stamp media freedom restrictions and buttress digital censorship efforts. For example, in April 2018, a Russian district court ordered the popular social media platform Telegram to be blocked for refusing to comply with the Yarovaya Law, which requires apps to provide encryption keys to the government upon request.

In contrast, Beijing has constructed its censorship apparatus grounded on the belief that a state exerts complete control over the digital network within its borders, actively campaigning for 'cyber sovereignty' at the United Nations. The key elements to achieve these institutional conditions are: (i) legislation regulating digital content; (ii) regulatory bodies that police content in the digital space; and (iii) authoritarian governance.

Legislation and regulatory bodies give censorship an air of legitimacy in China, while authoritarian governance ensures the state can control these processes without obstructions. These conditions allow the state to control technical aspects needed to censor digital media, such as controlling telecommunications infrastructure like internet service providers (ISPs) either directly or by proxy. Beijing's ultimate aim is for individuals, the media, journalists, and businesses to self-censor.

For years, the number of countries using technology to monitor and track their citizens has been growing, with China and Russia being the most active in applying these technologies. Beijing increasingly uses surveillance methods within its own country, while Moscow engages in extensive hacking of other countries' systems, and both nations aggressively sell surveillance technology and training to foreign governments.[25]

The Chinese and Russian surveillance models, while similar in scope, differ by method. China uses more advanced techniques, while Russia relies on older strategies. In 1995, the Russian government began laying the legal framework for extensive surveillance, including intercepting calls, monitoring the internet, social media, and Wi-Fi, and regulating blogging, encryption, and data storage.

The Russian government has paid less attention to censorship than China, failing to establish domestic media substitutes to foreign outlets and allowing foreign apps, social media platforms, and search engines. While Russian authorities conduct online filtering, it is less pervasive than in China. 'Russians don't have as many options for technological surveillance, so they rely mostly on traditional methods of controlling their population through intimidation or passing laws to intimidate people or by extensive (harassing) of journalists', according to Valentin Weber, research affiliate at the University of Oxford.

China, in contrast, is leveraging its technological expansion around the world by building and adapting tech tools for conducting surveillance on its own population and exporting those models abroad. Citizens, including children, are monitored through apps, facial recognition cameras, and other technologies. Beijing also engages in dispelling information critical of the regime or tied to controversial subjects and actively posts on social media to steer public attention.

Bots are commonly used on social media platforms to spread false information, promote particular stories or viewpoints, and push specific agendas in an organised manner. This can be done by sharing fake news or engaging in behaviours like trying to get something to trend, artificially amplifying conversations through multiple accounts, generating fake engagements, or using hashtags in a spammy way.

Research shows that malicious bots can deceive and manipulate public opinion, influence stock markets, and spread misinformation and fake news on social media dialogues. For example, Twitter has around 23 million social bots, accounting for 8.5% of total users, and over two-thirds of tweets are estimated to come from these bots. This highlights how social bots can be vectors for spreading misinformation and shaping public opinion on social networking sites.

Bots can shape public opinion by triggering actions from human users through various mechanisms, such as repeatedly sharing misinformation, creating an illusion of widespread support for a particular stance, or skewing poll results. This can influence people's perceptions, attract them to fringe political views, or even lead to radicalisation in extreme cases.

Bots have been shown to retweet articles within seconds of their first being posted, contributing to the articles going viral.[26] Moreover, 33% of the top sharers of content from low-credibility sources were likely to be bots, significantly higher than the proportion of bots among top sharers of fact-checked content. Bots also employ the strategy of mentioning influential users in tweets linking to false or misleading articles, in the hope that these users will share the article with their many followers, contributing to its spread and boosting its credibility.

In light of findings that humans are largely unable to distinguish social bots from genuine (human) accounts,[27] it is likely that humans unknowingly contribute to the spread of misinformation as well. One study found that in regard to low-credibility content, humans retweet bots and other humans at the same rate. Fake news articles spread faster on Twitter than true news articles because humans, not bots, were more likely to retweet fake articles. Given human susceptibility to both automated accounts and fake news, some have warned that intelligent social bots could be leveraged for mass deception or even political overthrow.

There is evidence that bots have already infiltrated political conversations online. Leading up to the 2016 presidential election in the United States, 20% of all political tweets originated from accounts that were likely to be bots. While it did not specifically implicate bots, one study found that a majority of fake or extremely biased news articles relating to the 2016 election were shared by unverified accounts – that is, accounts that were not confirmed to be human. Bots have also been used to spread misinformation in the 2017 French presidential election, though ultimately the bot campaign was unsuccessful, in part because the human users who engaged with the bots were mostly foreigners with no say in the election outcome. Bot strategies specifically relevant to political campaigns include hashtag hijacking, in which bots adopt an opponent's hashtags in order to spam or otherwise undermine them, as well as flagging their opponent's legitimate content in the hopes it gets removed from the platform.

Online trolling, harassment, and distraction, especially by highly active automated accounts, are a key component of the modern disinformation purveyor's toolkit. These techniques push independent voices out of public spaces and are sometimes considered a new form of political censorship.

In the early to mid-2000s, the Russian government began recruiting human commenters before later adopting the use of automated 'bot' accounts. One study suggests that on Twitter more than half of tweets in Russian are produced by automated accounts.[28] Aiming to avoid detection, many disinformation campaigns now avail themselves of accounts that are partially automated, partially controlled by human users; these are often referred to as cyborg or sock puppet accounts.

In recent years, the use of bots and trolls to shape online discussion has become so common across countries that it could be considered a widely exploited bug in the digital public square extending far beyond conflict or authoritarian settings. In Mexico, paid political consultants orchestrated the theft of campaign secrets and the large-scale distribution of disinformation to voters. Such activity continues to this day, as pro-government accounts swarm political hashtags, threaten the lives of activists, and marginalise protesters.

In the Philippines, where the public square faces significant threats both online and off, interview-based research has explored a sophisticated 'underground' public relations industry in which digital strategists, social media influencers, and paid commenters compete to deliver their clients the greatest degree of control over political narratives on the internet. In a stroke of market innovation, the subcontracting of digital disinformation in the Philippines has tied the financial and career incentives of competing freelancers to the objectives of national political parties, to devastating effect.

Digital disinformation often promotes xenophobic sentiment, and hate speech is common. In India, far-right religious figures used messaging applications to spread false claims about religious minorities, sparking communal violence. In Indonesia, political and religious leaders have decried the spread of hate speech and rumours over social media, which played a pivotal role in the Jakarta mayoral election.

Mass media have been used to spread disinformation and hate speech in the past and have played a key role in modern genocides. Social media is now playing a similar role in contemporary atrocities: in Burma, for instance, ultranationalist Buddhist monks have used social media to mobilise supporters and instigate violence against the Rohingya, a persecuted Muslim minority group.

Social media has generated a wealth of propaganda and disinformation surrounding the Russia-Ukraine War, becoming a veritable information battleground as both countries use social media to discredit each other and influence global opinion.[29]

As the Russia-Ukraine conflict unfolded, it became clear that both sides are using social media to manipulate the truth, and many examples abound. Fake news about the war on the ground plays a role in influencing the outcome of the conflict and can easily mislead the public who are desperate to know what is happening. Another propaganda technique uses emotive footage to foster suspicion.

Social media users, including those in the Arab World, are not merely unwitting victims of misleading information. A large number believe false narratives because of their political realities and in order to meet their own political views, known as Uses and Gratifications Theory (UGT). With this theory in mind, the Russia-Ukraine War has provoked a debate among Arabs. According to Egyptian writer and researcher Amr Salah at the Carnegie Endowment for International Peace, although many Arabs intuitively empathise with the Ukrainian people, social media reveals significant support for Putin in spite of the evidence of the horrors of the conflict and its global economic impact.

Salah finds that supporters of this counter-narrative mostly view the Ukrainian president as a Western puppet who initiated hostilities and threatened Russia. On the other hand, they see the Russian president as the creator of a new nation, a leader challenging Western hegemony, and a commander who runs a powerful home-grown military able to lend support to Arab and Muslim countries. Accordingly, people consume certain television channels or social media platforms because these outlets frame information or directly convey messages which support their pre-existing beliefs and views.

Most Arabs may have no stance on the Russia-Ukraine conflict due to the geographical distance of the war. Additionally, Arab public opinion might also reflect the perspectives of their respective governments, which view the conflict as European. This type of audience, one which holds no strong opinions, might be more easily influenced by propaganda and disinformation in the media and needs to be trained in dissecting information.[30]

Seeing the daily realities of war has led to a sentiment of guilt on social media that perpetuates mass posting. Many feel pressure to raise awareness and share posts about ongoing conflicts as a salient form of activism.[31] While this may have helped put Western public opinion in Ukraine's court from the outset, mass posting has not always worked in Ukraine's favour.[32]

The speed of online updates born from millions of users and the scale of Russian aggression have pushed mainstream media outlets to rush and break stories that compete with the current pace of social media cycles before they have finished developing. This has undermined the value of legitimate open-source investigations being carried out to debunk Russian claims and unintentionally helped propagate misinformation that ultimately aids the Kremlin.[33]

Moreover, as other pressing conflicts continue to unfold in the world and ordinary citizens are confronted by their own problems, attention is bound to be diverted elsewhere, manifesting in a form of compassion fatigue (dubbed 'Ukraine Fatigue'), where users become weary of the Ukrainian struggle for freedom on social media. It is under these conditions that the Russian capabilities in the information war begin to thrive.[34]

As compassion fatigue sets in, Russian disinformation against Ukraine can permeate social media spaces more effectively.[35] One of Russia's most successful information tactics on global public opinion about the war in Ukraine is a particular brand of misinformation that simply draws attention to Western faults. Despite currently engaging in an active occupation, Russia has incited anti-Western sympathy and used it to gain ground through social media – particularly in countries that suffered from Western colonisation, such as those in Africa and across Latin America. By reminding citizens of this painful history and stoking renewed anger against Western responses to current events, Russia continues to fuel a mistrust of Western narratives on social media.

As the world becomes more polarised and the Russian invasion continues, anger towards Western governments can play a pivotal role in shaping the narrative of this conflict. Arguments surrounding double standards and hypocrisy have inflamed Ukraine fatigue, distract from the Ukrainian plight, and can further shift the way social media users engage with this conflict. Such deflection is not an uncommon tactic for occupying powers, and artificial intelligence (AI) has been an enabling factor.[36]

What follows is a transcript of a discussion with a person who has first-hand experience of disinformation and is shared for understanding its impact and context.

Author: Thank you for joining me today to discuss your experiences with Russian disinformation during the war with Ukraine. Can you start by explaining how you first became aware of these disinformation efforts?

Victim: We have seen such disinformation from Russia all our lives but not on this scale. I first noticed something was off when I started seeing a lot of conflicting information online about political events and news stories. It seemed like there were deliberate attempts to spread false information and create confusion. As the situation in Ukraine became more tense, it became clear that these were part of Russia's Active Measures, which are covert operations aimed at influencing public opinion and destabilising societies.

Author: That must have been quite unsettling. How did you feel when you realised that you were being targeted by these disinformation campaigns?

Victim: It was a mix of anger, frustration, and a sense of betrayal. Knowing that my perception of reality was being manipulated by foreign entities was deeply unsettling. It made me question the information I was consuming and the sources I trusted. It also made me feel vulnerable, realising that my opinions and beliefs could be influenced without my knowledge.

Author: How did these disinformation efforts affect your trust in media and information sources?

Victim: My trust in media took a significant hit. I became much more sceptical of the information I encountered, especially from sources that I previously considered reliable. It made me realise the importance of verifying information from multiple sources and being critical of sensationalist headlines. It also highlighted the need for media literacy and the ability to discern credible information from propaganda.

Author: Can you describe the psychological toll these disinformation campaigns took on you?

Victim: It was mentally exhausting. Constantly questioning the validity of the information I was exposed to create a sense of paranoia and anxiety. It was like living in a state of constant doubt, never knowing what to believe. This took a toll on my mental health, making me feel more isolated and distrustful of others.

Author: How did you cope with these feelings and the impact of the disinformation campaigns?

Victim: I sought support from friends and family, who helped me navigate through the confusion. I also made a conscious effort to educate myself about disinformation tactics and how to identify them. This empowered me to be more critical of the information I encountered and to share this knowledge with others. It was a way to regain some control and reduce the anxiety I felt.

Author: What advice would you give to others who might find themselves targeted by disinformation campaigns?

Victim: My advice would be to stay informed and vigilant. Always verify information from multiple sources before accepting it as truth. Be critical of sensationalist headlines and be aware of the tactics used in disinformation campaigns, such as spreading false information and creating confusion. It's also important to seek support from trusted individuals and to engage in conversations about media literacy and critical thinking.

References

1. https://en.wikipedia.org/wiki/Russian_disinformation.
2. https://dgap.org/system/files/article_pdfs/meister_isolationpropoganda_apr16_web_1.pdf.
3. Ziemer, C.T., Schmid, P., Betsch, C. and Rothmund, T., 2024. Identity is key, but Inoculation helps–how to empower Germans of Russian descent against pro-Kremlin disinformation. *advances.in/psychology*, *2*, p. e628359.
4. Wenzel, M., Stasiuk-Krajewska, K., Macková, V. and Turková, K., 2024. The penetration of Russian disinformation related to the war in Ukraine: Evidence from Poland, the Czech Republic and Slovakia. *International Political Science Review*, *45*(2), pp. 192–208.
5. https://freedomhouse.org/country/russia/freedom-net/2023.
6. https://www.hrw.org/news/2020/06/18/russia-growing-internet-isolation-control-censorship.
7. https://www.hrw.org/news/2020/06/18/russia-growing-internet-isolation-control-censorship.
8. https://www.nytimes.com/2022/03/04/world/europe/russia-censorship-media-crackdown.html.
9. https://freedomhouse.org/report/freedom-net/2018/rise-digital-authoritarianism.
10. https://www.cfc.forces.gc.ca/259/290/317/305/salloum.pdf.
11. https://www.nytimes.com/2022/03/04/world/europe/russia-censorship-media-crackdown.html.

12. https://www.anura.io/blog/how-can-social-media-bots-influence-public-opinion.
13. https://young.scot/get-informed/ysdigiknow-fake-news-bots/.
14. https://cronfa.swan.ac.uk/Record/cronfa58271/Download/58271__21479__e1c3c3909c3347f7b4c69a09ae6cc392.pdf.
15. https://www.thecairoreview.com/essays/social-media-as-a-propaganda-tool-in-the-russia-ukraine-conflict/.
16. https://gjia.georgetown.edu/2024/02/02/russia-ukraine-through-the-eyes-of-social-media/.
17. https://www.oecd.org/ukraine-hub/policy-responses/disinformation-and-russia-s-war-of-aggression-against-ukraine-37186bde/.
18. https://ejpr.onlinelibrary.wiley.com/doi/10.1111/1475-6765.12646.
19. https://www.oecd.org/coronavirus/policy-responses/transparency-communication-and-trust-the-role-of-public-communication-in-responding-to-the-wave-of-disinformation-about-the-new-coronavirus-bef7ad6e/.
20. https://www.brookings.edu/articles/misinformation-is-eroding-the-publics-confidence-in-democracy/.
21. https://www.ncbi.nlm.nih.gov/pmc/articles/PMC11065866/.
22. https://epjdatascience.springeropen.com/articles/10.1140/epjds/s13688-023-00414-5.
23. https://eprints.lse.ac.uk/64065/1/Russia_China.pdf.
24. https://docs.aiddata.org/ad4/pdfs/Innovators-and-Emulators--China-and-Russias-Compounding-Influence-on-Digital-Censorship.pdf.
25. https://www.usnews.com/news/best-countries/articles/2019-09-20/china-russia-spreading-surveillance-methods-around-the-world.
26. https://www.sciencedirect.com/science/article/abs/pii/S0736585323001156.
27. https://www.ncbi.nlm.nih.gov/pmc/articles/PMC10166499/.
28. https://www.ned.org/wp-content/uploads/2018/06/How-Disinformation-Impacts-Politics-and-Publics.pdf.
29. https://www.thecairoreview.com/essays/social-media-as-a-propaganda-tool-in-the-russia-ukraine-conflict/.
30. https://researchbriefings.files.parliament.uk/documents/POST-PN-0719/POST-PN-0719.pdf.

31. https://gjia.georgetown.edu/2024/02/02/russia-ukraine-through-the-eyes-of-social-media/.
32. https://apnews.com/article/russia-crackdown-surveillance-censorship-war-ukraine-internet-dab3663774feb666d6d0025bcd082fba.
33. https://apnews.com/article/disinformation-election-interference-russia-china-2925ca62c1ba8c1893454ccb2f76785a.
34. https://demtech.oii.ox.ac.uk/wp-content/uploads/sites/12/2017/06/Casestudies-ExecutiveSummary.pdf.
35. https://www.cambridge.org/core/elements/evolution-of-authoritarianism-and-contentious-action-in-russia/3C9C2565E6956AC2E0FF8F4F6BAABC29.
36. https://www.cambridge.org/core/books/social-media-and-democracy/bots-and-computational-propaganda-automation-for-communication-and-control/A15EE25C278B442EF00199AA660BFADD.

CHAPTER 11

Russian Hacking Operations and Cyberattacks

Villalón-Huerta et al. (2024) argue that the Russian Federation intelligence community is a complex ecosystem with distinct agencies having formal assignments defined by Russian law. Other actors, such as criminal gangs or patriotic hackers, have close ties with the government intelligence services. All of these actors possess the capability to conduct hostile operations within cyberspace.[1]

An Advanced Persistent Threat (APT) is defined by NIST as an adversary that possesses sophisticated levels of expertise and significant resources that allow it to create opportunities to achieve its objectives by using multiple attack vectors including, for example, cyber, physical, and deception.[2] These objectives include establishing and extending footholds within the IT infrastructure of targeted organisations for purposes of exfiltrating information, undermining or impeding critical aspects of a mission, programme, or organisation; or positioning itself to carry out these objectives in the future. The advanced persistent threat pursues its objectives repeatedly over an extended period of time, adapts to defenders' efforts to resist it, and is determined to maintain the level of interaction needed to execute its objectives.

Takamaa and Lehto (2024) researched cyberattacks, where the target has been the Ukrainian state and its critical infrastructure. They analysed the traits of state-affiliated attacks in Ukraine, which helped uncover emerging patterns of Russian involvement. The main objective of these

T. Singh, *Digital Psychological Warfare*,
https://doi.org/10.1007/978-3-032-15294-7_11

cyber operations has been to undermine the functioning of Ukrainian society. The attack targets follow similar patterns with Russian information warfare strategies and doctrines throughout the years. Offensive cyber operations aimed at fundamentally weakening the ability to operate in Ukraine.[3]

Aljohani (2024) contends that Russia added cyber operations as a crucial component in its wartime doctrine. Ukrainian cyber teams have consistently had to counter persistent attempts by Russian hackers to disrupt critical infrastructure (CI).[4]

Russian hackers employ a range of sophisticated strategies and tactics to carry out cyberattacks. Spear phishing is a highly targeted form of phishing attack, where hackers impersonate trusted contacts or use insider lingo to trick victims into revealing sensitive information or clicking malicious links.[5] The Russian security service has used spear phishing techniques to compromise private conversations of high-profile politicians, civil servants, and others in attempts to meddle in British politics since 2015. A notable example is the 2018 hack on the Institute for Statecraft think-tank and the leak of US-UK trade documents used in the 2019 general election campaign. Campaigns by Russian hacking groups like Gamaredon have targeted Ukrainian government agencies and NGOs through spear phishing emails containing malware.[6] These emails often include tracking pixels to inform the attackers if they have been opened.

Once initial access is gained through phishing or other means, Russian cyber actors can deploy sophisticated malware capabilities. They adapt their techniques to target cloud infrastructure, stealing system-issued access tokens, enrolling new devices via credential reuse, and using password spraying and brute-forcing against weak passwords.[7]

Russian hackers conduct thorough research and preparation, including impersonating contacts through social engineering tactics. Their attacks involve sophisticated techniques like selectively leaking and amplifying stolen information. Reducing the risk surface by adopting the Principle of Least Privilege and implementing security measures like phishing analysers can help mitigate these threats.

Cyberwarfare by Russia includes denial of service attacks, hacker attacks, dissemination of disinformation and propaganda, participation of state-sponsored teams in political blogs, internet surveillance using SORM technology, and persecution of cyber-dissidents and other active measures. According to investigative journalist Andrei Soldatov, some of these activities were coordinated by the Russian signals intelligence, which was part of the FSB and formerly a part of the 16th KGB department.

An analysis by the Defence Intelligence Agency outlined Russia's view of 'Information Countermeasures' or IPb (*informatsionnoye protivoborstvo*) as 'strategically decisive and critically important to control its domestic populace and influence adversary states', dividing 'Information Countermeasures' into two categories of 'Informational-Technical' and 'Informational-Psychological' groups. The former encompasses network operations relating to defence, attack, and exploitation, and the latter to 'attempts to change people's behaviour or beliefs in favour of Russian governmental objectives'.

Propaganda tactics are key methods. US journalist Pete Earley described his interviews with former senior Russian intelligence officer Sergei Tretyakov, who defected to the United States in 2000. Tretyakov would send an officer to a branch of the New York Public Library where he could access the internet anonymously and post propaganda on various websites and send it in emails to US publications and broadcasters, sometimes disguised as educational or scientific reports.

According to a publication in Russian computer weekly *Computerra*, 'just because it became known that anonymous editors are editing articles in English Wikipedia in the interests of UK and US intelligence and security services, it is also likely that Russian security services are involved in editing Russian Wikipedia, but this is not even interesting to prove it – because everyone knows that security bodies have a special place in the structure of our [Russian] state'.[8]

Some of the prominent Russian black hat hacker groups include Cozy Bear, also known as APT29 or The Dukes, is a Russian hacker group believed to be associated with one or more Russian intelligence agencies.[9] They have been active since at least 2008 and are known for targeting government agencies, think tanks, and other high-profile organisations.[10]

Sandworm, also known as Unit 74,455, is a Russian cyber military unit of the GRU (Russia's military intelligence agency). They are responsible for the devastating NotPetya ransomware attack in 2017, which caused billions of dollars in damage globally.[11]

Turla is one of the most sophisticated hacker groups supporting the Russian government. They have been active since at least 2008 and are known for their advanced techniques, including the use of rootkits and complex malware.

Noname057(16) is a Russian-speaking hacker group whose attacks have been aligned with Russia's invasion of Ukraine. They have been involved in defacing Ukrainian websites and launching distributed denial-of-service (DDoS) attacks.

Wizard Spider, also known as Trickbot, is a Russian/Ukrainian hacker group suspected of being behind the Ireland Health Service Executive cyberattack in 2021. They are known for their use of the Trickbot malware, which is often used as a precursor to ransomware attacks.

UNC1151 is a hacker group believed to be based in Belarus, a close ally of Russia. They have been involved in various cyber operations, including the targeting of Ukrainian organisations during the Russian invasion.

Killnet is a group of Russian hacktivists that has been targeting European governments, infrastructure, and even the Eurovision song contest with cyberattacks and disinformation campaigns in support of Russia's war efforts in Ukraine. While not as sophisticated as state-sponsored groups, they have been successful in setting narratives about the war.

Other common techniques employed by Russian hackers include Distributed Denial of Service (DDoS) attacks. Russian crowdsourced DDoS attacks are mounting against Ukraine and NATO members' critical infrastructure.[12] A DDoS attack floods a website or server with traffic, overwhelming the target and causing it to slow down or crash. In the run-up to Russia's invasion of Ukraine, the number of DDoS attacks originating in Russia rose by 450% year-on-year.

A key actor in Russia's DDoS offensive is the hacker group NoName057(16). Rather than carry out attacks themselves, NoName recruits hackers by offering rewards in cryptocurrency for successful DDoS attacks. The platform automates user registration via the messaging service Telegram and had over 45,000 subscribers as of June 2023.

Despite their lack of technical sophistication, NoName's DDoS attacks create significant disruption, targeting sectors like finance, transportation, and healthcare across Europe. In February 2022, a suspected Russian DDoS attack shut down IT systems at a healthcare facility in Tallahassee, Florida.

Russian threat actors like Turla and APT28 have exploited zero-day vulnerabilities in Microsoft Office products against European diplomatic and military agencies. FireEye identified three new zero-day vulnerabilities exploited by these groups in 2023.[13]

Microsoft revealed a zero-day vulnerability (CVE-2023–36,884) in Office and Windows being actively exploited by the Russian cybercriminal group Storm-0978 to target defence and government entities. The attacks use lures related to Ukraine and NATO to deliver malicious attachments.[14]

Russia has effectively propagated distorted narratives surrounding key events like the annexation of Crimea and the war in Ukraine through disinformation campaigns. These efforts sow discord, justify Russia's actions, and erode trust in democratic institutions.[15]

Russian disinformation tactics include establishing a presence for 'freedom fighters', portraying military interventions as defending Russian-speaking people, and invoking the Russian Orthodox Church. The Kremlin also constructs enemy images, creates historical myths, and downplays its crimes through state media and anonymous websites.

One method is to plant fabricated news articles and social media posts that promote American isolationism, stir fears over border security, and amplify economic and racial tensions in the US. Russian content is translated, shared on platforms like X (Twitter), and amplified through a network of Telegram channels.[16]

The disinformation seeks to decrease support for Ukraine, undermine public trust, and polarise society in the USA and Europe. It has influenced a segment of the Republican base and some members of Congress.

Global interference campaigns are key methods. Russia's meddling isn't limited to the USA. The Kremlin has a pattern of using political, economic and social tactics to affect policy, hacking into websites and interfering with elections on a global scale.[17]

Germany faced a social media-fuelled propaganda attack in 2016. Looking to exploit tensions over Germany's acceptance of refugees, Russia fabricated a story about Arab immigrants raping a teenage girl, known as the Lisa case. This and other false narratives promoted by Russia helped to divide Germany over its immigration and refugee policies.

Researchers at the Oxford Internet Institute found evidence of bot activity and hashtag campaigns for three days during the second round of the 2017 French presidential election campaign. They noted that 25% of news links on Twitter were based on misinformation, identified as deliberately false and expressing ideologically extreme, hyper-partisan or conspiratorial views with logical flaws and opinions presented as facts.

In another study, the Institute determined that Sweden was flooded with false news reports in the run up to its election. Researchers found that 22% of shared URLs linked to junk sites, but only 1% of them could be traced to Russia.

Intelligence officials have reportedly found that Russia is interfering in the 2020 elections to try to support President Trump's re-election, while also meddling in the Democratic primaries to help Sen. Bernie Sanders' campaign.

Some strategies and tactics for election interference were the same as before. Russia's trolls pretended to be American people, including political groups and candidates. They tried to sow division by targeting both the left and right with posts to foment outrage, fear, and hostility. Much of their activity seemed designed to discourage certain people from voting. And they focused on swing states.

The IRA targets both sides of the ideological spectrum to sow division. This strategy is unique to Russian election campaigns, making it different than conventional persuasion-oriented propaganda or other foreign countries' election interference strategies.

The divide between the police and the Black community has been a running theme of the IRA's influence campaigns, as exhibited in activities between 2014 and 2017 through posts around 'Blue Lives Matter' vs. 'Black Lives Matter'. Furthermore, the IRA exaggerated a sharp division in the African American community.

Geographically, these accounts specifically targeted battleground states including Michigan, Wisconsin, Florida, Ohio, and Arizona. Drawing upon the literature, voter suppression is defined as a strategy to break the coalition of the opposition. Four types of voter suppression messages were identified: election boycott, deception (lying about voting details), third-party candidate promotion (e.g., promoting Jill Stein targeting likely Hillary Clinton voters), and same-side candidate attack (e.g., attacking Clinton targeting likely Clinton voters).

Among the posts captured in September 2019, third-candidate promotion (e.g., Rep. Tulsi Gabbard) and same-side candidate attacks, both targeting likely Democratic supporters, were found. In particular, the same-side candidate attack tactic centring around major Democratic candidates like former Vice President Joe Biden (portraying him as engaging in inappropriate touching) and Sen. Kamala Harris (heavy attacks on her) was very common.

Despite tech platforms' transparency measures, the IRA tactics aimed at the 2020 elections appear to have become even more brazen than those from 2016. In 2016, the IRA created 'shell groups' mimicking grassroots advocacy groups, which were relatively easy to detect. However, in the newer posts, fake accounts pretended to be official Democratic candidate or campaign committee accounts, with only subtle changes in names or addresses that are harder to notice (e.g., mimicking 'bernie2020' with 'bernie.2020__').

Among the reviewed IRA posts touching on the 2020 election, many used the identity of legitimate, relatively popular nonprofits, political action committees (PACs), or grassroots organisations, even in their original posts (not reposts). Similarly, there was an apparent increase in the use of nonpolitical content and seemingly apolitical or commercial materials to conceal the political nature of the campaigns.

Looking at the history of Russian cyber operations, the Kremlin employs cyber means to engage in long-term competition with rivals.[18] Before 2014, Moscow's campaigns tended to focus on political warfare and espionage. Massive denial-of-service operations sought to punish Estonia in 2007 after the country moved the Russian monument known as the Bronze Soldier.[19] During the Russo-Georgian conflict of 2008, Russia leveraged cyberattacks to enable information operations (IO) against Georgia.[20] Russian's IO operations aimed 'to influence, disrupt, corrupt, or usurp the decision-making of adversaries and potential adversaries while protecting [their] own'.[21]

In a harbinger of its military campaign to destroy Ukrainian critical infrastructure, Moscow also used cyber operations to target Kyiv's power supply. Following the illegal annexation of Crimea in 2014, advanced persistent threat (APT) groups such as Sandworm were implicated in the 2015 BlackEnergy campaign targeting Ukrainian power generation and distribution.[22] While the attacks captured headlines, they produced limited effects.[23] In 2017, Russian-linked groups launched the NotPetya campaign, which produced effects that spilled over from the intended targets, Ukrainian companies, to affect global logistics.[24]

Firdini et al. (2024) argue cyberattacks used by Russia in the war with Ukraine show how Russia leverages cyber operations in hybrid warfare against the West, aiming to avoid direct military responses. Russian groups are suspected of cyber-attacks on other countries' infrastructure over the past 20 years including in 2007 where cyber-attacks were targeted at Estonia's parliament, banks, and TV stations. In 2007, Russia's intelligence agency was accused of hacking into the US Democratic National Committee's email system and weaponising this information as part of efforts to influence the 2016 US presidential election. In

2015, a Russian group attacked Ukraine's power grid. In 2017, the NotPetya malware, developed by Russian intelligence, spread to A.P. Møller-Maersk's systems, one of the world's largest shipping companies, resulting in losses of up to $300 million. In 2020, the SolarWinds cyber-attack targeted SolarWinds' Orion software product used by companies to manage IT resources. The attack went undetected for months, allowing hackers to spy on SolarWinds customers and install malware on their systems. Targets included cyber security firms, US government institutions, and Microsoft.[25]

Russia has also used cyber operations as a form of political warfare, using a mix of propaganda to polarise societies and influence political elections. Of note, these efforts included parallel disruption campaigns seeking to deface websites and portray supporters for Ukraine as Nazis. This campaign was followed by the even more audacious attempt to undermine confidence in US democracy through the 2016 operations targeting the presidential election, where the effects are still debated. In 2018, US Cyber Command used Russia's past behaviour as well as other indicators and warnings that Moscow was about to repeat its efforts as justification for launching a pre-emptive operation against the Internet Research Agency, a Russian propaganda and influence operation firm, designed to forestall attacks during the midterm elections.[26]

More recently, Russian operations have combined a mix of sophisticated espionage and criminal malware campaigns. For most of 2020, the Russian hacking group APT29, or Cozy Bear, exploited a supply chain vulnerability in the SolarWinds Orion program to exfiltrate data and digital tools from an extensive list of targets. The operation raised alarm bells since neither the NSA nor major firms such as Microsoft detected the intrusion and because it likely involved a combination of human intelligence and cyber operations to insert malicious code deep into servers. In 2021, criminal actors known as DarkSide, likely linked to the Russian state, were successful in deploying ransomware against Colonial Pipeline, the system that moves much of the fuel used across the United States' East Coast.

Russia's motivations behind its cyber operations can be broadly categorised into three main areas: political agenda, economic gains, and strategic dominance.

Russia sees activities in cyberspace as a subset of the overarching framework of 'information confrontation', derived from the Russian understanding of relations between states and the struggle between great powers for global influence. Cyber operations play an essential role in this confrontation, compensating for conventional force by disabling critical civil infrastructure and weakening an adversary's war-fighting capabilities.

Russia has used cyber operations as a form of political warfare, employing propaganda to polarise societies and influence political elections. These efforts included parallel disruption campaigns seeking to deface websites and portray supporters of Ukraine as Nazis. The 2016 operations targeting the US presidential election were an audacious attempt to undermine confidence in American democracy, with effects still being debated.

Globally, Russia wages 'narrative warfare' in cyberspace to erode global confidence in Ukraine. This involves creating fake social media accounts, using bots, and targeting content prompts to unique user groups to change public attitudes.

While economic motives are not as prominent as political and strategic ones, Russia has recognised the potential economic benefits of cyber operations. By targeting sectors like finance, transportation, and healthcare across Europe, Russian cyber actors can create significant disruptions that may provide economic leverage.

The Kremlin's offensive stance assumes a systemic, continuous struggle between great powers, necessitating the defence against consistent influence operations by the West. Russia aims to exploit the vulnerabilities of strategic challengers, even in peacetime, as demonstrated by the annexation of Crimea and interference in the 2016 US election, which reaffirmed the effectiveness of information weapons in achieving strategic objectives without triggering military confrontation.

The overall goal of the 'information confrontation' is to achieve strategic effects and gain superiority over opponents, whether through military or non-military means. Russian military thinkers posit that by targeting not only the leadership and military but also the entire mass consciousness of the population, strategic effects may be achieved.

Russia has recognised that aspiring for military parity with the USA is costly and must be avoided, given the fate of the Soviet Union and Russia's economic stagnation. Therefore, the Kremlin is eager to exploit cyber vulnerabilities to achieve strategic objectives without escalating to direct military confrontation.

The UK and its international allies have accused Russia of being behind a series of cyberattacks since the start of its renewed invasion of Ukraine. The most recent attack targeted Viasat on February 24th, approximately

1 hour before Russia launched its major offensive against Ukraine. The UK's National Cyber Security Centre (NCSC) assesses that Russia was almost certainly responsible for this attack.

Although the primary target is believed to have been the Ukrainian military, the attack affected other customers as well, including personal and commercial internet users across Europe. Wind farms in central Europe were also impacted by the Viasat attack.

Additionally, the NCSC assesses that Russian military intelligence was almost certainly involved in defacing Ukrainian government websites on January 13th and deploying the destructive Whispergate malware. These cyberattacks had significant consequences for ordinary citizens and businesses in Ukraine and across Europe.

Several key events spurred the development of Russia's cyber capabilities and the use of disinformation campaigns.

In the second Chechen War (1999), Russia dominated traditional media but struggled against the global perception of Chechen independence due to rebels' use of the internet. This prompted Russian security services to harness the internet for influence operations.

Russo-Georgian War (2008), Georgia gained an upper hand by reporting Russian airstrikes on civilians, leading to discussions on creating 'Information Troops' within the Russian military.

During the 2011–2013 Moscow protests, social media's role in generating unrest demonstrated its potential for regime change, contributing to the Kremlin's anxieties. This led to investments in human capabilities like the Internet Research Agency troll farm.

These events facilitated the development of information campaign capabilities used in the 2014 annexation of Crimea.

Russia has been implicated in numerous high-profile cyberattacks and hacking campaigns over the years.

2007 Cyber Attacks on Estonia: Following a diplomatic row, Estonia faced massive denial-of-service attacks targeting financial, media, and government websites.

2008 Cyber Attacks on Georgia: During the Russo-Georgian War, Georgian government websites were defaced, and denial-of-service attacks were launched.

2015 TV5Monde Attack: The French broadcasting service was hit by a cyberattack linked to the Russian hacker group APT28, taking all channels off the air.

2017 Emmanuel Macron Email Leak: On the eve of the French presidential election, emails from Macron's campaign were leaked, with evidence pointing to APT28's involvement.

2017 NotPetya Ransomware Attack: The devastating NotPetya ransomware attack, attributed to the Russian hacking group Sandworm, caused billions in global damage.

2018 Winter Olympics Cyber Attack: US intelligence officials believe Russia was likely behind the cyberattacks targeting the 2018 Winter Olympics in South Korea.

2014–2016 Android Malware Targeting Ukrainian Army: The Russian APT group Fancy Bear used Android malware to target Ukraine's Rocket Forces and Artillery during this period.

2015 Ukrainian Power Grid Attack: A cyberattack caused a power outage in Ukraine, affecting over 200,000 people. The Russian groups, Sandworm and Fancy Bear, were suspected.

2021 SolarWinds Supply Chain Attack: The Russian hacking group APT29 or Cozy Bear exploited a vulnerability in SolarWinds software to infiltrate numerous US government agencies and private companies.

2021 Colonial Pipeline Ransomware Attack: The DarkSide ransomware gang, believed to have links to Russia, carried out a crippling attack on the Colonial Pipeline system in the USA.

These incidents highlight Russia's extensive use of cyber operations for political, economic, and strategic objectives against various targets worldwide.

Hacking tools and software are essential components of the hacking process, as they enable hackers to gain unauthorised access, exploit vulnerabilities, and carry out various malicious activities.[27] Hackers often utilise a wide range of tools and software, including network scanners, vulnerability scanners, password crackers, and exploit kits, to identify and exploit weaknesses in computer systems and networks. The use of hacking tools and software is a critical aspect of the hacking process, as it allows hackers to gather information, gain access, and execute their malicious plans.

Russian cyber actors have demonstrated their ability to target and disrupt communication networks and infrastructures. In March 2023, Swedish authorities accused Russia of deliberately targeting the country's satellite networks with 'harmful interference' shortly after Sweden's accession to NATO.[28] The interference, originating from Russia and Crimea, targeted three different Sirius satellite networks crucial for satellite services in Nordic countries and eastern Europe.

This incident is part of a broader pattern of Russian attempts to disrupt European communication systems since its invasion of Ukraine in 2022, seen as tests of the European Union and NATO's preparedness. European satellite companies have reported months of Russian radio frequency interference, resulting in broadcast interruptions and even instances of violent programming replacing content on children's channels.

Hackers may also target and manipulate the psychological aspects of their victims, such as their emotions, biases, and decision-making processes, in order to gain access or influence their behaviour. Psychological manipulation techniques, such as social engineering, can be used to trick individuals into revealing sensitive information or performing actions that compromise the security of a system or network.

The United States' National Cyber Security Centre (NCSC) has accused Russia of being behind the cyberattack on Viasat, which disabled satellite communication across Europe.[29] To support this accusation, the NCSC cited the following evidence:

The Russian security service utilised spear phishing techniques to gain initial access to the satellite network. Specifically, they exploited a vulnerability in the satellite network to disable communication across the region. By disabling communication across the entire network, they were able to disrupt communication for many customers. The hack demonstrates Russia's ability to cause major disruptions through cyberattacks. The attack highlights the threat posed by Russia's cyber capabilities and Russia's ability to disrupt critical systems.

The Russian Security Services (formerly the KGB) have long-standing ties to Russian national criminal and hacktivist communities. A decade ago, the Russian state demonstrated its reach into these informal communities with the large-scale DDoSing of Estonia.[30]

Repeatedly over the last 6 years, Russia has demonstrated the capability and utility of patriotic organisations in combined arms campaigns. The hybridisation that results in the use of an open-source malware kit to attack the Ukrainian power grid or patriotic hackers taking part in attacking a foreign government's networks as part of a kinetic attack demonstrates the extent to which outsourcing can empower and obfuscate nation-state actions.

Furthermore, the crossing of official state-sponsored hacking with cybercriminal outfits has created a spectre of Russian state hacking that is far larger than their actual program. This hybridisation of tools, actors, and missions has created one of the most potent and ill-defined advanced threats that the cybersecurity community faces. It has also created the most technically advanced and bold cybercriminal community in the world.

Even in the case of the Yahoo hack, Belan was using his official task, gain access to Yahoo accounts for FSB intelligence and Counterintelligence purposes, and using it to turn a profit by manipulating search algorithms to drive web traffic and credit card skimming.

Positive Hack Days is organised by Russian cybersecurity company Positive Technologies – which the US government sanctioned in April 2021 for supporting Russian government cyber operations. Reportedly, it discovers vulnerabilities in technology products, develops exploits for those vulnerabilities, and provides them to Russia's Federal Security Service (FSB). It plays a key role in Russia's national cyber threat response program (GosSOPKA), too.[31]

Positive Hack Days appears to be one such gathering where Russia's FSB and military intelligence agency (GRU) survey company talks, capture-the-flag competitions, and other hacking challenges to identify talent. Dmitry Sergeyevich Badin, an officer in the GRU unit that would go on to hack the Democratic National Committee, attended in 2014.

Maria Zakharova, the infamous spokesperson for Russia's Ministry of Foreign Affairs, headlined a discussion on 'Creating a Multipolar World' at Positive Hack Days. The conversation was laden with nationalistic talking points about tech isolation, accusing Western countries and corporations of pursuing 'a policy of exclusion' and arguing that 'we need to stop protecting the Western platforms and websites and hosting platforms'.

Russia's Minister of Digital Development, Communications, and Mass Media, Maksut Shadayev, also spoke at the event, arguing for incentives to keep developers in Russia, which the Kremlin has rapidly expanded since February (such as exempting some IT workers from military conscription and IT companies from income taxes).

In a panel on technological independence through 'import substitution', featuring representatives from Russian technology firms, the participants discussed how tech isolation and the resulting need for domestic technology is 'an irreversible process'. These conversations underscore a ratcheting-up of this rhetoric in Russia's cybersecurity community.

One participant noted that 'suddenly, you see companies that were developing some huge products for one, two customers, but now, they are going national, they are going big-time, and it's one of the, probably, benefits of the current situation'. Another speaker was even blunter about the Russian government's push to eradicate foreign technology, stating: 'It's irreversible, and it's ambitious. Because we all now enter a new field of opportunities. There is demand from the market, there is regulation, there is support from the state, there is cyber war – I want to say, thank god there is cyber war, but, well, there is cyber war. Everything we are doing now is not going to be tested on a virtual mock-up at The Standoff; it's going to be tested in real-life settings. And if we can demonstrate the infosec maturity of Russian solutions, then it's a big opportunity'.

Even on a panel with less outwardly nationalistic rhetoric, a theme of Russian technological isolation persisted – this time, with an eye towards the potential impacts of the war on Russia's cybersecurity sector. One Positive Technologies employee stated that 'Recent events became geopolitical' and 'Some countries don't like to use cyber software not from their own countries, not from their own locations'. Hence, he said, it is important for Russia to cultivate *the open-source software community, because opening code can improve trust*.

Russian hacking forums and marketplaces have proliferated.

XSS.is prides itself on offering several security features, including disabling IP address logs and encrypting private messages, aimed at protecting its users' anonymity. Members of the forum gain access to a plethora of information on credential access, exploits, and valuable zero-day vulnerabilities.[32]

Exploit.in serves as a networking platform for career cybercriminals looking to collaborate on illegal ventures, including hacking, scamming, and Ransomware-as-a-Service (RaaS) schemes. The forum is also a marketplace for threat actors to auction initial access to organisations, complete with detailed pricing structures for bidding.

Originally known as Payload.bin, RAMP was a marketplace for illegal goods, predominantly drugs, within Russia. It also built a reputation for selling FortiNet VPN and sharing hacking tools used in infiltration operations. The forum's new avatar, RAMP 2.0, is a near clone of the old portal, attracting new users and creating a special 'partners program' for ransomware groups to conduct their activities.

After the Hydra Market's takedown, RuTor experienced a surge in activity, rapidly transforming from a forum into a bustling marketplace. The integration of the OMGOMG marketplace into RuTor's platform demonstrates its adaptability in the ever-changing dark web landscape.

These forums and marketplaces serve as hubs for Russian cybercriminals, facilitating the exchange of information, tools, and services related to various illegal activities, including hacking, ransomware, and cyberattacks.

There are few examples of the disaster scenario of an attempt to 'steal' an election. More often, attacks are now about undermining public trust in the system, rather than trying to change election results. But it is difficult to measure the impact of disinformation, for example, on votes.[33]

People assume when they see a headline that says 'election hacked' that it is about changing the results. But if your goal is about undermining the credibility and trust in elections, attacks can take many forms. That includes direct attacks on campaign security, such as hacking and releasing emails, or election infrastructure, such as the websites used to register to vote. They can be launched independently by hackers or be sponsored by a state, with Russia frequently accused of being behind such disruption campaigns.

However, simple attacks on vulnerable targets can be carried out by anyone with basic technical knowledge, and disinformation can be created and spread by anyone with a social media account. It's not illegal to be an idiot, given free speech protections.

Cyberattacks and disruption more broadly give people who are already sceptical about democracy, elections, or 'the quality of their politicians', another argument to say, 'this system isn't working for us'. This is much easier to achieve and only takes small attacks that anyone could do, for example, a distributed denial of service (DDoS) attack on a political party's website.

This is what happened to the UK Labour Party during the 2019 election. In Latvia's 2018 elections, a popular social network, Draugiem.lv, was targeted and its homepage filled with pro-Russia content. All of this contributes to a general environment of suspicion and doubt. 'It's all about trust', said van der Staak.

The infamous Russian hacking group Fancy Bear, a part of Russia's GRU military intelligence service, hacked the German Social Democratic Party last year.[34] It's the latest intrusion showing how Moscow has actively disrupted European politics ahead of a crucial EU election.

Poland has also experienced an increase in Russian cyberattacks over the past few months. Russia-linked hackers published a false article about military mobilisation on the news feed of Poland's state news agency, PAP, as part of a disinformation campaign. Russian state-sponsored hackers also targeted Polish government institutions in an espionage campaign attributed to the Fancy Bear hacker group associated with Russia's military intelligence agency, the GRU.[35]

Russia is a distinct case as it is a nondemocratic state that uses *sharp power* – it takes advantage of the asymmetry between open and democratic political systems and restricted nondemocratic political systems. In an open society, freedom of speech and freedom of the press can facilitate disinformation and misinformation while restricted political systems where speech and press are limited can restrict intervention through cyber information warfare.[36]

Russia undermines the democratic nature of its adversaries, dividing their societies between competing groups – supporters of the right and supporters of the left, liberals and conservatives, and even racial divisions. Any social rift can be used to divide and incite. Therefore, divisions created or amplified harm the governance of Russia's adversaries.

In Russia's domestic arena, however, legislation is used strategically to ensure domestic obedience. For instance, the Yarovaya Law allows Russia to restrict the flow of undesirable information. Russian authorities perceive cyberspace as a major threat to Russian national security, stability, and regime legitimacy as the free flow of information could undermine the regime.

Recent cyberattacks have caused alarm.

May 2024: Poland and the Czech Republic accused Russian cyber spies of targeting government and infrastructure networks. Both countries claim the attacks occurred around the same time Russian hackers attacked the German government. Hackers gained access by exploiting a Microsoft Outlook vulnerability, and the extent of the compromised data is currently unknown.

May 2024: Germany accused Russian hackers of breaking into the emails of Germany's Social Democrats, the leading party in its governing coalition, and recalled its ambassador from the country. The campaign started in March 2022 when hackers exploited vulnerabilities in Microsoft Outlook to target the party's executive committee, as well as German defence and aerospace companies.

March 2024: Russian hackers launched phishing attacks against German political parties. Hackers concealed ransomware in a fake dinner invitation from Germany's Christian Democratic Union to install a backdoor in their victims' computers.

March 2024: Russian hackers leaked an intercepted conversation between German military officials about the country's support for

Ukraine. In the call, the head of Germany's Air Force discussed the possibility of supplying Taurus missiles to Ukraine and commented on German Chancellor Olaf Scholz's hesitance to send the missiles. Germany announced it would investigate the incident and believes the leak was intended to inflame divisions in Germany.

January 2024: Russian hackers launched a ransomware attack against Sweden's only digital service provider for government services. The attack affected operations for 120 government offices and came as Sweden prepared to join NATO. Sweden expects disruptions to continue for several weeks.

December 2023: Russian hackers hit Ukraine's largest mobile phone provider, Kyivstar, disabling access to its 24 million customers in Ukraine. Hackers claim to have destroyed more than 10,000 computers and 4,000 servers, including cloud storage and backup systems. The attack began hours before President Zelenskyy met with President Biden in Washington, D.C.

December 2023: Denmark suffered its largest cyberattack on record when Russian hackers hit 22 Danish power companies. The attack began in May 2023 and appeared to be aimed at gaining comprehensive access to Denmark's decentralised power grid. Hackers exploited a critical command injection flaw and continued to exploit unpatched systems to maintain access.

September 2023: Russian forces in occupied Crimea reported a cyberattack on Crimean Internet providers. The attack happened around the same time as a Ukrainian missile strike aimed at Russian naval headquarters in the area. Ukrainian officials have yet to comment.

September 2023: Russian cybercriminals breached the International Criminal Court's IT systems amid an ongoing probe into Russian war crimes committed in Ukraine.

September 2023: Russian hackers stole thousands of documents from the British Ministry of Defence and uploaded them to the dark web. The documents contained accessibility details for a nuclear base in Scotland, high-security prisons, and other national security details. Hackers acquired the documents by breaking into a British fencing developer and gaining backdoor access to Ministry files.

August 2023: Russian hacktivists launched several DDoS attacks that knocked the Polish government's website offline, as well as the Warsaw Stock exchange and several Polish national banks.

August 2023: Russian hacktivists disabled Poland's rail systems by gaining access to the system's railway frequencies and transmitted a malicious signal that halted train operations. Attackers blasted Russia's national anthem and a speech from Putin on Russia's military operation in Ukraine during the attack.

June 2023: Pro-Russian hacktivists attacked several European banking institutions, including the European Investment Bank, in retaliation against Europe's continued support of Ukraine. The hacktivists used a DDoS attack to disrupt EIB.

June 2023: Pro-Russian hackers targeted several Swiss government websites, including those for Parliament, the federal administration, and the Geneva airport. The DDoS attacks coincided with preparations for Ukrainian President Volodimir Zelensky's virtual address before the Swiss parliament.

Cyberwarfare by Russia includes denial of service attacks, hacker attacks, dissemination of disinformation and propaganda, participation of state-sponsored teams in political blogs, internet surveillance using SORM technology, and persecution of cyber-dissidents and other active measures. According to investigative journalist Andrei Soldatov, some of these activities were coordinated by the Russian signals intelligence, which was part of the FSB and formerly a part of the 16th KGB department.

In April 2007, following a diplomatic row with Russia over a Soviet war memorial, Estonia was targeted by a series of cyberattacks on financial, media, and government websites, which were taken down by an enormous volume of spam being transmitted by botnets in what is called a distributed denial-of-service attack.

In 2015, the Paris-based French broadcasting service TV5Monde was attacked by hackers who used malicious software to attack and destroy the network's systems and take all twelve of its channels off the air. The attack was initially claimed by a group calling themselves the 'Cyber Caliphate' however a more in-depth investigation by French authorities revealed the attack on the network had links to APT28, a GRU-affiliated hacker group.

In May 2017, on the eve of the French presidential election, more than 20,000 emails belonging to the campaign of Emmanuel Macron were dumped on an anonymous file-sharing website, shortly after the campaign announced they had been hacked. An analysis by Flashpoint, an American cybersecurity firm, determined with 'moderate confidence' that APT28 was the group behind the hacking and subsequent leak.

On 20 July 2008, the website of the Georgian president, Mikheil Saakashvili, was rendered inoperable for 24 hours by a series of denial-of-service attacks. Shortly after, the website of the National Bank of Georgia and the parliament were attacked by hackers who plastered images of Mikheil Saakashvili and former Nazi leader Adolf Hitler. During the war, many Georgian government servers were attacked and brought down, reportedly hindering communication and the dissemination of crucial information.

From 2014 to 2016, according to CrowdStrike, the Russian APT Fancy Bear used Android malware to target the Ukrainian Army's Rocket Forces and Artillery. They distributed an infected version of an Android app whose original purpose was to control targeting data for the D-30 Howitzer artillery. The app, used by Ukrainian officers, was loaded with the X-Agent spyware and posted online on military forums.

The US government concluded after a study that a cyberattack caused a power outage in Ukraine which left more than 200,000 people temporarily without power. The Russian hacking group Sandworm or the Russian government were possibly behind the malware attack on the Ukrainian power grid as well as a mining company and a large railway operator in December 2015.

In February 2021, Ukraine accused Russia of attacking the System of Electronic Interaction of Executive Bodies a web portal used by the Ukrainian government to circulate documents by uploaded documents that contained macroscripts which if downloaded and enabled would lead to the computer to secretly download malware that would allow hackers to take over a computer.

In January 2022, a cyberattack on Ukraine took down the website of the Ministry of Foreign Affairs and other government agencies. Although an investigation has not been conclusive the cyberattacks coincide with the Russo-Ukrainian crisis.

In February 2022, before and after Russian troops entered eastern Ukraine amid an environment of escalating tensions between Ukraine and Russia, several major Ukrainian governmental and business websites were taken down by a series of cyberattacks. US officials attributed the attacks to Russian attackers, although the Russian government denied involvement.

Pro-Russian hackers launched a series of cyberattacks over several days to disrupt the May 2014 Ukrainian presidential election, releasing hacked emails, attempting to alter vote tallies, and delaying the final result with distributed denial-of-service (DDOS) attacks.

In the run up to the 2016 referendum on the United Kingdom exiting the European Union ('Brexit'), Prime Minister David Cameron suggested that Russia 'might be happy' with a positive Brexit vote, while the Remain campaign accused the Kremlin of secretly backing a positive Brexit vote.

In 1999, Moonlight Maze was the US investigation of a 1996–1999 Russian cyberattack against NASA, the Pentagon, the US military, civilian academics and government agencies. The cyberattack was attributed to Russian-state-sponsored hackers.

In 2015, CNN reported that 'Russian hackers' had 'penetrated sensitive parts of the White House' computers in 'recent months'. It was said that the FBI, the Secret Service, and other US intelligence agencies categorised the attacks as 'among the most sophisticated attacks ever launched against US government systems'.

In 2016, the release of hacked emails belonging to the Democratic National Committee, John Podesta, and Colin Powell, among others, through DCLeaks and WikiLeaks was said by private sector analysts and US intelligence services to have been of Russian origin.

Over several months in 2020, a group known as APT29 or Cozy Bear, working for Russia's Foreign Intelligence Service, breached a top cybersecurity firm and multiple US government agencies including the Treasury, Commerce, and Energy departments and the National Nuclear Security Administration.

The UK government has long highlighted the threat from malicious Russian cyber activities aimed at interfering in British democratic processes.[37] The Russian Federal Security Service (FSB), the successor agency to the KGB, has conducted a sustained effort to target and interfere in UK politics. Their targets include politicians from multiple political parties since at least 2015, civil servants, journalists, nongovernmental organisations (NGOs), and other civil society organisations that play a crucial role in UK democracy.

The FSB-linked hacking group known as Callisto Group, SEABORGIUM, or COLDRIVER has selectively leaked and amplified the release of information to undermine trust in politics in the UK and like-minded states. Notable incidents include the hack of UK-US trade documents leaked ahead of the 2019 General Election, the 2018 hack of the Institute for Statecraft think tank, and the more recent compromise of its founder Christopher Donnelly's account from December 2021.

While some attacks resulted in documents being leaked, the UK government judges that Russia's attempts to interfere in UK politics and democracy have ultimately failed. However, these actions demonstrate a clear and persistent pattern of hostile behaviour by Russia.

The UK government views Russia's cyber activities targeting Members of Parliament, civil servants, journalists, and NGOs as an attack on British democracy itself and the public they represent. Democracy is built on trust, and Russia's actions undermine the confidence that politicians can conduct democratic processes free from interference.

This revelation is part of a long pattern of hostile activities by Russia and other states like Iran and North Korea against Britain and its allies. Russia's malign activities go beyond just cyber-attacks and digital interference, extending to the use of artificial intelligence, deepfakes to seed false narratives, spread lies, and foment divisions through disinformation, misinformation, and misinformation across mainstream and social media.

In response to Russia's sustained attempts at political interference, the UK's Foreign, Commonwealth, and Development Office has sanctioned individuals involved in the FSB hacking group's activities and summoned the Russian Ambassador to express deep concern. The UK government has stated that Russia's attempts to interfere in UK politics are completely unacceptable and seek to threaten democratic processes.

The UK has vowed to continue working with allies to expose Russian covert cyber activities and hold Russia accountable for its actions. Furthermore, the National Security Act aims to make the UK a harder operating environment for those seeking to interfere in democratic institutions, as an attack against these institutions is an attack on fundamental British values and freedoms.

What follows is a transcript from an interview held with representatives of an organisation that was hit hard by a ransomware attack. It is shared for context and emphasising the point that ransomware attacks are extremely hard to defend against and have serious human consequences.

Author: Thank you for joining me to discuss your experience with a devastating NotPetya ransomware attack in 2017. Can you start by explaining how your company first became aware of this cyberattack?

Victim: It was a typical workday when our systems suddenly started crashing and displaying ransom messages. We quickly realised that we were under attack by a ransomware called NotPetya. It spread rapidly through our network, encrypting files and causing widespread disruption. We soon learned that this attack was linked to Russia's Sandworm, a cyber military unit of the GRU.

Author: That must have been incredibly alarming. How did your company respond to the attack?

Victim: We immediately activated our incident response team and began isolating affected systems to prevent further spread. We also notified law enforcement and cybersecurity experts to assist us in mitigating the attack. Despite our efforts, the damage was extensive, and it took us weeks to restore our systems and resume normal operations.

Author: What was the immediate impact on your company and its operations?

Victim: The impact was devastating. Not only did we lose access to critical data and systems, but the attack also disrupted our supply chain and caused significant financial losses. We estimated that the damage amounted to billions of dollars globally, not just for us but for many other affected organisations. It was a wake-up call about the destructive potential of cyber warfare.

Author: How did this experience affect you and your colleagues personally and professionally?

Victim: Personally, it was a very stressful and anxiety-inducing experience. Watching our systems being compromised and knowing the potential consequences for our company and employees was incredibly distressing. Professionally, it forced us to reevaluate our cybersecurity measures and invest heavily in improving our defences. It also highlighted the importance of having robust incident response plans in place.

Author: Let's explore the psychological toll this cyberattack had on you and your colleagues a little bit more. How did you cope with the aftermath of such a significant breach?

Victim: It was an incredibly challenging time. Personally, I felt a tremendous amount of stress and anxiety. The uncertainty of not knowing the full extent of the damage and the fear of potential future attacks weighed heavily on me. Many of my colleagues experienced similar feelings of fear and helplessness. The constant pressure to recover and restore our systems added to the overall mental strain.

Author: How did the attack impact your employees?

Victim: The human impact was devastating. Many employees lost their jobs due to the financial losses we incurred. Watching colleagues and friends face unemployment was heartbreaking. The sense of guilt and responsibility for their well-being was overwhelming. It created a ripple effect of stress and uncertainty within the company, affecting everyone from executives to frontline staff.

Author: What about the reputational damage? How did the attack affect your company's image and relationships with clients and partners?

Victim: The reputational damage was significant. Our clients and partners lost confidence in our ability to safeguard their data. Rebuilding that trust has been an uphill battle. We had to invest considerable resources in improving our cybersecurity measures and reassuring our stakeholders that we were taking every possible step to prevent future incidents. The attack also attracted negative media attention, which further damaged our reputation.

Author: How did you and your team cope with the emotional and psychological impact of the attack over the long term?

Victim: We focused on fostering a supportive work environment and encouraging open communication. Providing access to mental health resources and support for employees was crucial. We also organised regular check-ins and counselling sessions to help employees process their experiences and cope with the ongoing stress. Building a sense of community and solidarity was essential in helping us recover as a team.

Author: What lessons have you learned from this experience, both personally and professionally?

Victim: One of the most important lessons I've learned is the critical importance of cybersecurity. Protecting our systems and data must always be a top priority. I've also learned the value of resilience and adaptability. Facing such a significant challenge forced us to rethink our strategies and become more innovative in our approach. On a personal level, it taught me the importance of self-care and seeking support when needed. Balancing professional responsibilities with personal well-being is essential in navigating through such crises.

Author: What steps has your company taken since the attack to prevent future incidents?

Victim: We've implemented several measures to strengthen our cybersecurity posture. This includes regular security audits, employee training on recognising phishing attempts, and upgrading our IT infrastructure. We've also invested in advanced threat detection and response technologies to identify and mitigate potential threats more effectively.

Author: What advice would you give to other companies to help them prepare for and respond to similar cyberattacks?

Victim: My advice would be to take cybersecurity seriously and invest in comprehensive measures to protect your systems and data. Regularly update and patch your software, conduct frequent security assessments, and educate your employees about the latest threats. Having a well-defined incident response plan is crucial, as it can make a significant difference in minimising the impact of an attack.

Author: Thank you for sharing your experience.

References

1. Villalón-Huerta, A., Ripoll-Ripoll, I. and Marco-Gisbert, H., 2024. Provisioning the external infrastructure for Cyberspace Operations. A spotlight on Russian APT groups. *International Journal of Information Security Science, 13*(2), pp. 1–32.
2. https://nvlpubs.nist.gov/nistpubs/SpecialPublications/NIST.SP.800-171r3.pdf.
3. Takamaa, M. and Lehto, M., 2024, June. Cyber Operations in Ukraine: Emerging Patterns in Cases. In *European Conference on Cyber Warfare and Security* (Vol. 23, No. 1, pp. 788–794).
4. Aljohani, T.M., 2024. Cyberattacks on Energy Infrastructures as Modern War Weapons – Part I: Analysis and Motives. *IEEE Technology and Society Magazine.*
5. https://news.sky.com/story/russian-hackers-used-spear-phishing-to-steal-information-from-uk-politicians-13024300.
6. https://therecord.media/russia-state-hackers-deploying-malware-nato.
7. https://www.tessian.com/blog/examples-of-social-engineering-attacks/.
8. https://thehackernews.com/2023/08/microsoft-exposes-russian-hackers.html.
9. https://en.wikipedia.org/wiki/List_of_hacker_groups.
10. https://www.nsa.gov/Press-Room/Press-Releases-Statements/Press-Release-View/Article/3616384/russian-cyber-actors-are-exploiting-a-known-vulnerability-with-worldwide-impact/.
11. https://www.politico.eu/article/meet-killnet-russias-hacking-patriots-plaguing-europe/.
12. https://cepa.org/article/russia-ukraine-launch-cyber-offensives/.
13. https://cofense.com/blog/fireeye-russians-others-exploiting-zero-day-microsoft-office-vulnerabilities/.
14. https://www.techtarget.com/searchsecurity/news/366544596/Russia-based-actor-exploited-unpatched-Office-zero-day.

15. https://aspeniaonline.it/russian-disinformation-in-europe-justifying-violence-and-spreading-propaganda/.
16. https://www.voanews.com/a/how-russia-s-disinformation-campaign-seeps-into-us-views-/7566503.html.
17. https://www.brennancenter.org/our-work/analysis-opinion/new-evidence-shows-how-russias-election-interference-has-gotten-more.
18. https://www.gov.uk/government/news/uk-exposes-attempted-russian-cyber-interference-in-politics-and-democratic-processes.
19. https://www.csis.org/programs/strategic-technologies-program/significant-cyber-incidents.
20. https://www.ncsc.gov.uk/collection/annual-review-2023/threats-risks/case-study-russia.
21. https://carnegieendowment.org/2024/02/05/russia-s-countervalue-cyber-approach-utility-or-futility-pub-91534.
22. https://stratcomcoe.org/cuploads/pfiles/Nato-Cyber-Report_11-06-2021-4f4ce.pdf.
23. https://www.csis.org/analysis/cyber-operations-during-russo-ukrainian-war.
24. https://www.ncsc.gov.uk/news/russia-behind-cyber-attack-with-europe-wide-impact-hour-before-ukraine-invasion.
25. Firdini, Firdini, Jeffri Urbanus Panggabean, and Syaiful Anwar. "The Role of Russian Cyber Operations in The Russian–Ukraine War in Achieving Russia's Strategic Objectives." *Jurnal Perencanaan Pembangunan: The Indonesian Journal of Development Planning* 8, no. 1 (2024): 118–131.
26. https://en.wikipedia.org/wiki/Cyberwarfare_by_Russia.
27. https://www.reuters.com/world/fbi-says-it-has-sabotaged-hacking-tool-created-by-elite-russian-spies-2023-05-09/.
28. https://www.telecomstechnews.com/news/2024/jun/21/nordic-satellites-targeted-by-russia-after-sweden-nato-accession/.
29. https://www.ncsc.gov.uk/news/uk-allies-expose-evolving-tactics-of-russian-cyber-actors.
30. https://www.cybereason.com/blog/blog-russia-nation-state-hacking-the-countrys-dedicated-policy-of-strategic-ambiguity.
31. https://www.brookings.edu/articles/russias-largest-hacking-conference-reflects-isolated-cyber-ecosystem/.
32. https://socradar.io/top-5-russian-speaking-dark-web-forums/.

33. https://www.newstatesman.com/spotlight/tech-regulation/cybersecurity/2023/08/hacking-democracy-electoral-commission-cyber-attacks.
34. https://www.politico.eu/article/olaf-scholz-social-democratic-party-russian-hackers-fancy-bear/.
35. https://therecord.media/poland-blames-russia-ddos-euro-2024-online-broadcast.
36. https://www.usmcu.edu/Outreach/Marine-Corps-University-Press/MCU-Journal/JAMS-vol-12-no-1/Russian-Cyber-Information-Warfare/.
37. https://hansard.parliament.uk/commons/2023-12-07/debates/D3F22078-B63B-4279-A459-97CE8738AD81/CyberInterferenceUKDemocracy.

CHAPTER 12

China: Mass Surveillance, Censorship, and Robot Police

China's interference operations were part of larger efforts by foreign adversaries to undermine American election integrity and capitalise on lessons learned by Russia during its efforts in 2016.[1] Like Russia, China is spearheading digital disinformation campaigns to erode Americans' faith in democratic institutions.[2]

Beraja et al. (2023) argue that Chinese surveillance has penetrated deeper into society in the Xi era because the ideology rationalising its use has expanded. The Xi strategy is to restrain certain attitudes and movements but also to positively encourage behaviours that produce social stability. Political ideology is important because it sets the boundaries of social control and penetration of the State into the everyday lives of citizens. Chinese mass surveillance is of concern especially since this is now being exported as a service internationally. China's surveillance AI technology is now being exported into markets in Latin America.[3]

Vila Seoane and Velasco (2024) contend that there is ample evidence of China's expansion into digital surveillance markets in Brazil, Argentina and Ecuador among others.[4]

Min-Cheng (2024) maintains as authoritarian regimes like China increasingly employ sophisticated information warfare tactics, democratic societies face urgent challenges in countering cognitive influence operations. The Chinese Communist Party strategically disseminate misleading narratives through social media platforms to sway public opinion, erode

T. Singh, *Digital Psychological Warfare*,
https://doi.org/10.1007/978-3-032-15294-7_12

trust in democratic institutions, and advance the People's Republic of China's geopolitical agendas. Leveraging techniques such as coordinated inauthentic behaviour, algorithmic manipulation, and emerging technologies like deepfakes, these operations exacerbate societal divisions and undermine national resilience.[5]

China has been found to operate troll farms generating thousands of fake accounts to disseminate disinformation during election years. Chinese hackers target demographic groups with specially tailored disinformation meant to exacerbate these users' distrust towards other social and political groups.[6]

In the 2022 midterms, China spearheaded a social media campaign targeting Democratic and Republican voters. Chinese hacker groups identified by companies like Recorded Future and Mandiant posted social media videos that promoted 'civil war' as a solution to America's political divides.

China uses disinformation operations to discredit political leaders and to deter the Taiwanese electorate who may be supportive of Taiwan proclaiming *de jure* independence. In the Philippines, China has pushed the narrative of it being a positive regional actor and has cast doubt on the US leadership in an attempt to drive a wedge in US-Philippine relations.[7]

China's disinformation operations can be considered part of its public-opinion and psychological warfare, wherein it seeks to weaken Taiwan's will to announce *de jure* independence and also undermine the Philippines' maritime claims in the South China Sea.

There are various tactics of disinformation being used. It is increasingly common to see fabricated content which is completely false, and manipulated content where genuine information or imagery that has been distorted, e.g., a sensational headline or populist 'click bait'. Imposter content is rife with impersonation of genuine sources, e.g., using the branding of an established agency. Misleading information is presented as fact. False context is provided with factually accurate content combined with false contextual information, e.g., when the headline of an article does not reflect the content. Humorous but false stories are passed off as true, with no intention to harm, but readers may be fooled. False connections are used where headlines, visuals, or captions do not support the content. Advertising or PR is disguised as editorial content. Propaganda is used to manage attitudes, values, and knowledge.

State-sponsored disinformation campaigns are being deployed.[8] China has employed overt military manoeuvres, foreign-influence operations and disinformation against the Philippines in pursuit of its strategic objectives in the South China Sea.

China has also conducted disinformation campaigns in Taiwan. One China-linked disinformation actor named DRAGONBRIDGE, also known as Spamouflage Dragon, began its activity in 2019 and was described by Google's Threat Analysis Group in 2022 as the most prolific information-operations actor it has tracked.

Ahead of the 2024 presidential elections in Taiwan, Joseph Wu, Taiwan's foreign minister, revealed that 'the PRC has been making unprecedented efforts to meddle in the democratic process in Taiwan'.

China is conducting targeted disinformation campaigns across social-media platforms in the Asia-Pacific, alongside other operations, to achieve its strategic objectives.

A wide range of government and military actors have played key roles in China's disinformation strategy. The PLA, including its Nanjing Political Institute, has been at the forefront of efforts and has been particularly active in pushing propaganda and false news in Taiwan.[9]

Arms of the CCP, including its propaganda department, as well as the party's UFWD, play a critical role. Also important are bodies of the government's State Council, including its Taiwan Affairs Office, the State Council Information Office (SCIO), and the Cyberspace Administration of China.

China's state-run media, including the People's Daily, CCTV, and the Global Times, have played key roles drumming up nationalism at home by attacking Hong Kong protesters and Taiwan's DDP government.

Chinese social media companies like Sina Weibo and WeChat have developed a vast internal censorship apparatus and have played a critical role in spreading news denigrating the US electoral system.

The world's biggest social media platforms, including Facebook, Twitter, and YouTube, have also been used by Chinese government officials to forcefully promote China's rise.

China has increasingly used non-state actors like the '50 Cent Army' to push propaganda and disinformation in Hong Kong and beyond, piggybacking on their social media platforms.

Taiwan is a key operating environment for China's UFWD, whose mandate is to try to influence non-party groups and individuals to alter their behaviour to suit the CCP's interests.

Advances in artificial intelligence (AI) are amplifying a crisis for internet freedom and human rights online. While AI technology offers exciting and beneficial uses for science, education, and society at large, its uptake has also increased the scale, speed, and efficiency of digital repression.[10]

Restrictions on information access is rife. Innovations in the AI field have allowed governments to carry out more precise censorship that is less detectable, minimising public backlash and reducing the political cost to those in power. A record number of governments blocked websites with content that should be protected under free expression standards within international human rights law.

The Great Firewall is the world's most sophisticated internet censorship apparatus. Content that contains criticism of individuals, policies, or events that are considered integral to the one-party system is blocked. Most international social media and messaging platforms are blocked, including Facebook, WhatsApp, Twitter, Instagram, Signal, Clubhouse, YouTube, Telegram, Snapchat, Line, and Pinterest.[11]

Surveillance and censorship mechanisms are highly sophisticated. Online surveillance refers to governments' ongoing automated efforts to gather, store, and analyse digital traces of particular individuals or the entire population. The looming threat of social media surveillance in societies may deter citizens from engaging in political debates and diminish the mobilising power of online news content.[12]

Automated systems have enabled governments to conduct more precise and subtle forms of online censorship. Legal frameworks in at least 21 countries mandate or incentivise digital platforms to deploy machine learning to remove disfavoured political, social, and religious speech. In at least 22 countries, social media companies were required to use automated systems for content moderation, effectively forcing them to detect and remove banned speech more efficiently.

Monitoring content on social networking sites (SNSes) leads to constrained behaviour on these sites. The monitoring inhibits the freedom of expression, as users are cautious about expressing their political leanings honestly for fear of grave consequences such as online harassment and its reverberating effects on their work and personal lives.

Disinformation by China spreads through a complex interaction of social media, online news sites, traditional media, and offline spaces. Academic, government, and industry stakeholders attribute the connectivity of social media and the ability to build global networks as central in the circulation of mis/disinformation.

In November 2023, market research company Ipsos surveyed internet users across 16 countries and found that 56% use social media as their primary source of news, and 68% say that disinformation was most widespread there. The prevalence of disinformation differs across platforms. Social media algorithms may increase the spread of disinformation by amplifying content with high user engagement. Social media 'bots', automated programmes that simulate human behaviour online, can also be used to like or click disinformation at scale to boost engagement metrics ('like/click farming').

One study tracked the spread of fact-checked false news stories on Twitter (now X) between 2006 and 2017. Within their sample, inaccurate news stories spread faster and more widely than credible information online. Social media provides an environment in which individuals can exchange personal, group, or popular interests to build relationships with people who have similar and/or diverging beliefs and values. Social media platforms are also channels for recruiting interested parties for the continuity and propagation of a long-held ideology.

Moreover, people with common demographic attributes use the instant messaging services on social media to communicate more than those without such shared demographics. Social media platforms are thus online services that mirror real-world activities (e.g., dating services from Facebook, live Instagram feeds from parties). The expansion of multiple access points for information and news sharing on social media platforms contributes more to the spread of falsity than reducing its impact.

Disinformation news sites may pose as legitimate news sources, and produce or amplify false and/or misleading content. Since February 2022, NewsGuard has identified 471 illegitimate news sites amplifying disinformation related to the Russia-Ukraine war. By March 2024, they had identified 750 AI-generated sites propagating false narratives that operated with little or no human oversight.

Social media is being used as a medium to accelerate or prop up sociopolitical movements. Network effects enhance participation in social media platforms, which in turn spread information (good or bad) at a faster pace compared to traditional media. Due to a massive surge in online content consumption primarily through social media, both business organisations and political parties have begun to share content that is ambiguous or fake to influence online users and their decisions for financial and political gains.

Platforms' structure and algorithms also have an essential role in spreading misinformation.[13] Business models of these platforms are based upon maximising user engagement. For example, in the case of Facebook or Twitter, user feed is based on their existing belief or preferences. User feeds provide users with similar content that matches their existing beliefs, thus contributing to the echo chamber effect. Platform architecture makes the transmission and retransmission of misinformation easier.

Apart from platform politics, users have an essential role in creating or distributing disinformation. In China, both bots and users are being pushed to share disinformation. Disinformation has the power to influence the decisions of its audience. It can change the perceptions of citizens domestically and abroad.[14]

Digital platforms host distinct actors that learn to abuse infrastructures to drive traffic. Influencer industry, which often uses controversial content to game the algorithm to drive engagement. Audience fragmentation, monetisation schemes, and user-data extraction are supercharging conditions for the spread of misinformation. The reason is that the digital market monetises highly engaging content through ad revenue-sharing programmes.

AI and bots are being used in sophisticated ways. Social media platforms have become more than mere tools for communication. They've evolved into bustling arenas where truth and falsehood collide. Among these platforms, X (formerly Twitter) stands out as a prominent battleground. It's a place where disinformation campaigns thrive and China is using X in campaigns perpetuated by armies of AI-powered bots programmed to sway public opinion and manipulate narratives.

AI-powered bots on social media and chat platforms are pushing messages on behalf of the Chinese State designed to mimic human behaviour.[15] Bots and conversational AI are being crafted with malicious intent. Bots constitute a significant portion of X's user base.[16] In 2017, it was estimated that there were approximately 23 million social bots, accounting for 8.5% of total users. More than two-thirds of tweets originated from these automated accounts, amplifying the reach of disinformation and muddying the waters of public discourse.[17]

Social influence is now a commodity that can be acquired by purchasing bots. Companies sell fake followers to artificially boost the popularity of accounts, with many celebrities among the purchasers. Research has detected bots that had posted tweets offering followers for sale. Using AI methodologies and actor-network theory, researchers have dissected how malicious social bots manipulate social media, influencing what people think and act with alarming efficacy. It is possible to identify if fake news was generated by a human or a bot with an accuracy rate of 79.7%.

Chinese state-sponsored actors use networks of bots to amplify false narratives, manipulate trends, and swiftly disseminate misinformation. Users should exercise caution when encountering accounts exhibiting suspicious behaviour, such as excessive posting or repetitive messaging.

Disinformation campaigns, online trolls, and other 'bad actors' used by China are increasingly using generative AI to fuel election falsehoods to undermine democracy in the West. Based on prior studies of cyber and automated algorithm attacks, AI is projected to help spread toxic content across social media platforms on a near-daily basis in 2024.[18]

Disinformation in previous elections in the West has pinpointed how bots can spread malicious content across social media, manipulating online discussions and eroding trust. While earlier bots would repeat messages created by humans or programs, modern large language models (LLMs) enhance those bots with machine-written text that sounds convincingly human.

The rise of synthetic media and deepfakes presents new opportunities but has also ushered in new challenges in combating misinformation and fraud. Synthetic media is describing any content, whether video, image, text, or voice, that has been partially or fully generated using artificial intelligence or machine learning.

Deepfakes are a specific subset of synthetic media that focus on manipulating or altering visual or auditory information to create convincing fake content, ranging from images, audio, and video. Deepfakes can often be created with malicious intent to deceive viewers and are becoming highly realistic and difficult to distinguish from genuine recordings or images. The number of deepfake videos published online has risen exponentially, with the majority coming from the UK in Q1 2023, according to global verification platform Sumsub. Additionally, 51.1% of online misinformation comes from manipulated images. Deepfakes are likely to spread as malicious actors based in China seek to exploit their capabilities to sway public opinion, erode trust in democratic institutions, and spread misinformation about politicians.

Western companies and individuals critical of China are at risk of reputational damage from disinformation and deepfakes. The most worrying risk is the potential for deepfakes to assist criminals in committing fraud against western businesses.

A review of numerous forensic investigations, think tank reports, platform transparency reports, and media coverage points to a disconcerting if unsurprising trend: Beijing-linked actors are continually engaging in covert disinformation or other online influence operations. And they are experimenting with tactics that are more sophisticated, harder to detect, and potentially more effective than in previous years, while also tackling issues that cut to the heart of public debate in democracies.

The network identified in last month's Meta takedown – a persistent revival of a previously exposed and thwarted network known as Spamouflage – notably extended beyond Facebook and Instagram. Links were found to some 50 other applications, including TikTok, Reddit, Pinterest, and Medium, as well as local online forums in Asia and Africa. Meta suggested that the pivot to smaller platforms may have been a deliberate response to larger firms' increased monitoring, detection, and removals.

A separate report published by Microsoft uncovered a range of influence efforts, from networks of fake accounts to a corps of Chinese state-linked influencers who masquerade as independent commentators. The company counted at least 230 such state media employees or affiliates across multiple platforms, with accounts that reached 103 million people using 40 different languages. The report described an expansion to new languages – like Indonesian, Croatian, and Turkish – and new platforms – including Vimeo, Tumblr, and Quora – by both human influencers and automated accounts over the past year.

Among the most striking discoveries from the recent set of investigations are the various ways in which proxy entities or accounts on multiple platforms are used to 'launder' content, increasing its credibility and obfuscating its origins to the point that even some people involved in its production are unaware.

The network that was active on Meta platforms sought to harass or discredit journalists in the USA (such as Jiayang Fan), political commentators and dissidents (such as Chen Pokong), and occasionally elected officials (including Republican Representative Jim Banks and Democratic Representative Nancy Pelosi). In an incident from May that was exposed in August by the Canadian government, a network on Tencent's WeChat platform engaged in a coordinated campaign to smear the reputation of Parliament member Michael Chong, whose father is from Hong Kong and who has been a vocal critic of the increasing repression there and in China.

The disinformation networks have also taken aim at think tanks and other nongovernmental organisations whose investigations of the CCP's transnational repression and disinformation campaigns have been especially effective at spurring public awareness and policy responses. These include the Madrid-based Safeguard Defenders and ASPI, which have been subjected to aggressive and wide-ranging campaigns of harassment, threats, and impersonations. ASPI found that 70% of the top 50 Chinese-language search results for the organisation's name on YouTube had been 'posted by CCP-linked inauthentic accounts'.

During the 2019 Hong Kong protests, China employed a disinformation campaign primarily on Twitter. The campaign featured hastily constructed tactics without an integrated strategy. It involved repurposing spam accounts to disseminate messaging and leveraging an influence-for-hire network.[19] The predominant use of the Chinese language suggests that the target audiences were Hong Kongers and the overseas diaspora. Three main narratives emerged: condemnation of the protesters, support for the Hong Kong police and the 'rule of law', and conspiracy theories about Western involvement in the protests.

On TikTok, there have been suspected instances of censorship across the app, though a lack of transparency makes it challenging to prove. Within Douyin, the Chinese version of TikTok, state-endorsed propaganda and patriotic messages are commonplace, as the platform is legally required to censor controversial content.

Facebook has been a platform where China is suspected of buying followers to increase legitimacy and lend credibility to disinformation. Additionally, China has purchased Twitter ads to promote propaganda related to the Xinjiang situation.

During the COVID-19 pandemic, China employed tactics such as using hacked accounts to post propaganda and disinformation on Twitter, as well as utilising public relations companies. China has also placed ads in mainstream US newspapers like The New York Times, The Wall Street Journal, and The Washington Post to promote narratives surrounding issues like the Uyghur camps and Hong Kong protests.

In some instances, China has signalled government power through its disinformation campaigns, though the platforms used are not specified. On local news portals managed by the propaganda department, like Ganzhou Net, adoring messages have been posted as part of disinformation efforts.

A study analysed the tactics of the '50c party', a group of government employees engaged in online propaganda efforts. The study found that their posts focused on cheerleading and distracting rather than combative debating. It also noted that 'Most 50c posts from our data appear in highly coordinated bursts around events with collective action potential – either after unexpected events or before periods of time such as Qingming festival and political meetings when collective action is perceived by the regime to be more likely'.

During the COVID-19 pandemic, Beijing's disinformation efforts included a 'massive state-sponsored disinformation campaign, prominent "third-party spokespeople" and the expulsion of some of the most experienced American journalists in China'. As China's state-sponsored messages proliferated across various media platforms worldwide, it demonstrated the success of China's long-standing attempt to build its 'discourse power overseas'.

One COVID-19 disinformation campaign operated across multiple platforms, starting on Facebook and then using screenshots from Facebook as 'evidence' on Twitter and Weibo to generate further engagement. The campaign showed 'clear signs of coordination, both in accusing the Tsai government of hiding cases of coronavirus, identical wordings, similar structures of messages, and usage of mainland Chinese phrasings'.

China has also employed an agency called OneSight to manage overseas social media accounts as part of its disinformation efforts. Regarding inward-facing propaganda during COVID-19, China focused on highlighting positives, heroisms, and benchmarking its performance against countries perceived as faring worse.

In a notable instance, propaganda videos were uploaded to the adult website Pornhub during the Hong Kong protests.

China has been found to operate troll farms generating thousands of fake accounts to disseminate disinformation during election years. Chinese hackers target demographic groups with specially tailored disinformation meant to exacerbate these users' distrust towards other social and political groups.

China further spreads such disinformation through artificial intelligence (AI) and has already done so to interfere in foreign elections. In the weeks leading up to the January 2024 Taiwan elections, researchers from Doublethink Lab determined that the Chinese Communist Party (CCP) created dozens of videos on social media platforms that disseminated disinformation targeting the Taiwanese president. Through what the Taiwan foreign ministry calls 'cognitive warfare', China uses a combination of troll farms and AI to stoke divisions in rival countries.

These disinformation operations pair their generation of fake social media accounts with AI. Experts have determined that AI-generated content, including deepfakes, is being utilised by foreign adversaries like China to disseminate disinformation about political candidates. UC Berkeley computer science professor Hany Farid claims that deepfakes are becoming more 'sophisticated and compelling', allowing adversaries to deploy multiple mechanisms to dupe voters. A Department of Homeland Security memorandum further conveyed that generative AI capabilities 'may amplify existing risks for election infrastructure', thereby making election offices, officials, and vendors more vulnerable to disinformation attacks.

Disinformation actors create networks of fake personas and websites to increase the believability of their message with their target audience.[20] Such networks may include fake academic or professional 'experts', journalists, think tanks, and/or academic institutions. Some fake personas are even able to validate their social media accounts (for example, a blue or grey checkmark next to a username), further confusing audiences about their authenticity. Fake expert networks use inauthentic credentials to make their content more believable.

Disinformation actors also increase the credibility of these fake personas by generating falsified articles or research papers and sharing them online. Sometimes, these personas and their associated publications are intentionally amplified by other actors. In some instances, these materials are also unwittingly shared by legitimate organisations and users. The creation or amplification of content from these fake personas makes it difficult for audiences to distinguish real experts from fake ones.

Adversaries have demonstrated a 'long game' approach with this tactic by building a following and credibility with seemingly innocuous content before switching their focus to creating and amplifying disinformation. This lends a false credibility to campaigns.

Synthetic media content may include photos, videos, and audio clips that have been digitally manipulated or entirely fabricated to mislead the viewer. Cheapfakes are a less sophisticated form of manipulation involving real audio clips or videos that have been sped up, slowed down, or shown out of context to mislead. In contrast, deepfakes are developed by training artificial intelligence (AI) algorithms on reference content until it can produce media that is nearly indistinguishable from real life.

Deepfake technology makes it possible to convincingly depict someone doing something they haven't done or saying something they haven't said. While synthetic media technology is not inherently malicious, it can be deployed as part of disinformation campaigns to share false information or manipulate audiences.

Conspiracy theories attempt to explain important events as secret plots by powerful actors. Disinformation actors capitalise on conspiracy theories by generating disinformation narratives that align with the conspiracy worldview, increasing the likelihood that the narrative will resonate with the target audience. By repeating certain tropes across multiple narratives, malign actors increase the target audience's familiarity with the narrative and therefore its believability. Conspiracy theories can also present a pathway for radicalisation to violence among certain adherents.

Disinformation campaigns will often post overwhelming amounts of content with the same or similar messaging from several inauthentic accounts, either created by automated programs known as bots or by professional disinformation groups known as troll farms. By consistently seeing the same narrative repeated, the audience sees it as a popular and widespread message and is more likely to believe it. This practice, known as astroturfing, creates the impression of widespread grassroots support or opposition to a message, while concealing its true origin.

A similar tactic, flooding, involves spamming social media posts and comment sections with the intention of shaping a narrative or drowning out opposing viewpoints, often using many fake and/or automated accounts. Flooding may also be referred to as 'firehosing'. This tactic is used to stifle legitimate debate, such as the discussion of a new policy or initiative, and discourage people from participating in online spaces. Information manipulators use flooding to dull the sensitivity of targets through repetition and create a sense that nothing is true. Researchers call these tactics 'censorship by noise', where artificially amplified narratives are meant to drown out all other viewpoints. Artificial intelligence and other advanced technologies enable astroturfing and flooding to be deployed at speed and scale, more easily manipulating the information environment and influencing public opinion.

Disinformation actors often seek opportunities for their narratives to gain traction among smaller audiences before attempting to go viral. While alternative social media platforms are not inherently malicious, disinformation actors may take advantage of less stringent platform policies to intensify belief in a disinformation narrative among specific user groups. These policies may include fewer user protections, less stringent content moderation policies, and fewer controls to detect and remove inauthentic content and accounts than some of the other social media platforms.

Data voids, or information gaps, occur when there is insufficient credible information to satisfy a search inquiry, such as when a term falls out of use or when an emerging topic or event first gains prominence (e.g., breaking news). When a user searches for the term or phrase, the only results available may be false, misleading, or have low credibility. While search engines work to mitigate this problem, disinformation actors can exploit this gap by generating their own influence content and seeding the search term on social media to encourage people to look it up.

Disinformation campaigns target prominent individuals and organisations to help amplify their narratives. These secondary spreaders of disinformation narratives add perceived credibility to the messaging and help seed these narratives at the grassroots level while disguising their original source. Targets are often unaware that they are repeating a disinformation actors' narrative or that the narrative is intended to manipulate. The content is engineered to appeal to their and their follower's emotions, causing the influencers to become unwitting facilitators of disinformation campaigns.

Disinformation actors conduct surveillance over a targeted online community to understand its worldview, interests, and key influencers and then attempt to infiltrate it by posting tailored influence content likely to resonate with its members. By starting with entertaining or non-controversial posts that are agreeable to targeted communities, disinformation actors gain 'insider' status and grow an online following that can make future manipulation efforts more successful. This tactic often takes a 'long game' approach of spreading targeted content over time to build trust and credibility with the target audience.

Information operations undermine trust in information more broadly.[21] Studies have shown that exposure to falsehoods online, even if they have low levels of credibility, can affect perceptions of truth over time. With trust in information eroding, democracies which draw their authority from an informed public could be further destabilised.

The Chinese Communist Party (CCP) and, by extension, the People's Liberation Army (PLA) conduct information operations for political power. The CCP considers each of these warfare methods to have the potential to establish favourable conditions for battlefield success and eventual victory. China's disinformation operations can be considered part of its public-opinion and psychological warfare, wherein it seeks to weaken Taiwan's will to announce *de jure* independence and also undermine the Philippines' maritime claims in the South China Sea.

China has employed overt military manoeuvres, foreign-influence operations and disinformation against the Philippines in pursuit of its strategic objectives in the South China Sea. China has also conducted disinformation campaigns in Taiwan. One China-linked disinformation actor named DRAGONBRIDGE, also known as Spamouflage Dragon, began its activity in 2019 and was described by Google's Threat Analysis Group in 2022 as the most prolific information-operations actor it has tracked.

Ahead of the 2024 presidential elections in Taiwan, Joseph Wu, Taiwan's foreign minister, revealed that 'the PRC has been making unprecedented efforts to meddle in the democratic process in Taiwan'. The elections on 13 January 2024 resulted in a win for the independence-leaning Democratic Progressive Party. While it is still too early to confidently assess the extent of China's cyber and information operations against Taiwan during this period, initial reports suggest that there is evidence that the CCP conducted a broad range of information operations, including disinformation, against Taiwan during this period.

Fake news is 70% more likely to be retweeted than true stories. China is conducting targeted disinformation campaigns across social-media platforms in the Asia-Pacific, alongside other operations, to achieve its strategic objectives. While it is difficult to assess the impact and influence of an operation such as DRAGONBRIDGE, the overt and covert proliferation of narratives designed to reinforce China's sovereignty claims in the Asia-Pacific and to favourably shape opinions online in its favour should encourage regional governments to limit this spread, enhance the debunking of false narratives, de-incentivise a blooming disinformation industry and improve the digital literacy of their populations.

Governments need to establish a firm understanding of how their populations could be manipulated into furthering other parties' strategic objectives, and have near-real-time collaboration with the platforms in question, which also need to have the necessary tools to identify what is likely to be a growing wave of inauthentic content and behaviour.

There is increasing evidence of disinformation-for-hire operations. This can come in the form of state-sponsored propagandists, click armies, troll farms, commercially motivated data-analytics firms selling toolkits to politicians, fake news factories, as well as content farms (content designed to be clickbait and highly ranked on search engines). The hiring of private entities to carry out inauthentic behaviour on behalf of a state makes it harder to identify the source of their funding and thereby more difficult to hold the hiring actor to account.

National security officials are examining disinformation campaigns operated by CCP-supported Chinese officials. One prominent Chinese campaign, known as 'Spamouflage', networks hundreds of thousands of disinformation accounts to push anti-American messages and discredit American politicians. In April 2023, the Department of Justice charged 34 Chinese government officials for their involvement in a foreign interference operation believed to be Spamouflage.

Algorithms and the spread of disinformation are inexorably linked. Algorithmic recommender systems that suggest new content to users may serve as a vector between disinformation producers and social media users, potentially delivering false and harmful content.[22] Understanding these systems, their effects, and public perceptions of algorithms is vital to forming legislation that responds to such threats.

Artificial intelligence has turbocharged state efforts to crack down on internet freedoms over the past year. Governments and political actors around the world, in both democracies and autocracies, are using AI to generate texts, images, and video to manipulate public opinion in their favour and to automatically censor critical online content.

As generative AI tools grow more sophisticated, political actors are continuing to deploy the technology to amplify disinformation. Authoritarian regimes, in particular, are using AI to make censorship more widespread and effective.

Freedom House researchers documented 22 countries that passed laws requiring or incentivising internet platforms to use machine learning to remove unfavourable online speech. Chatbots in China, for example, have been programmed not to answer questions about Tiananmen Square. And in India, authorities in Prime Minister Narendra Modi's administration ordered YouTube and Twitter to restrict access to a documentary about violence during Modi's tenure as chief minister of the state of Gujarat, which in turn encourages the tech companies to filter content through AI-based moderation tools.

Mass surveillance in China emerged in the Maoist era after the establishment of the People's Republic of China in 1949. Mao invented this mechanism of control that encompassed the entire nation and its people in order to strengthen his power in the newly founded government. In the early years, when technology was relatively undeveloped in China, mass surveillance was accomplished through disseminating information by word of mouth. Chinese people kept a watchful eye on one another and reported inappropriate behaviours that infringed upon the dominant social ideals of the time.

In 2005, the Chinese government created a mass surveillance system called Skynet. The government revealed Skynet's existence in 2013, by which time the network included over 20 million cameras. In addition to monitoring the general public, cameras were installed outside mosques in the Xinjiang region, temples in Tibet, and the homes of dissidents. Feminists and LGBT rights groups are subject to increased scrutiny.[23]

In 2017, the Chinese government encouraged the use of various mobile phone apps as part of a broader surveillance push. Local regulators launched mobile apps for national security purposes and to allow citizens to report violations.[24]

As of 2018, the most notable surveillance mechanisms were mass camera surveillance on the streets, Internet surveillance, and newly invented surveillance methods based on social credit and identity.[25] As of 2018, the Chinese central government had also adopted facial recognition technology, surveillance drones, robot police, and big data collection targeting online social media platforms to monitor its citizens.[26]

In 2019, NSA whistleblower Edward Snowden said China's mass surveillance mechanisms and machinery of private communications was 'utterly mind-boggling'. As of 2019, it was estimated that 200 million monitoring CCTV cameras of the 'Skynet' system had been put to use in mainland China, four times as many as the surveillance cameras in the USA. State media in China claim that Skynet is the largest video surveillance system in the world, utilising facial recognition technology and big data analysis.[27] In 2019, Comparitech reported that 8 out of the 10 most monitored cities in the world are in China, with Chongqing, Shenzhen and Shanghai being the world's top 3. In 2019, China supplied surveillance technology to most of the world, and positioned the country in control over the mass surveillance industry.[28]

According to industry researcher IHS Markit, at the end of 2019, there were 770 million surveillance cameras in the world, with approximately 415.8 million of them located in China. If these trends continue, by the end of 2021 there will be about 1 billion in the world and 540 million in China.[29] The government says this prevents crime, but citizens worry that their data and privacy could be compromised.

The facial recognition technology has technological and systematic limitations. For example, a supervisor at an AI firm that provides research support for this technology has stated that the system of activity profile can only look for a maximum of a thousand people in one search. Additionally, the system cannot work continuously for long periods of time, requiring reactivation in cases of extreme need.

China has highly advanced facial recognition technology. The technology is integrated with others, such as big data and AI, to build a national surveillance and data sharing platform. The smart system is equipped with facial recognition technology to record jaywalkers and non-motor vehicles that break traffic rules. When shopping in the self-service markets of Alibaba and Jingdong, two top Chinese e-commerce companies, customers can use electronic payments through the facial recognition system, which links them with their bank cards. Moreover, Baidu, a Chinese multinational technology company, cooperated with China Southern Airlines to install the facial recognition technology in Nanyang Jiangying Airport, Henan, for boarding.

Robot police have been installed in public places such as train stations, museums, and tourist attractions. Furthermore, the Chinese government uses big data technology in order to analyse and monitor people's online behaviour, such as Sesame Credit, which ranks its users based on their online activities along with its previously mentioned functions.

The Chinese government uses short videos for information disclosure, image construction, distribution of legal information propaganda, and social governance.

The Chinese government employs numerous individuals to sway public opinion on the Internet.[30] This has led to a backlash in popular opinion. The Chinese Communist Party (CCP) uses the Internet to censor, set agendas, and frame stories to ensure that expressions and activities of mass nationalism in the public sphere are controlled. Social media has become a new tool that the government can use to manage information and control public opinion.

The Chinese government is widely known for its adept use of mass media for propaganda. Chinese propaganda has been used to consolidate governmental control, stabilise the country, and defend national interests through self-promotion and self-advocacy.[31]

The Chinese government uses soft propaganda to mobilise emotions, entertain the public, and call for unity. The Chinese government often uses visual propaganda. Visual nationalist propaganda is generally effective in mainland China. Generally, nationalist ideologies involve several features that provide citizens with a sense of common identity and establish common feelings and actions among them.

The Xinhua News Agency and People's Daily, both entities governed by the Chinese government, deliver stories concerning foreign governments with seriousness and a unified voice, ensuring a coherent narrative that fosters a grassroots nationalist sentiment. This strategic use of visual propaganda not only reinforces a consistent political narrative but also cultivates a sense of national identity and unity among the populace.

The Chinese government has been strengthening its tight control over the Internet and digital communication. There are more than 750 million Internet users in China, and their online actions are strictly regulated. In 2017, the Cyberspace Administration of China (CAC) released a new regulation, which imposed restrictions on the production and distribution of online news. The regulation required all platforms, such as online blogs, forums, websites, and social media apps, to be managed by party-sanctioned editorial staff. These staff must obtain approval from the national or local government Internet and information offices and be trained by the central government.

Launched in 2011, WeChat, China's most popular messaging app, is under surveillance by Internet police. Any message sent through a WeChat group is monitored by the Chinese technology giant Tencent, the application's operator. All conversations are stored for six months. Even conversations deleted by WeChat users can be retrieved back by Tencent, especially when government authorities seek evidence of a suspect's illegal activities. Authorities have admitted that they can retrieve archived messages once sent on WeChat.

In 2017, the Chinese government required all users of Sina Weibo, a microblogging site, to register with their real names and identity numbers by September 15 of that year. Weibo users who refused to register their accounts with real names were not able to post, repost, or comment on the site.

Chinese Internet users have several ways to circumvent censorship. Netizens generally rely on virtual private networks (VPNs) to access blocked websites and messaging apps. However, in July 2017, the Chinese government required telecommunications carriers including China Mobile, China Unicom, and China Telecom to block individual access to VPNs by February 1. In August 2017, more than 60 VPNs, such as Astrill and Express VPN, were removed from China's App Store. VPNs that are allowed to be used in China must be approved by state regulators and use the state network infrastructure.

Disinformation causes confusion and has a chilling effect on freedom of expression and information.[32] It directly impacts the level of trust in the public sphere as a space for democratic deliberation. People no longer feel safe to express their ideas for fear of online harassment and being targeted by disinformation campaigns; others feel paralysed and silenced by the puzzlement and uncertainty created by the surrounding information pollution and remove themselves from public debate concerning key issues of public interest.[33]

Freedom of expression is being violated in China. Disinformation is a human rights issue because the spread of disinformation can cause harm to a range of human rights.[34] It threatens:

- The right to free and fair elections (Article 25, International Covenant on Civil and Political Rights [ICCPR]): for elections to be free and fair, voters need accurate information about parties, candidates and other factors when voting. Incorrect information may influence how individuals vote, and disinformation can impact election and referendum results.
- The right to health (Article 12, International Covenant on Economic, Social and Cultural Rights): inaccurate health information, like false claims about vaccine risks, may deter people from making healthcare decisions that protect their health, putting them and others at greater risk. During the COVID-19 pandemic, health misinformation increased vaccine hesitancy and negatively impacted public health worldwide.
- The right to freedom from unlawful attacks upon one's honour and reputation (Article 17, ICCPR): disinformation often targets individuals, particularly political figures, public personalities, and journalists, aiming to harm their reputation.
- The right to non-discrimination (Articles 2(1) and 26, ICCPR): Disinformation sometimes focuses on particular societal groups, like migrants or ethnic minorities, inciting violence, discrimination, or hostility.

Disinformation threatens freedom of thought, the right to privacy, the right to democratic participation, and endangers economic, social, and cultural rights.[35] It diminishes indicators of democratic quality by distorting free and fair elections, fomenting digital violence and repression, and unsettling citizens' faith in democratic institutions.

However, inappropriate policy responses to disinformation can also pose risks to human rights, particularly the right to freedom of expression (Article 19, ICCPR). As highlighted by a previous UN Special Rapporteur on freedom of expression, 'the penalisation of disinformation is disproportionate, failing to achieve its goal of tamping down information while instead deterring individuals from sharing what could be valuable information'.

Laws like Singapore's Protection from Online Falsehoods and Manipulation Act (POFMA) criminalise publishing and circulating 'fake news' detrimental to areas like national security, public health, international relations, electoral integrity, and public confidence in authorities. In 2019, the UN Special Rapporteur on freedom of expression raised concerns about POFMA's overbroad definition of falsehood, lack of guidance on assessing statements as detrimental to public interests, and severe penalties for sharing false news. The Special Rapporteur noted such provisions may have a chilling effect on freedom of expression and be used to criminalise criticism of the government or expression of unpopular, controversial or minority opinions. Similar concerns exist for laws and policies in other regions like Sub-Saharan Africa.

During the 2019 Hong Kong protests, China employed a disinformation campaign primarily on Twitter. The campaign featured hastily constructed tactics without an integrated strategy. It involved repurposing spam accounts to disseminate messaging and leveraging an influence-for-hire network. The predominant use of the Chinese language suggests that the target audiences were Hong Kongers and the overseas diaspora. Three main narratives emerged: condemnation of the protesters, support for the Hong Kong police and the 'rule of law', and conspiracy theories about Western involvement in the protests.

On TikTok, there have been suspected instances of censorship across the app, though a lack of transparency makes it challenging to prove. Within Douyin, the Chinese version of TikTok, state-endorsed propaganda and patriotic messages are commonplace, as the platform is legally required to censor controversial content.

Facebook has been a platform where China is suspected of buying followers to increase legitimacy and lend credibility to disinformation. Additionally, China has purchased Twitter ads to promote propaganda related to the Xinjiang situation.

During the COVID-19 pandemic, China employed tactics such as using hacked accounts to post propaganda and disinformation on Twitter, as well as utilising public relations companies. China has also placed ads in mainstream US newspapers like The New York Times, The Wall Street Journal, and The Washington Post to promote narratives surrounding issues like the Uyghur camps and Hong Kong protests.

In some instances, China has signalled government power through its disinformation campaigns, though the platforms used are not specified. On local news portals managed by the propaganda department, like Ganzhou Net, adoring messages have been posted as part of disinformation efforts.

Drawing insights from Taiwan's proactive counter measures, there are whole-of-society approaches that other nations can take to protect themselves from Chinese State-sponsored disinformation campaigns such as enhancing media literacy, fostering societal resistance, and 'vaccinating' the public against hostile influence campaigns. By strengthening cognitive defences and fortifying the information environment, democratic nations can safeguard their values, uphold sovereignty, and maintain strategic advantages over revisionist authoritarian powers in an era of relentless information confrontation.[36]

Below is a transcript from an interview held with a person who had first-hand experience and was able to share the impact of surveillance on them.

Author: Thank you for joining me today to discuss your experiences. Can you start by explaining how you first became aware of Chinese surveillance?

Victim: As an activist in Hong Kong, I was always cautious about surveillance and censorship, but it became more pronounced during the height of the pro-democracy protests. I started noticing that some of my social media posts were being deleted or flagged, and I received warnings about sharing certain content. It was clear that Chinese authorities were actively monitoring and controlling the information that activists were sharing.

Author: That must have been incredibly frustrating. How did you feel when you realised that you were being targeted by these surveillance and censorship efforts?

Victim: It was a mix of anger, fear, and a sense of helplessness. Knowing that my online activities were being monitored and that my voice was being silenced was deeply unsettling. It made me question the safety of my digital presence and the integrity of the platforms I was using. The sense of being constantly watched created a feeling of vulnerability and stress.

Author: How did these surveillance and censorship efforts affect your ability to organise and participate in pro-democracy activities?

Victim: The impact was significant. It became much harder to communicate and coordinate with fellow activists. We had to resort to more secure communication methods and be extremely cautious about what we shared online. The constant threat of surveillance made it challenging to plan protests and share information with the public. It felt like a constant battle to find ways to stay connected and keep our movement alive.

Author: Can you describe the psychological toll these surveillance campaigns took on you and your fellow activists?

Victim: It was mentally and emotionally exhausting. The constant stress of being watched and the fear of repercussions took a toll on our mental health. Many of us experienced anxiety, paranoia, and a sense of isolation. The pressure to stay vigilant and protect ourselves and our information added to the overall strain. It was a difficult balance to maintain our activism while also taking care of our well-being.

Author: How did you cope with these feelings and the impact of the surveillance and censorship campaigns?

Victim: We relied heavily on the support of our community and fellow activists. Sharing our experiences and supporting each other helped us cope with the stress. We also sought out support services to help manage our anxiety and fear. Educating ourselves about digital security and finding ways to protect our online activities gave us a sense of control. It was important to stay connected and remind ourselves of the importance of our cause.

Author: What advice would you give to other activists who might find themselves targeted by surveillance and censorship campaigns?

Victim: My advice would be to stay informed and vigilant. Always be aware of the risks and take steps to protect your digital presence. Use secure communication tools and be cautious about the information you share online. Build a strong support network and lean on your community for support. It's also important to prioritise your mental health and seek help when needed. Remember that you are not alone and that there are resources and people who can help you navigate these challenges.

Author: Thank you for sharing your experience.

References

1. https://www.bbc.com/news/56364952.
2. https://www.unhcr.org/innovation/wp-content/uploads/2022/02/Factsheet-4.pdf.
3. Beraja, M., Kao, A., Yang, D.Y. and Yuchtman, N., 2023. *Exporting the surveillance state via trade in AI* (No. w31676). National Bureau of Economic Research.
4. Vila Seoane, M. F., and C. M. Álvarez Velasco. 2024. The Chinese surveillance state in Latin America? Evidence from Argentina and Ecuador. *The Information Society* 40 (2): 154–167.
5. Min-Cheng, H.S.U., 2024. Inoculating Society against Authoritarian Influence in the Digital Age: Fortifying the Barracks against Authoritarian Cognitive Warfare. Journal of Indo-Pacific Affairs, 7(3).
6. https://www.atlanticcouncil.org/wp-content/uploads/2020/12/CHINA-ASI-Report-FINAL-1.pdf.
7. https://www.americansecurityproject.org/the-red-wave-how-china-weaponizes-disinformation/.
8. https://akademie.dw.com/en/disinformation-current-definitions-and-examples/a-67786912.
9. https://www.politico.eu/newsletter/digital-bridge/chinas-kremlin-style-disinformation-playbook/.
10. https://freedomhouse.org/report/freedom-net/2023/repressive-power-artificial-intelligence.
11. https://freedomhouse.org/country/china/freedom-net/2023.
12. https://www.ncbi.nlm.nih.gov/pmc/articles/PMC10106894/.
13. https://crestresearch.ac.uk/comment/addressing-algorithms-in-disinformation/.
14. https://www.techuk.org/resource/synthetic-media-what-are-they-and-how-are-techuk-members-taking-steps-to-tackle-misinformation-and-fraud.html.
15. https://thediplomat.com/2023/09/chinas-increasingly-aggressive-tactics-for-foreign-disinformation-campaigns/.

16. https://www.technologyreview.com/2023/10/04/1080801/generative-ai-boosting-disinformation-and-propaganda-freedom-house/.
17. https://theconversation.com/election-disinformation-how-ai-powered-bots-work-and-how-you-can-protect-yourself-from-their-influence-227174.
18. https://www.scientificamerican.com/article/how-ai-bots-could-sabotage-2024-elections-around-the-world/.
19. https://medium.com/doublethinklab/collection-of-cases-on-dis information-campaigns-from-china-c34074274dd3.
20. https://www.cisa.gov/sites/default/files/publications/tactics-of-disinformation_508.pdf.
21. https://www.iiss.org/publications/strategic-dossiers/asia-pacific-regional-security-assessment-2024/chapter-5/.
22. https://link.springer.com/article/10.1007/s10796-022-102 42-z.
23. https://www.rand.org/content/dam/rand/pubs/research_rep orts/RR4300/RR4373z3/RAND_RR4373z3.pdf.
24. https://www.isdglobal.org/disinformation/.
25. https://www.weforum.org/agenda/2022/08/four-ways-disinf ormation-campaigns-are-propagated-online/.
26. https://www.tandfonline.com/doi/full/10.1080/10242694.2024.2302236.
27. https://thehill.com/changing-america/opinion/581002-how-alg orithms-are-amplifying-misinformation-and-driving-a-wedge/.
28. https://en.wikipedia.org/wiki/Mass_surveillance_in_China.
29. https://www.technologyreview.com/2022/10/10/1060982/china-pandemic-cameras-surveillance-state-book/.
30. https://www.nature.com/articles/s41599-024-03059-5.
31. https://demtech.oii.ox.ac.uk/wp-content/uploads/sites/12/2017/06/Comprop-China.pdf.
32. https://www.ohchr.org/Documents/Issues/Expression/disinf ormation/2-Civil-society-organisations/APC-Disinformation-Sub mission.pdf.
33. https://www.weforum.org/agenda/2024/06/ai-combat-online-misinformation-disinformation/.
34. https://www.gp-digital.org/a-human-rights-based-approach-to-disinformation/.

35. https://www.europarl.europa.eu/RegData/etudes/STUD/2021/653635/EXPO_STU(2021)653635_EN.pdf.
36. Min-Cheng, H.S.U., 2024. Inoculating Society against Authoritarian Influence in the Digital Age: Fortifying the Barracks against Authoritarian Cognitive Warfare. Journal of Indo-Pacific Affairs, 7(3).

CHAPTER 13

India: Bots, Ballots, and Bullets

India's psychological warfare efforts include propaganda and psychological operations to influence opinions and attitudes of its enemies. The goal is to create discontent against the government and communal discord. There is widespread use of propaganda using false media to negatively affect the enemy's psychological well-being. Covert military operations, misleading the enemy and causing mental fatigue. Encouraging desertion or providing instructions on how to surrender. Shock and awe, using military strategy to project repetitive and disturbing noises and music towards groups under siege. They closely partner with social media platforms to effectively fact-check and spread pro-India narratives. The Indian Government are investing in information warfare, psychological operations, electronic, and cyber warfare. Psychological warfare on this scale causes mental health issues such as mistrust, suspicion, and a sense of hopelessness.[1]

India has significant countermeasures enshrined in its constitution to enable it to control the populace and its diaspora. India's constitution, unlike its US counterpart, is not designed to limit political power and secure public freedom. Instead, it is dominated by the idea of constituting and enabling political power, and channelling it for socioeconomic reform. The constitution enshrined centralisation, executive supremacy, and retained the '*bureaucratic authoritarianism*' of its colonial predecessor.[2]

T. Singh, *Digital Psychological Warfare*,
https://doi.org/10.1007/978-3-032-15294-7_13

It empowered the centre over the states, allowing it to create, dismember provinces at will (Articles 2 and 3), or impose president's rule under Article 356. It also empowered the executive over the legislature, permitting the executive to usurp legislative functions through ordinances (Article 123) and dictate when the legislature is summoned or prorogued. Furthermore, it empowered the state over citizens by qualifying the fundamental rights guaranteed in Part III in pursuit of state security and social uplift.

The concentration of power and its use by the executive are baked into India's constitutional order and institutional structure. The broadly defined social goals and nebulous criteria of 'security of the state' are vessels into which multiple contemporary ideas can be poured or removed, subject to creative interpretation. What matters is the facilitation, generation of legitimacy, and harnessing of executive power.

India's constitution enables a vast armoury of coercive laws at the executive's disposal, creating a political structure dedicated to promoting executive power. Every government, to the extent that it can command a legislative majority, has used state force to push its agenda for social transformation and state security. Yesterday it was Indira Gandhi, today it is Narendra Modi, and tomorrow may be someone else, but the same concentration of power is available if a leader can muster a legislative majority.

The period between 1989 and 2014, referred to as the coalition era, generally seems to form the backdrop against which arguments for India's democratic deficit – or its drift into electoral autocracy are made. This, however, skews perceptions about the nature of democracy and political power in India, providing a powerful rhetorical tool to direct attention to the post-2014 period but saying little about why the coalition era proved especially profitable for the extra-parliamentary aspects of democracy.

In the states, where mandates were not splintered, things were very different. There, with concentration of power made even more acute by the Tenth Schedule, and thus largely secured against backbench rebellion and intraparty conflict, chief ministers – especially those from regional parties who also doubled as party bosses – quickly transformed themselves into 'supreme leaders' and pioneered a 'Chief Minister model of governance'.

Given this structural situation, it is unsurprising to find governments using these powers to maximum effect. Recent assessments argue that India's democratic deficits lie not just in the electoral arena, but in the erosion of non-electoral freedoms and civil liberties, especially the freedoms of expression and association.

The boundaries of the playing field have yet to be altered, and this movement is part of a continuum within which Indian democracy has historically oscillated without going out of bounds at either end.

Lewis and Lall (2024) argue India and Russia have simplified decolonial discourse in higher education to reject 'Western-influenced' critiques of development, inequality, and authoritarianism. Under political pressure from their authoritarian regimes, universities have helped to embed repressive majoritarian politics through anti-Western rhetoric disguised as de-linking, enabling democratic backsliding by discrediting opposition. This is done to protect a new identity based upon state conceptions of traditional values, paradoxically erasing minority voices that do not fit neatly into the unified national narrative. When universities are branded as Western agents for being critical of local traditions and schools of thought, the space for critical thinking and democratic debate is removed.[3]

Mukherji (2024) contends Modi's government has been squeezing civic space, attacking the press, political opponents, nongovernmental organisations (NGOs), and stoking ethnic tensions. The State has used legislation to harass critics. Yet there is a chance the power of the vote could lead to a democratic revival.[4]

Mostofa et al. (2024) argue that the BJP government have systematically used religious sentiments as a potent tool, altering national identities and citizenship criteria. This manipulation, driven by majoritarian ideologies, has marginalised religious minorities, leading to discrimination, violence, and legal persecution against them.[5]

Batool (2024) argues the targeting of minorities by the BJP, through controversial citizenship laws and Hindu nationalist rhetoric, has intensified in recent years. Economic growth under Modi's governance has not translated into improvements for the impoverished masses. Persecution, economic inequality, and erosion of democratic freedoms persist. Substantive changes are needed to prevent further division, inequality, and authoritarianism in India.[6]

Das (2024) contends that the fascist-influenced BJP government is making full use of digital controls to persecute minorities.[7] Duberstein (2024) laments the alarming erosion of India's democratic institutions, under the guidance of the Bharatiya Janata Party (BJP) holding far-reaching implications for the future of Indian society.[8]

Internet freedom in India has undergone a gradual evolution, with the government imposing strict controls and censorship measures. The state exercises significant authority over traditional media outlets, such as print and broadcast media.[9] The Indian constitution guarantees various fundamental rights, including freedom of speech and expression, but these rights are often curtailed under the pretext of 'national security' and 'public order'.[10]

Journalists and media professionals face numerous challenges, including preventive detentions, arrests under security laws, and threats for their reporting. The government has employed tactics like communications shutdowns and surveillance to monitor and restrict the flow of information. Female journalists have been particularly targeted with gendered abuse and online harassment, reflecting the deeply unequal access to the internet in India.[11]

With use of the internet and digital media, India witnessed marginal change in internet freedom. Efforts to bridge the digital divide and expand internet access contributed. However, the government continues to impose internet shutdowns and use intelligence agencies to monitor, influence and control its citizens.[12]

Legal challenges to laws enabling government censorship, such as the Information Technology (Intermediary Guidelines and Digital Media Ethics Code) Rules, 2021, resulted in slight limitations on the state's powers. However, the government still blocks online content, and internet users risk arrest for posts critical of the authorities.

Misinformation and disinformation remain prevalent online, and journalists, nongovernmental organisations, and marginalised groups continue to face hate speech and online harassment. The government has also attempted to expand its control over the media through measures like the Digital Personal Data Protecting Act 2023, which restricts the information that can be disclosed through Right to Information requests.

Despite these challenges, India's multiparty electoral democracy and constitution provide a framework for internet freedom. However, the concentration of power in the executive branch and the broadly defined criteria for state security have enabled the government to impose restrictions on online content and activities.

The Indian government has implemented various legislative measures to regulate and restrict internet content and activities. One key mechanism is the licensing requirements for Internet Service Providers (ISPs). ISPs seeking licenses from the Department of Telecommunications

(DOT) 'shall *block* Internet sites and/or individual subscribers, as identified and directed by the Telecom Authority *from time to time*' in the interests of '*national security*'. Additionally, license agreements mandate that ISPs prevent the transmission of obscene or objectionable material.

In 2003, the government established the Indian Computer Emergency Response Team (CERT-IN) to oversee internet security. CERT-IN's mission is 'to enhance the security of India's Communications and Information Infrastructure through proactive action and effective collaboration'. This agency reviews and approves requests to block specific websites, and all licensed ISPs must comply with CERT-IN's decisions without any review or appeals process.

The Information Technology (IT) Rules 2011, adopted as a supplement to the 2000 Information Technology Act (ITA), require internet companies to remove any content deemed objectionable by authorities within 36 hours of notification. The objectionable content includes material that is 'defamatory'" 'hateful', 'harmful to minors', or 'infringes copyright' but has been used more broadly than this.

The government has taken active measures to enforce its internet restrictions and censorship policies. In 2007, Indian law enforcement entered an agreement with the social networking site Orkut to track down content deemed defamatory, including criticism of political figures. The government requested the removal of 236 items from Orkut and 19 items from YouTube, citing reasons such as defamation, privacy and security concerns, impersonation, hate speech, pornography, and national security.

Furthermore, the IT Rules 2011 impose stringent requirements on cybercafé owners. They must photograph customers, ensure computer screens are in plain sight, maintain records of customer IDs and browsing histories for a year, and forward this data to the government monthly.

The government has also increased pressure on US tech companies like Facebook, Twitter, and WhatsApp to comply with its regulations or risk losing access to the Indian market. The new rules force companies to remove content deemed objectionable or illegal by the government within 3 days, including any content that threatens 'the interests of the sovereignty and integrity of India', public order, decency, morality, or incites offences. Platforms must also provide user information to law enforcement upon request.[13]

The Indian government has a long history of political disinformation and digital hate speech designed to cause communal tensions so that extreme politics can capitalise. Representatives and proxies of the BJP government made numerous hate speeches against minorities in the run up to the 2024 general elections. Narendra Modi himself made numerous inflammatory statements against minorities in the build-up to the Gujarat riots. People linked to the Congress party made hate speeches in the build up the anti-Sikh pogrom in 1984.

Encrypted messaging services like WhatsApp are required to keep records of the 'first originator' of any message and provide this information to the government on demand. Additionally, companies must appoint a resident Indian citizen as a 'chief compliance officer' who will be criminally liable for any non-compliance with the rules. Digital publications are subject to oversight by government-run committees with the power to block, remove, or shut down entire websites.

Disinformation and the abundance of 'fake news' generated by groups allegedly linked to the Indian state are degrading trust in institutions and fragmenting worldviews with conflicting ideas about what constitutes reality, making it difficult to reach consensus on public policy. The more divisive India becomes as a society, the more radical representation it will seek in its legislative bodies, effectively destroying the concept of common ground in the parliamentary democracy of India, where it prides itself on the principles of 'unity in diversity'.[14]

Demagogues and profiteers are exploiting powerful emerging technologies to amplify their own voices for personal gain. Addiction to mobile devices is resulting in isolation and depression. The existing political environment is responsible for political and other categories of disinformation. Two political conditions are usually conducive to disinformation: polarisation of society and populist communication. Both tendencies are present in contemporary India.

Disinformation is being used to influence the election of governments by manipulating citizens' political attitudes. This could be seen in the 2016 USA Presidential election and 2017 French elections.[15] Disinformation was abundantly relied upon in the Indian elections in 2019 and 2024 where there were lots of examples where misinformation influenced the election process.

During the 2024 Indian elections, false information was presented as if it was from an authorised source. Confirmation bias had a dominant role in social media disinformation related to politics. Readers were more likely to read and engage with information that confirmed their pre-existing beliefs and political affiliations and reject information that challenges it. Misinformation spreads quickly among people who have similar ideologies.

In 2018, the BBC published a report based on extensive research in India, Kenya, and Nigeria into how ordinary citizens engage with and spread fake news. According to the report, 'facts were less important to some than the emotional desire to bolster national identity. Social media analysis suggested that right-wing networks are much more organised than [those] on the left, pushing nationalistic fake stories further. There was also an overlap of fake news sources on Twitter and support networks of Prime Minister Narendra Modi'.[16]

India as a democracy has had a mixed and chaotic track record in combatting fake news. Governments have shown to be continuously working with big technology companies to restrict the spread of fake news on the one hand, yet at the same time they are deciding what constitutes the truth, using threats of a ban from Indian markets and legislation to block criticism, threaten critics and politicians have continued to spread unproven and inaccurate information.

Ahead of its annual Davos Summit, the World Economic Forum released its Global Risks Report for 2024, analysing challenges countries will face in the coming decade. The report placed mis- and disinformation at the top of the list in terms of posing a risk – and India was ranked first as the country facing the highest risk in the world.

Research conducted in 2019 found high levels of concern among respondents over hyper-partisan content and the political context of disinformation, and evidence that some political groups have actively disseminated falsehoods. Interestingly, when those heightened levels of concern and exposure were examined by political leaning, there were no partisan differences. Concerns over disinformation and false news were similar across all respondents regardless of the party they supported. In other words, people in India were worried about disinformation across political lines.

According to Freedom House's annual Freedom on the Net report, which assesses the level of internet freedom in 70 countries around the world, India is classified as having a 'Partly Free' internet with an overall score of 50 out of 100. The scores for 'Obstacles to Access', 'Limits on Content' and 'Violations of User Rights' are 13, 20, and 17, respectively.[17]

The Indian Constitution has fundamental rights, including freedom of speech and expression, freedom of religion, rights to form associations, and the right to privacy. However, the government led by Prime Minister Narendra Modi and the Bharatiya Janata Party (BJP) has presided over discriminatory policies and increased violence affecting the country's Muslim population. Muslims, scheduled castes (Dalits), and scheduled tribes (Adivasis) remain economically and socially marginalised.[18]

India has been the global leader in the number of internet shutdowns imposed for the last 5 years, and local authorities have restricted connectivity since at least 2010. Authorities typically justify shutdowns as cautionary measures to maintain law and order, quell potential violence or communal tensions, restrict protests, prevent the spread of disinformation, or stop cheating in school exams.

India leads the world in the number of internet shutdowns, with over 100 reported incidents in 2018 alone.[19] Between 2014 and November 2022, there were 680 government-imposed internet shutdowns across India, the highest number in the world. In 2021, there were 101 forced internet shutdowns. The worst example was the internet shutdown in Kashmir for almost a year after the stripping of its special status on August 5, 2019.[20]

The government has also censored online content critical of its handling of the COVID-19 crisis, including tweets criticising the Prime Minister for his negligence and inefficiency in combating the virus. Additionally, the government has issued numerous blocking orders to Twitter, particularly targeting Kashmir-related content and accounts supporting the farmer protests.

Journalists, particularly Muslim journalists, have faced consistent threats of arrest and prosecution for their work. In June 2022, the Delhi state police arrested Zubair, the owner of the fact-checking website Alt News, over a 4-year-old post. Siddique Kappan, a journalist, was arrested in October 2020 while trying to cover a murder and rape case and remained in jail despite being granted bail by the Supreme Court.

Human rights organisations, civil society, political parties, and retired security officials have raised concerns about the government's actions, citing violations of freedom of expression and access to information.

Many candidates in India's recent elections have used AI-powered 'avatars' to engage with individual citizens in an electorate with 968 million registered voters. Such 'hyper-personalised' engagement is believed to enhance candidates' political appeal by showing voters that the candidates are attuned to each voter's specific concerns. However, the two biggest national-level parties – the ruling Bharatiya Janata Party (BJP) and the opposition Congress Party – accused each other of unfairly influencing voters by spreading 'fake news' through 'deepfakes', or digitally manipulated audio, images, or video.

Recent examples include fake videos of the deceased former Tamil Nadu chief minister, M. Karunanidhi, praising the leadership of his son M.K. Stalin, the state's current chief minister. Meta, the parent company of WhatsApp and Facebook, reportedly approved 14 AI-generated electoral ads that contained Hindu supremacist language and called for the killing of Muslims and a key opposition leader while elections were underway. Some of the videos contained the false claim that the leader 'wanted to erase Hindus from India'.[21]

The Indian government has implemented several policies and regulations that enable digital authoritarianism and limit internet freedom. The government has regularly shut down the internet to suppress protests against the Citizenship Amendment Act, the scrapping of Jammu and Kashmir's special status, farm laws, and to target critical voices with spyware. It has also pressured international social media platforms to remove content critical of the government's Hindu nationalist/populist agenda.

The Information Technology Rules 2021 have significantly reduced social media platforms' freedom to operate and their immunity from prosecution. These rules require intermediaries to remove content identified as illegal by the government within 3 days and provide user information to law enforcement officials. Additionally, companies must increase their data retention period to 180 days, putting end-to-end encryption at risk.

The government has also introduced a Central Monitoring System (CMS), a surveillance system that monitors electronic communications, including phone calls, text messages, and social media engagement. This system raises privacy concerns as individuals may not know when their data has been intercepted, leading to mass surveillance.

Legal challenges to laws enabling the government to censor online content in India have seen slight limits imposed on some powers. However, the state continues to block online content at an increasing pace, and Indian internet users risk arrest for posts critical of the government. Misinformation and disinformation are frequently shared online, and journalists, nongovernmental organisations (NGOs), and members of marginalised groups remain at risk of being targeted by hate speech and harassment online.

The government of Punjab restricted access to the internet across the state for 4 days in March 2023, while authorities in Manipur imposed a statewide shutdown in May 2023 that lasted for several months. The government released the draft Indian Telecommunication Bill, 2022 and the draft Digital Personal Data Protection Bill, 2022 (DPDPB), which together would overhaul India's existing legal architecture for internet regulation.

India has witnessed a troubling rise in internet shutdowns, particularly outside the conflict-prone region of Jammu and Kashmir. These shutdowns are issued by various state governments, often in response to protests or to suppress dissent. The Hindu-nationalist Bharatiya Janata Party (BJP) is both directly and indirectly responsible for many of these shutdowns.[22]

BJP-run state governments issue more internet shutdowns than non-BJP states, primarily to suppress protests (the direct responsibility). Additionally, the party's polarising rhetoric and policies, coupled with the BJP-built limited regulatory framework governing the issuance of shutdowns, contribute to an environment in which these shutdowns can thrive (the indirect responsibility).

Quantitative analyses from 2012 to 2020 reveal that districts in BJP-ruled states experience significantly more internet shutdowns, primarily in response to protests, while Hindu-Muslim conflicts trigger internet shutdowns across the country. Rather than a centrally coordinated, top-down campaign from the central government, India's 28 state governments are largely responsible for issuing these shutdowns.

In September 2022, new rules requiring virtual private network (VPN) providers to store information about their users for 5 years came into effect, prompting a few providers to remove their servers from the country. Government officials increasingly ordered content removed from social media platforms under the emergency provisions of the Intermediary Guidelines, including a British Broadcasting Corporation (BBC) documentary about communal violence during Modi's tenure as chief minister of Gujarat.

In recent years, India's minority communities have been repeatedly targeted by misinformation spread through digital platforms. Data suggests that 2020 was a particularly bad year. A 2019 survey found that six in ten Indian respondents had come across fake news online, placing the country 6th out of 22 surveyed.

A key reason for the perennial issue of minority misinformation in India is the role that such false stories play in servicing the Indian government's agenda. '[Misinformation targeting minorities] highlights the growing discrimination and attacks against Muslims and other minorities since the Hindu nationalist Bharatiya Janata Party (BJP) government led by Prime Minister Narendra Modi was first elected in 2014', said Meenakshi Ganguly, the South Asia director at Human Rights Watch (HRW).[23]

Modi has interwoven a more secular agenda, including economic modernisation, with *Hindutva* – a 100-year-old Hindu nationalist ideology. Fake news stories allege that Muslim men who marry Hindu women are motivated by 'love jihad', or Christians are forcibly converting Hindus. These stories play into fears that Hindus, who make up 80% of the population, are being outbred by minorities or that Hindus are second-class citizens.

Elections and legislative shifts – ideal moments to accelerate the government's divisive nationalist agenda – tend to trigger surges in anti-minority misinformation. The first wave of the COVID-19 pandemic similarly triggered another wave of anti-minority misinformation, with the government linking the outbreak of the virus to a gathering of the Muslim missionary organisation Tablighi Jamaat, giving rise to claims that Muslims were super spreaders and were deliberately trying to infect Hindus.

Although Muslims have borne the brunt of misinformation, Sikhs, Christians, and Dalits have also been targeted. The sophisticated deliberate disinformation strategies of the BJP and affiliated Hindutva groups, such as the paramilitary volunteer organisation Rashtriya Swayamsevak Sangh (RSS), make anti-minority myths yet more dangerous. The government's actions, such as internet shutdowns, censorship of online content, and surveillance measures, have contributed to a decline in public trust in democratic institutions.[24]

The selective enforcement of laws and the subjective interpretation of rules have raised concerns about the government's commitment to transparency and accountability. The incident involving the suspension of accounts covering the farmer protests on X (formerly Twitter) and the platform's statement about complying with government orders under the threat of penalties, including imprisonment, exemplifies the government's heavy-handed approach. Such actions undermine the public's confidence in the free flow of information and the ability to hold authorities accountable.[25]

The amendments to existing laws and the introduction of new regulations have raised concerns about the curtailment of freedom of expression in India. The broad rules that give the government discretion without parallel efforts to understand their impact on citizens are particularly worrisome.

The government's rebukes to platforms like Google and the requirement for AI models and algorithms to seek explicit permission before deployment on the Indian internet have set off alarm bells among AI start-ups and experts. These measures could stifle innovation and limit the free exchange of ideas in the digital realm.

The Editors Guild of India has criticised the government's attempts to determine what constitutes fake news, stating that it could result in censorship of the press and give sweeping powers to government agencies to force online intermediaries to take down content deemed problematic. This raises concerns about the potential suppression of dissenting voices and the erosion of press freedom.

The targeting of journalists, particularly those from minority communities, through threats of arrest and prosecution, further undermines the principles of a free press and freedom of expression. The arrests of individuals like Zubair, the owner of the fact-checking website Alt News, and journalist Siddique Kappan, highlight the risks faced by those who seek to hold the government accountable.

The Indian government has employed various mechanisms to exert control over the digital sphere and enable digital authoritarianism. These mechanisms can be broadly categorised into surveillance techniques and censorship mechanisms.

Highly sophisticated surveillance techniques are being used in India. India has heightened the use of artificial intelligence-enabled facial recognition technology in urban centres for identifying criminals and tracking persons of interest. While this technology may have legitimate law enforcement applications, the lack of appropriate checks and balances raises concerns about its potential misuse against political dissidents and human rights activists.[26]

The government has also introduced a sweeping surveillance order that gives ten government agencies the authority to 'tap, intercept, and decrypt all personal data on computers and networks'. This order stems from a provision in the Information Technology Act (2009), which lacks robust oversight mechanisms for data use by law enforcement and intelligence services.

Furthermore, India's telecommunications regulator has sought feedback on rules that would mandate companies like WhatsApp to 'trace and remove objectionable content' within 24 hours. This proposal is reminiscent of practices in China and Russia, where governments demand access to encryption keys, effectively creating backdoors into digital systems and devices.

Another concerning development is the Central Monitoring System (CMS), a surveillance system that monitors electronic communications, including phone calls, text messages, and social media engagement. This system raises privacy concerns as individuals may not know when their data has been intercepted, potentially leading to mass surveillance.

A complex web of censorship mechanisms is used to stifle freedoms of expression. India leads the world in the number of internet shutdowns, with over 100 reported incidents in 2018 alone. Between 2014 and November 2022, there were 680 government-imposed internet shutdowns across India, the highest number in the world. These shutdowns are often justified as measures to halt the flow of disinformation and incitement to violence during riots and protests.

However, shutdowns are a blunt instrument for interrupting the spread of disinformation online, as they deny entire cities and provinces access to communication tools at a time when they may need them the most. In practice, shutdowns serve as a substitute for more effective policymaking to counter online manipulation without disproportionate restrictions on freedom of expression and access to information.

The government has also pressured international social media platforms to remove content critical of its Hindu nationalist/populist agenda. The Information Technology Rules 2021 require intermediaries to remove content identified as illegal by the government within 3 days and provide user information to law enforcement officials.

During the COVID-19 crisis in 2021, the Indian government made an emergency order to censor tweets criticising the government for its negligence and inefficiency in combating the virus. This specifically referred to a tweet from a politician in West Bengal holding Prime Minister Modi directly responsible for Coronavirus deaths, and from an actor criticising PM Modi for holding political rallies while the virus raged.

The government also issued numerous blocking orders to Twitter, particularly targeting Kashmir-related content and accounts supporting the farmer protests. On August 11 and August 12, 2020, Twitter was asked to take down eight accounts, claiming that they were 'circulating fake news' and that the language used was a 'clear indication' that they were either being run by the ISI or the Pakistan Army. This is a typical tactic used to disavow the dissent as somehow foreign.

Additionally, the government has introduced website blocking mechanisms under Sect. 69A of the IT Act and the 2009 Blocking Rules, which allow the reasons for banning websites to be kept confidential. In 2021, a total of 6,096 websites were blocked, a significant increase from 633 websites banned in 2016.[27]

The Aadhaar system, an ambitious biometric identity system implemented in India, has been criticised for enabling mass surveillance. The system requires every Indian citizen to undergo fingerprint and retinal scans to create a massive central database that can uniquely identify every person in the country. While supporters argue that such an identity management system has the potential to facilitate government services, and enable Indians to enter the formal economy, critics view it as a project that may be the core infrastructure for a surveillance state, allowing the government to better monitor and track many aspects of citizens' lives.[28]

The internet and social media can push citizens into polarised echo chambers and fuel hostility between different communities. Over the past years in India, false rumours and hateful propaganda spread online have incited jarring outbreaks of violence against ethnic and religious minorities. Such rifts often serve the interests of antidemocratic forces in society, the government, or hostile foreign states, which have actively encouraged them through content manipulation.[29]

Exposed to these ideas, many segments of the public mirror the state's overt aggression towards 'the others' within the cyber realm. There are instances where things go beyond cyberbullying, leading to actual physical attacks due to the spread of news on social networking sites. In India, hate speech, false news, and misinformation shared on social media have been linked to increased violence and hatred towards non-Hindu religious groups.

Specifically, WhatsApp users among a section of rural and urban upper- and middle-class Hindu men are predisposed to believe populist disinformation and share misinformation about 'othered' and 'impure' groups in face-to-face and WhatsApp networks. This discrimination culminates in widespread distrust, hatred, contempt, and suspicion towards Muslims, Dalits, Sikhs, and other minority dissenting citizens.

An example of such social media-led violence can be found in incidents of lynching of Muslims and Dalits fuelled by rumours spread on social media. Since 2015, there have been more than a hundred instances of lynching, targeting individuals from discriminated groups (Dalits, Muslims, Christians, Adivasis) based on allegations of cow slaughter, cow trafficking, and cattle theft, leading to extreme mob violence and lynching that have resulted in death and trauma.

There is a 'thematic alignment' between those who propagate and believe in conspiracy theories and populists. Both do not believe in mainstream media or the government and are paranoid – afraid of minorities, refugees, and other groups plotting against them. Their basic assumption is that the government and media are in cahoots to deceive the majority group, who are the victims.

Unsurprisingly, conspiracy theories promoted by the Hindutva against Muslims have gone viral on social media. During the COVID-19 pandemic, conspiracy theories blaming Muslims for the spread of the novel Coronavirus in India became viral, leading to incidents of violence against Muslims.

Similarly, there have been incidents of lynchings and beatings of Muslims after allegations of 'love jihad' – a conspiracy theory accusing Muslims of grooming Hindu women to deceitfully convert them to Islam – spread on social media, resulting in the killing of 62 people and forced displacement of over 50,000 Muslims in the northern Indian town of Muzaffarnagar.[30]

Securing internet freedom against the rise of digital authoritarianism is fundamental to protecting democracy as a whole. Technology should empower citizens to make their own social, economic, and political choices without coercion or hidden manipulation. The internet has become the modern public sphere, and social media and search engines have a weighty responsibility to ensure that their platforms serve the public good. If antidemocratic entities effectively capture the internet, citizens will be denied a forum to articulate shared values, debate policy questions, and peacefully settle intersocietal disputes.

Democracies are famously slow at responding to crises due to their systems of checks and balances, open deliberation, and public participation. However, this built-in caution has helped some semi democratic countries fend off authoritarian-style internet controls. In May, Kenyan bloggers challenged the constitutionality of criminal provisions against the spread of false news, winning a suspension of the rules pending a final court judgment. That same month, Malaysians voted in a prime minister who promised to rescind a recently adopted law against fake news that was used by his predecessor in a failed attempt to sway the elections.

The 2019 Indian General Elections served as a stark reminder of the susceptibility of electoral processes to cyber threats. During this period, reports emerged of disinformation campaigns proliferating on social media platforms, attempting to influence public opinion by disseminating false narratives. Additionally, concerns were raised about the security of electronic voting machines (EVMs), with allegations of tampering and hacking swirling around.

State elections in India have also witnessed their fair share of cyber threats, with notable instances occurring in Maharashtra and Haryana. Threat actors, in these cases, employed phishing attacks and malware to compromise the email accounts of political figures, seeking unauthorised access to sensitive information.

In recent years, India's minority communities have been repeatedly targeted by misinformation spread through digital platforms. Data suggests that 2020 was a particularly bad year. A 2019 survey found that six in ten Indian respondents had come across fake news online, placing the country 6th out of 22 surveyed.

A key reason for the perennial issue of minority misinformation in India is the role that such false stories play in servicing the Indian government's agenda. '[Misinformation targeting minorities] highlights the growing discrimination and attacks against Muslims and other minorities since the Hindu nationalist Bharatiya Janata Party (BJP) government led by Prime Minister Narendra Modi was first elected in 2014', said Meenakshi Ganguly, the South Asia director at Human Rights Watch (HRW).

Modi has interwoven a more secular agenda, including economic modernisation, with *Hindutva* – a 100-year-old Hindu nationalist ideology. Fake news stories allege that Muslim men who marry Hindu women are motivated by 'love jihad', or Christians are forcibly converting Hindus. These stories play into fears that Hindus, who make up 80% of the population, are being outbred by minorities or that Hindus are second-class citizens.

Elections and legislative shifts – ideal moments to accelerate the government's divisive nationalist agenda – tend to trigger surges in anti-minority misinformation. The first wave of the COVID-19 pandemic similarly triggered another wave of anti-minority misinformation, with the government linking the outbreak of the virus to a gathering of the Muslim missionary organisation Tablighi Jamaat, giving rise to claims that Muslims were super spreaders and were deliberately trying to infect Hindus.

Although Muslims have borne the brunt of misinformation, Christians, Sikhs, and Dalits have also been targeted. The sophisticated deliberate disinformation strategies of the BJP and affiliated Hindutva groups, such as the paramilitary volunteer organisation Rashtriya Swayamsevak Sangh (RSS), make anti-minority myths yet more pervasive.

Many candidates in India's recent election have used AI-powered 'avatars' to engage with individual citizens in an electorate with 968 million registered voters. Such 'hyper-personalised' engagement is believed to enhance candidates' political appeal by showing voters that the candidates are attuned to each voter's specific concerns. However, the two biggest national-level parties – the ruling Bharatiya Janata Party (BJP) and the opposition Congress Party – accused each other of unfairly influencing voters by spreading 'fake news' through 'deepfakes', or digitally manipulated audio, images, or video.[31]

Some examples include fake videos of the deceased former Tamil Nadu chief minister, M. Karunanidhi, praising the leadership of his son M.K. Stalin, the state's current chief minister. A few Bollywood celebrities have filed police complaints about their 'presence' in viral 'deepfake' videos circulating on social media. These videos routinely feature misleading electoral messaging. Meta, the parent company of WhatsApp and Facebook, reportedly approved 14 AI-generated electoral ads that contained Hindu supremacist language and called for the killing of Muslims and a key opposition leader while elections were underway. Some of the videos contained the false claim that the leader 'wanted to erase Hindus from India'.

While India's Election Commission issued an advisory to parties warning against AI-generated deepfakes, the government's generally hands-off approach to regulating the AI landscape extends to its possible misuse in elections. Today's large language models are enhancing bots with new features and efficiency, imbuing them with a deceptive human-like persona, according to a 2024 analysis published in PNAS Nexus. 'Generative AI alone is not more dangerous than bots. It's bots plus generative AI', said computational social scientist Kathleen Carley of Carnegie Mellon University's School of Computer Science in an interview.[32]

The 2019 and 2024 General Elections were fought on social media. A majority of campaigns by leading parties incorporate online disinformation into their campaign strategies, which included both lies about their opponents as well as propaganda. The researchers identified sophisticated campaigns using forwarded WhatsApp messages and the mass deployment of IT bots on Facebook to disseminate doctored photos, publish coordinated content and post fake videos. The vast majority of erroneous information came from the Bharatiya Janata Party (BJP) and the Indian National Congress (INC); 'both parties were also sources and targets of misinformation. Another report by the Digital Forensic Research Lab showed automated 'bots' were boosting hashtags and trying to manipulate traffic on Twitter in February 2019.

Parties are reportedly using AI to send messages, form digital avatars, translate speeches in real-time, create memes, generate songs from speeches, and auto-tune content. The appeal of leveraging AI is apparent: the technology is quick, cost-effective, expands the scope of reach and automates the grunt work party workers would generally have to do. A US-based digital marketing firm told Government Technology that AI could help 'level the playing field' between well-funded and leaner campaigns.

Born out of the SaveTheInternet.in movement for net neutrality, the Internet Freedom Foundation (IFF) works on a range of issues including net neutrality, free expression, privacy, and innovation IFF submitted its analysis to the UN Human Rights Committee ahead of India's 4th periodic review, where they deeply analysed the state of privacy, dignity, free speech, and other constitutional guarantees and their judicial interpretations between 2019 and 2024.[33]

Several international organisations and think tanks have closely monitored and reported on the state of internet freedom in India. The annual Freedom on the Net report by Freedom House examines internet freedom in 70 countries, including India. In its latest report, Freedom House classified India as having a '*Partly Free*' internet, with concerns over obstacles to access, limits on content, and violations of user rights.

The Carnegie Endowment for International Peace, a prominent think tank, has also analysed India's internet policies and their implications. In a report titled 'India's Digital Ambition and the Global Order', they examined how India's emphasis on promoting good governance through digital public infrastructure and the 'democratisation of technology' affects its foreign policy. The report highlighted concerns that an erosion of India's democratic credentials could prompt the West to review the nature and limits of its cooperation with India.[34]

Furthermore, the US State Department's Annual Country Reports on Human Rights Practices have consistently raised concerns about internet shutdowns, online censorship, and the arrest of internet users for critical posts in India. These reports underscore the international scrutiny and responses to the challenges facing internet freedom in the country.

Efforts to exploit technical, social, economic, and institutional configurations of media can catalyse social change, sow dissent, and challenge the stability of social institutions. Data & Society's Media Manipulation & Disinformation research examines how different groups use the participatory culture of the internet to turn the strengths of a free society into vulnerabilities, ultimately threatening expressive freedoms and civil rights.[35]

Broadly, this initiative takes a sociotechnical approach to understanding the social, political, and economic incentives to game information systems, websites, platforms, and search engines – especially in cases where the attackers intend to destabilise democratic, social, and economic institutions. Through empirical research, they identify the unintended consequences of socio-technical systems and track attempts to locate and address threats, with an eye towards increasing organisational capacity across fields, so that action can be taken as problems emerge.

One tactic employed in India is the creation of fake news websites that disseminate misinformation and disinformation. These websites often have domain names and branding designed to appear legitimate, but they publish false or misleading content with the intent to deceive readers. Some key techniques used in this regard include. Data voids occur with manipulations exploring the lack of natural content to induce search engines to return low-quality and problematic content.[36] Circular reporting occurs with information, originated by a single source, appearing to come from multiple independent sources and channels with minor modifications.

Social media platforms used in India have become a prime target for disinformation campaigns due to their widespread reach and the ease with which content can be shared and amplified. Various tactics are employed to manipulate social media.

Astroturfing is deployed as a practice of disguising the sponsors of a message to give the impression that it originated spontaneously, representing the public interest and community concerns. Web brigades are rife with users coordinated to undertake large-scale disinformation campaigns by exploiting the weaknesses of communities and systems. Sock-puppets ensure the use of false or misleading identities on the internet to interact with ordinary users on social media for purposes of deception. Click farms engage in operations in which a large group fraudulently interacts with a website to artificially boost internet traffic, deceiving online systems.

Additionally, the use of bots and deepfakes has become increasingly prevalent in social media manipulation efforts. Spam bots designed to post on online comment sections, spread advertisements, or extract contact information for spam mailing lists. Social bots designed to automatically spread messages and advocate ideas, thus influencing public opinion on a given topic. They can also create fake accounts and simulate the popularity of social media profiles (e.g., through a massive network of followers). Cyborgs or hybrid accounts engage in combining automatic and human curation. In such accounts, a human periodically takes over a bot account to disguise and increase the account's credibility. Sybils or impersonators try to connect with a real user's friends and take advantage of its reputation. Sybils accounts may be operated by bots to spread disinformation and reach a wider audience.[37] Deepfakes are used as manipulations created using deep learning techniques trained on a large number of samples to automatically map facial expressions and achieve face swapping.

These tools and techniques are being employed by various actors, including state-sponsored groups, political organisations, and individuals, to spread disinformation and manipulate public opinion on social media platforms.

The Indian government has employed various tactics to silence dissent and criticism, raising concerns about the erosion of democratic values and human rights violations.

Censorship practices are the norm. The government has used arcane regulatory enforcement actions to close the space for dissent across the country.[38] Critics of Prime Minister Modi, the ruling party, or the Hindu nationalist policies they champion are the prime targets of this censorship apparatus. In several cases relating to social media, there have been efforts to regulate or censor social media content on the dubious basis that it is 'offensive' or 'objectionable'.[39]

Indian civil society organisations face significant operational barriers, including tight restrictions on foreign funding under the Foreign Contribution Regulation Act (FCRA). Authorities have invoked the FCRA to investigate prominent organisations that have reported critically on the government, such as Amnesty International India, which has halted its activities due to the probe. The International Commission of Jurists found that some 19,000 FCRA licenses were cancelled between 2014 and 2020, noting that the cancellations were imposed 'selectively to silence critical voices'.

Individuals involved in civil society activism are also targeted. Prominent journalist Rana Ayyub, a vocal critic of Prime Minister Modi's Hindu nationalist agenda, has endured multiple rounds of legal and extra-legal harassment, including a years-long money-laundering investigation over alleged misappropriation of funds from a COVID-19 relief effort. BJP critic Harsh Mander, formerly affiliated with the Congress party, has seen his home raided and his nonprofit investigated over alleged FCRA violations, with fellow activists denouncing the enforcement actions as politically motivated.

Surveillance: The government has also employed tactics of surveillance and intimidation to silence dissent. Activists and their families are subjected to relentless surveillance, raids, and harassment, creating an atmosphere of fear and helplessness among those who dare to resist. The threat of being labelled a terrorist or facing arrest under draconian laws like the Unlawful Activities (Prevention) Act (UAPA) has a chilling effect on free speech, leading to self-censorship among journalists, activists, and intellectuals.[40]

The UAPA, originally intended to combat terrorism, is increasingly being weaponised to stifle opposition. The 2019 amendment, which allows for individuals to be designated as terrorists without due process, raises grave concerns about its potential for abuse. The government's use of the UAPA to prosecute activists reveals a deliberate strategy to delegitimise dissent by branding dissenters as terrorists or criminals, discrediting their voices and instilling fear among others who might consider speaking out.

Bots, shorthand for software robots, come in a large variety of forms. Bots are typically automated in some fashion, either fully automated or human-in-the-loop. There is a common conception that all bots spam or spread malware, but this is not the case. Some bots are benign, like the Twitter account @big_ben_clock, which impersonates the real Big Ben clock by tweeting the time every hour.[41]

Groups of bots can function in coordination with each other, forming what are called botnets. One botnet of roughly 13,000 bot accounts was observed tweeting about Brexit, with most of these bot accounts disappearing from Twitter shortly after the vote.

Content polluters are one subclass; these are accounts that disseminate malware and unsolicited content. Traditional spambots, another subclass, are designed to be recognisable as bots. Social bots – a newer, more advanced type of bot – use a computer algorithm that automatically produces content and interacts with humans on social media, trying to emulate and possibly alter their behaviour. There are also hybrid human-bot accounts (often called cyborgs), which exhibit human-like behaviour and messages through loosely structured, generic, automated messages and from borrowed content copied from other sources.

Many features of bots enable them to be super spreaders of misinformation. Bots have been shown to retweet articles within seconds of their first being posted, contributing to the articles going viral. Moreover, the authors of this study found that 33% of the top sharers of content from low-credibility sources were likely to be bots, significantly higher than the proportion of bots among top sharers of fact-checked content. Similarly, a study of bots and anti-vaxxer tweets, found that bots were hyper-social, disproportionately contributing to content distribution. Bots also employ the strategy of mentioning influential users, in tweets linking to false or misleading articles, and are more likely to do so than their human counterparts. The hope is that these users will share the article with their many followers, contributing to its spread and boosting its credibility.

While the ability to investigate the origin and motive of social bots is difficult, the means to create a social bot are fairly easy to access. Social bots are available for purchase on the dark web, and there are tens of thousands of codes for building social bots on free repositories like GitHub.

The 2024 and 2019 General Elections in India were fought on social media. A majority of campaigns by leading parties 'incorporated online misinformation into their campaign strategies, which included both lies about their opponents as well as propaganda', according to a 2022 paper. The researchers identified sophisticated campaigns using forwarded WhatsApp messages and the mass deployment of IT bots on Facebook to disseminate doctored photos, publish coordinated content and post fake videos.

Information technology and social media in India play a crucial role in fostering polarisation, with a spillover effect on offline violence and protests. These platforms are not merely spaces of public discourse but also raise concerns over free speech, particularly when they contribute to the online amplification of the most radical and polarising content.[42]

Debates on free speech on platforms predominantly revolve around disinformation and hate speech, both of which are considered to exacerbate polarisation. Indian governments have taken a duplicitous approach with technology platforms pursuing stringent content moderation and censorship of critics while simultaneously using actors at an arm's length to exploit tech platforms to disseminate fake news and hate speech. Such practices are regarded as a threat to free speech and contribute to polarisation.

The role of fake news and hate speech in polarising societies is widely acknowledged in prior literature. Its crippling effects in India are now accompanied by rising calls for action on online disinformation, which threatens to polarise society and destroy democratic life.[43]

Politics remains a favoured breeding ground for disinformation and hate speech. While social media and online platforms have played a pivotal role in amplifying the spread of disinformation and hate speech, recent reports reveal the rampant misuse of these platforms by governments and political parties in over eighty countries engaged in political disinformation campaigns.

Likewise, there are global concerns over hate speech 'super-charged by the internet' in allowing falsehood and conspiracy theories to proliferate and provoke offline violence.

As this is their rice bowl, Social networking sites (SNSes) have made token efforts to 'detect and disinformation' all the while helping governments to step up measures to actively monitor social media users using sophisticated technology that enables them to monitor citizens' behaviours on these platforms. Indian governments have pushed the envelope further by imposing censorship on the internet. Such measures challenge the freedom of expression online and contribute to polarisation and political animosity among citizens.

Social media is using these attention-grabbing techniques, common in advertising and public relations exercises through existing consumer technologies, to create a polarised society, captured within their respective information echo chambers, living by divisive rhetoric and ideologies that are harmful to social unity and the ideals of democracy.

Misinformation and 'fake news' can degrade trust in institutions and fragment our worldviews with conflicting ideas about what constitutes reality, making it difficult to reach consensus on public policy. The more divisive we become as a society, the more radical representation we will seek in our legislative bodies, effectively destroying the concept of *common ground* in the parliamentary democracy of our country, where we pride ourselves on the principles of 'unity in diversity'.

Addiction to mobile devices can result in isolation and depression. Demagogues and profiteers can exploit powerful new technology to amplify their own voices for personal gain.

In India, political actors and parties are increasingly weaponising fake news and disinformation to effect polarisation among groups and reap electoral dividends in India, a deeply diverse and ethnically fragile country with a long history of communal tensions. Studies, in recent years, have found that such disinformation and polarising campaigns help the party to stay ahead of its opponents in electoral domination.[44]

The 2024 general elections in India had significant implications, with a highly engaged virtual space boasting over 750 million internet users and about 462 million social media users (around 32.2% of the total population) in January 2024. According to the World Economic Forum's 2024 Global Risks Report, misinformation and disinformation have risen rapidly to become a top risk that is likely to increase as elections take place.[45]

AI-generated campaign videos essentially have the potential to sway voters and incite protests. Even if platforms warn that the content is fabricated, there is still a risk of violence or radicalisation, and the impact of such campaigns could be far-reaching, possibly putting democratic processes at risk. While other parties also indulge in spreading fake news and conspiracy theories, the right-wing nationalists' ability to spread disinformation is unmatchable, according to a study of thousands of accounts by Reddit.

There are growing concerns that AI-generated and manipulative content undermine the democratic process and elections in India, potentially shaping the outcome. Further exploration of the relationship between political trust and misinformation consumption revealed a more complicated story, with moderates and conservatives finding exposure to fabricated news linked to higher trust in political institutions.

The worrying implications of AI-fuelled misinformation loomed over the 2024 general elections, threatening its integrity. For liberals, exposure to fabricated news is linked to lower political trust. A study conducted in 2019 found high levels of concern over hyper-partisan content and the political context of disinformation, with evidence that some political groups have actively disseminated falsehoods. Misinformation and 'fake news' degrade trust in institutions and fragment worldviews with conflicting ideas about what constitutes reality. This creates a hotbed of collusion which can benefit populist politicians and big tech.

Authoritarianism, disinformation, internet shutdowns, and the curtailing of freedoms are signals of deep-rooted systemic problems. The Indian government and its proxies monitor what we say and do online whether we are an Indian on Indian soil, a Non-Resident Indian born and brought up overseas in the West or person in the West who is a vocal critic. The digital trail of critics of the Indian government is monitored. There have been countless examples where citizens of the USA, UK, Europe, Australia, and Canada have been threatened in the real world for speaking out against human rights abuses in India. Freedom of expression and freedom of religion are basic human rights yet there have been examples where vocal critics on the internet or other digital media of the Indian Government have been assassinated in the real world.

There are several recent, notable assassination attempts and plots targeting Sikh activists abroad, particularly in the USA, Canada, and other Western countries.

Assassination Attempts and Methods were highly sophisticated with significant reconnaissance, preparation and intelligence sharing between Indian agents and the domestic criminal underworld.

According to the indictment, Nikhil Gupta allegedly told the undercover US law enforcement officer on an audio call that Hardeep Singh Nijjar 'was also the target' and 'we have so many targets'. Separately, US prosecutors state that Gupta confirmed Nijjar was the target he previously mentioned as the potential Canadian 'job', saying eventually 'some other guy did this job ... in Canada'. This suggests that Nijjar and Gurpatwant Singh Pannun were among the primary targets of the assassination plots orchestrated by Indian government agents. The targets were chosen for their support for running democratic balloting among the Sikh diaspora on independence.[46]

The indictment alleges that Gupta suggested posing as a client for Pannun so he could 'lure [him] to a place where he could be more easily executed'. He intended to meet a hitman in New York City, but instead met an undercover law enforcement officer who said he would carry out the killing for $100,000. Gupta paid $15,000 upfront via an associate on June 9th, and the indictment includes an apparent photograph of this payment.[47]

According to current and former US and Indian security officials, the assassination plot targeting Pannun was directed from within the Indian spy agency, the Research and Analysis Wing (RAW). An RAW officer named Vikram Yadav was identified as the one who wrote that the assassination was a 'priority now'. Hours after Nijjar was gunned down, Yadav sent a video clip to Gupta 'showing Nijjar's bloody body slumped in his vehicle'.

While the assassination attempt on Pannun was foiled by US authorities, the plot against Nijjar in Canada was successful, resulting in his death on June 18th outside a Sikh temple in Surrey, B.C. The foiled US assassination was part of an escalating campaign of aggression by RAW against the Indian diaspora in Asia, Europe, and North America, with the plot in the US coinciding with Nijjar's killing in Canada.[48]

Yadav indicated there would be more 'jobs' after Pannun, including one 'big target' in Canada, suggesting RAW was working with multiple criminal elements. Though Yadav served as RAW's point man, higher-ranking officials like then-RAW chief Samant Goel and India's national security adviser Ajit Doval are suspected of involvement or awareness, though no direct evidence of their complicity has emerged yet.

The back-to-back allegations by the US and Canada, both members of the Five Eyes intelligence alliance, have posed a huge diplomatic challenge for India, with Washington's accusations giving added weight to Ottawa's and raising questions about a larger campaign to target and silence Sikh leaders abroad.[49]

The White House has said it raised the issue of the alleged covert operation with India at the most senior levels and the Indian side responded with 'surprise'.[50]

A senior Biden administration official said that President Biden was so concerned by the murder-for-hire allegations that he dispatched top US intelligence leaders, including CIA director William Burns and director of national intelligence Avril Haines, to New Delhi to raise the issue.

The allegations are expected to loom large over US-India relations, with the Biden administration now saying it has been repeatedly raising its concerns with New Delhi during several leaders' meetings since the alleged plot was foiled.

The revelations have added to Western concerns about Modi, whose tenure has been marked by economic growth and rising global stature for

India, but also deepening authoritarianism. A recent report by Freedom House, a human rights organisation, listed India among the world's practitioners of 'transnational repression', a term for governments' use of intimidation or violence against their own citizens – dissidents, activists, journalists – in others' sovereign territory.

Canada, which has the world's largest Sikh population outside India, took a more forceful approach. Prime Minister Justin Trudeau publicly accused India of complicity in the killing of Nijjar and expelled RAW's station chief in Ottawa.

Relations between the countries went into a tailspin. Canada withdrew 41 diplomats from India after Modi's government threatened to revoke their legally protected status. Canadian officials who travelled to New Delhi for meetings with Doval and others said they were greeted with denials of Indian involvement.

Canadian intelligence agencies saw a surge in communications from Indian officials in Delhi to Indian diplomats in Ottawa conspicuously professing ignorance about who was responsible for Nijjar's killing – exchanges that Canadian officials came to regard as disinformation intended to be intercepted and confuse investigators, officials said.

In May 2023, an unnamed Indian government employee (referred to as CC-1) recruited Nikhil Gupta, an Indian national, to orchestrate the assassination of Gurpatwant Singh Pannun, a US citizen and vocal critic of the Indian government leading calls for democratic balloting among the Sikh diaspora over independence.

Around May 2023, Gupta and CC-1 met in Delhi to discuss the potential assassination plot.[51]

Gupta contacted an individual he believed to be a criminal associate but was actually a confidential DEA source (CS), seeking assistance in hiring a hitman to murder Pannun in New York City.[52]

The CS introduced Gupta to an undercover DEA officer (UC) posing as a hitman. CC-1 agreed to pay the UC $100,000 to assassinate Pannun.

On or about June 9, 2023, CC-1 and Gupta arranged for an associate to deliver $15,000 in cash to the UC as an advance payment for the murder in Manhattan.

In June 2023, CC-1 provided Gupta with personal information about Pannun, including his home address, phone numbers, and details about his daily conduct, which Gupta then passed to the UC.

On or about June 18, 2023, masked gunmen murdered Hardeep Singh Nijjar, an associate of Pannun and a leader of the Sikh independence movement, outside a Sikh temple in British Columbia, Canada.

On June 19, 2023, the day after Nijjar's murder, Gupta told the UC that Nijjar 'was also the target' and 'we have so many targets'.

On June 20, 2023, CC-1 sent Gupta a news article about Pannun and messaged him, 'It's [a] priority now'.

The first victim was Gurpatwant Singh Pannun, a US citizen of Indian origin and a vocal critic of the Indian government. He leads a US-based organisation that advocates for the democratic establishment of a sovereign Sikh state. The Indian government has banned Pannun and his organisation from India.

The second victim was Hardeep Singh Nijjar, an associate of Pannun and a leader of the Sikh movement. He was an outspoken critic of the Indian government and was murdered by masked gunmen outside a Sikh temple in British Columbia, Canada, on June 18, 2023.[53]

The first known perpetrator was Nikhil Gupta, an Indian national who resides in India and an associate of CC-1. Gupta was recruited by CC-1 to orchestrate the assassination of Pannun in the US. Gupta has described his involvement in international narcotics and weapons trafficking.

The other known perpetrator was CC-1, an employee of an Indian government agency, described as a 'senior field officer' with responsibilities in 'security management' and 'intelligence'. CC-1 directed the assassination plot from India and provided Gupta with Pannun's personal information and instructions.

We can consider evidence that is in the public domain. According to court documents, CC-1 worked with Gupta and others to direct an assassination plot against Pannun, a US citizen, on US soil. The US prosecutors linked the plot to the murder of Nijjar in Canada in June 2023, alleging that Gupta confirmed Nijjar was a target and stated, 'we have so many targets'. After Nijjar's murder, CC-1 sent Gupta a video clip showing Nijjar's 'bloody body slumped in his vehicle' and instructed Gupta that the assassination of Pannun was now a 'priority'. The indictment alleges that Gupta suggested posing as a client to lure Pannun to a place where he could be 'more easily executed'. Gupta intended to meet a hitman (the undercover UC) in New York City and paid $15,000 upfront as an advance payment for the murder. Gupta was arrested in the Czech Republic in June 2023 and is awaiting extradition to the USA, where he is charged with murder for hire and conspiracy to commit murder for hire.

The US government has raised the alleged assassination plot with India at the highest levels, with President Biden dispatching top intelligence officials to New Delhi to discuss the issue and press for accountability.[54]

Sikhs in Canada are not surprised by the allegations linking the Indian government to the killing of Nijjar, as they have long believed that India meddled in Canadian affairs. Chinese dissidents in Canada, especially human rights activists, are increasingly harassed and intimidated by Chinese authorities. Although the Islamic Revolutionary Guard Corps has been banned by Canada, several Iranian dissidents claim they are being monitored by the Iranian regime. This raises questions about whether the Canadian government and the RCMP have failed to take these signs more seriously and provide adequate security to prevent harassment, intimidation, and potential violence against Canadian citizens with migrant backgrounds. Certainly, it is evidence that the USA, Australia, UK, and Canada need to do more to protect its ethnic minority citizens from these attacks.[55]

Despite the violent racism that confronts many Sikhs in the diaspora, in many respects, they have become a 'model minority' in countries like USA and Canada. The success of many Sikh migrants in integrating into multicultural society can be seen in the election of a practicing turban-wearing Sikh, Jagmeet Singh, as the leader of the New Democratic Party, a crucial election partner of Prime Minister Justin Trudeau.

We can now consider the assassination cases in more detail.

US incidents have been considerable. In May 2023, an unnamed Indian government employee (referred to as CC-1) recruited Nikhil Gupta, an Indian national, to orchestrate the assassination of Gurpatwant Singh Pannun, a US citizen and vocal critic of the Indian government leading a Sikh organisation campaigning for self-determination.[56] Around May 2023, Gupta and CC-1 met in Delhi to discuss the potential assassination plot.[57] Gupta contacted an individual he believed to be a criminal associate but was actually a confidential DEA source (CS), seeking assistance in hiring a hitman to murder Pannun in New York City. The CS introduced Gupta to an undercover DEA officer (UC) posing as a hitman. CC-1 agreed to pay the UC $100,000 to assassinate Pannun. On or about June 9, 2023, CC-1 and Gupta arranged for an associate to deliver $15,000 in cash to the UC as an advance payment for the murder in Manhattan. In or about June 2023, CC-1 provided Gupta with personal information about Pannun, including his home address, phone numbers, and details about his daily conduct, which Gupta then passed to the

UC. Gupta directed the UC to carry out the murder as soon as possible but instructed the UC not to commit the murder around the time of anticipated engagements scheduled between high-level US and Indian government officials. On or about June 20, 2023, CC-1 sent Gupta a video containing the bloodied body of Pannun and messaged him, 'It's [a] priority now'.

Canadian incidents rang a similar tune. On or about June 18, 2023, masked gunmen murdered Hardeep Singh Nijjar, an associate of Pannun and a leader of the Sikh independence movement, outside a Sikh temple in British Columbia, Canada. On or about June 19, 2023, the day after Nijjar's murder, Gupta told the UC that Nijjar 'was also the target' and 'we have so many targets'. After Nijjar's murder, CC-1 sent Gupta a video clip showing Nijjar's 'bloody body slumped in his vehicle'. The indictment alleges that Gupta suggested posing as a client to lure Pannun to a place where he could be 'more easily executed'. US prosecutors linked the plot to the murder of Nijjar in Canada in June 2023, alleging that Gupta confirmed Nijjar was a target. Yadav, an RAW officer, indicated there would be more 'jobs' after Pannun, including one 'big target' in Canada, suggesting RAW was working with multiple criminal elements.

Australian incidents followed a similar pattern. Several Australian Sikhs have told Four Corners that Indian authorities have visited their families in India and threatened them due to their loved ones' activism overseas.[58] Two Australians said they were detained in India and questioned after accusations they were involved in the Khalistan movement – one said he was even stopped from returning to Sydney for several days. One man said he had received calls from an Indian intelligence officer while in Australia. Another man claimed he was slapped with criminal charges in India when he did not stop his Sikh activism in Australia. He said he was eventually granted a personal protection visa because the Australian government deemed his life would be in danger if he returned to India.

The impact on Sikhs in India, USA, Australia, and Canada is palpable. Trudeau made a public condemnation that the Indian government bore responsibility for Nijjar's death. Indo-Canadian relations long strained by Indian attacks on the Sikh population, had been maintained out of strategic necessity, largely over shared Canadian and Indian security interests in the Indo-Pacific. The diplomatic meltdown between India and Canada transcends Nijjar's death from an issue of law to a geopolitical crisis. Effectively, Trudeau's public condemnation was a key signal that

India had crossed the line by carrying out assassinations of ethnic minority leaders on Canadian soil.

The killing of Nijjar and the attempt against Pannun have confirmed attitudes among the Sikh diaspora in the West that India is targeting them and that they are not safe in any country. Sikhs are vocal on human rights and freedoms. While only a tiny minority of the Sikh diaspora is thought to support creating an independent Sikh state, the vast majority are clear on their disapproval of India and its repression of minorities. Memory of the 1984 anti-Sikh pogrom and riots in the wake of Indira Gandhi's assassination which left tens of thousands dead remains very much alive within the entire Sikh community to this day.

India's assassination plots in the USA and Canada are part of an expanding wave of aggression against minority groups seeking protection in other countries. Their home governments are increasingly willing to disregard the sovereignty of those nations and send agents across borders to assassinate political enemies.

The revelations have added to Western concerns about Narendra Modi, whose tenure has been marked by a rising global stature for India but also deepening authoritarianism. A recent report by Freedom House, a human rights organisation, listed India among the world's practitioners of 'transnational repression', a term for governments' use of intimidation or violence against their own citizens – dissidents, activists, journalists – in others' sovereign territory.

RAW's operations in Western countries during Modi's tenure have been overwhelmingly aimed at followers of the Sikh religion. There is no momentum or support for an independent Sikh state among the Sikh community. Even so, this is being constantly portrayed as a resurgent menace and overblown by Modi and his Hindu nationalist Bharatiya Janata Party in the desperate hope that the spectre of the 'bogeyman' among the Muslim, Sikh or other ethnic minority communities is enough to revive Modi's electoral chances. Regardless, ethnic minorities have been vocal on human rights abuses by the Indian government due to sustained attacks on their minority communities. Their voices in the digital realm increasingly mean they are being targeted for attacks in the real world.

A transcript of a discussion held with a person who has direct experience of harassment has been shared to add context to the points made in the chapter.

Author: Thank you for joining me today to discuss the challenges you've faced. Can you start by explaining how you first became aware of surveillance efforts?

Victim: I first noticed when I began receiving online harassment and threats. My social media accounts were being targeted by bots spreading false information about me. Deepfake audio and images were used to purport I had said outrageous things I would never say. This fuelled further public vitriol against me. It became evident that there was a coordinated effort to tarnish my reputation and silence my support for Punjabi and Kashmiri self-determination. As I dug deeper, I realised that these may have been orchestrated by RAW, India's intelligence agency.

Author: That must have been incredibly alarming. How did you feel when you realised that you were being targeted by surveillance and censorship efforts?

Victim: It was a mix of anger, fear, and helplessness. Knowing that my online activities were likely being monitored and that my voice was being systematically silenced was deeply unsettling. It made me question the safety of my digital presence and the integrity of the platforms I was using. The sense of being constantly watched and targeted created a feeling of vulnerability and stress.

Author: How did these efforts affect your ability to advocate for Punjabi and Kashmiri independence?

Victim: The impact was significant. It became much harder to communicate and coordinate with fellow activists. We had to resort to alternative communication methods and be extremely cautious about what we shared online. The constant threat of surveillance made it challenging to plan activities and share information with the public. It felt like a constant battle to stay connected and keep our movement alive.

Author: Can you describe the psychological toll these surveillance and censorship campaigns took on you?

Victim: It was mentally and emotionally exhausting. The constant stress of being watched and the fear of repercussions took a toll on my mental health. Many of us constantly experienced anxiety, paranoia, and a sense of isolation. The pressure to stay vigilant and protect ourselves and our information added to the overall strain. It was a difficult balance to maintain our activism while also taking care of our well-being.

Author: I understand that one of your colleagues was assassinated in America. How did that affect you?

Victim: That was a devastating blow. Losing a colleague in such a violent manner was a harsh reminder of the risks we face. It created a climate of fear among us, knowing that even living in America did not make us safe from such threats. It also fuelled our resolve to continue our activism, in honour of their sacrifice. But emotionally, it was a heavy burden to bear, knowing that our efforts could lead to such extreme consequences.

Author: How did you cope with these feelings and the impact of the surveillance, censorship, and the assassination of your colleague?

Victim: We relied heavily on the support of our community and fellow activists. Sharing our experiences and supporting each other helped us cope with the stress and fear. Some of us sought out mental health resources and counselling to help manage our anxiety and trauma. Some of us didn't want to seek out mental health support as we were aware that this information could be used to tarnish our reputations as well. We all had to improve our digital security and finding ways to protect our online activities to give ourselves some semblance of control. It was important to stay connected and remind ourselves of the importance of our cause.

Author: What advice would you give to other activists who might find themselves targeted by surveillance and censorship campaigns?

Victim: My advice would be to take appropriate measures to protect yourselves. Always be aware of the risks and take steps to protect your digital presence. Use secure communication tools and be cautious about the information you share online. Build a strong support network. Lean on your community for support. Don't be afraid to seek help. Remember that you are not alone and that there are resources and people who can help you navigate these challenges.

Author: Thank you for sharing your experience.

References

1. https://www.orfonline.org/expert-speak/indias-two-front-information-war.
2. https://www.journalofdemocracy.org/articles/the-authoritarian-roots-of-indias-democracy/.
3. Lewis, A. and Lall, M., 2024. From decolonisation to authoritarianism: the co-option of the decolonial agenda in higher education by right-wing nationalist elites in Russia and India. *Higher Education*, *87*(5), pp. 1471–1488.

4. Mukherji, R., 2024. How to Stop India's Authoritatarian Slide. *Journal of Democracy*, *35*(1), pp. 19–29.
5. Mostofa, S.M., Subedi, D.B. and Brasted, H., 2024. Introduction to the special issue: Authoritarianism and religion in South Asia: Trends and twists. *World Affairs*, *187*(2), pp. 130–136.
6. BATOOL, Z., 2024. Modi's Underwhelming Victory: A Precarious Path Ahead for India. *International Policy Digest*.
7. Das, R.J., 2024. The Right-Wing Attacks on the Academic Left in India. *Class, Race and Corporate Power*, *12*(1).
8. Duberstein, J., 2024. The Rise of Hindu Nationalism: A Catalyst for India's Strategic Pivot towards Israel. *The Macalester Street Journal*, *1*(2).
9. https://en.wikipedia.org/wiki/Internet_in_India.
10. https://en.wikipedia.org/wiki/Internet_censorship_in_India.
11. https://reutersinstitute.politics.ox.ac.uk/calendar/internet-freedom-and-independent-press-2023-view-india.
12. https://freedomhouse.org/country/india/freedom-net/2022.
13. https://time.com/5946092/india-internet-rules-impact/.
14. https://arxiv.org/pdf/2207.01508.
15. https://www.ncbi.nlm.nih.gov/pmc/articles/PMC8853081/.
16. https://reutersinstitute.politics.ox.ac.uk/news/ai-deepfakes-bad-laws-and-big-fat-indian-election.
17. https://freedomhouse.org/countries/freedom-net/scores.
18. https://freedomhouse.org/country/india/freedom-net/2023.
19. https://freedomhouse.org/report/freedom-net/2018/rise-digital-authoritarianism.
20. https://www.populismstudies.org/hindutva-civilisational-populist-bjps-enforcement-of-digital-authoritarianism-in-india/.
21. https://www.asiapacific.ca/publication/indian-election-use-of-ai-political-campaigns-voter-engagement.
22. https://pure.uva.nl/ws/files/121461566/The_authoritarian_practice_of_issuing_internet_shutdowns_in_India_the_Bharatiya_Janata_Party_s_direct_and_indirect_responsibility.pdf.
23. https://www.newstatesman.com/uncategorized/2021/10/misinformation-about-minorities-in-india-is-widespread-and-getting-worse.
24. https://arxiv.org/pdf/2207.01508.
25. https://reutersinstitute.politics.ox.ac.uk/news/ai-deepfakes-bad-laws-and-big-fat-indian-election.

26. https://www.justsecurity.org/62464/indias-digital-path-leaning-democratic-authoritarian/.
27. https://www.thehindu.com/opinion/lead/an-act-to-cement-digital-authoritarianism/article67202493.ece.
28. https://case.hks.harvard.edu/aadhaar-indias-big-experiment-with-unique-identification-a/.
29. https://thewire.in/rights/unfreedom-monitor-india-finds-mention-in-new-report-on-digital-authoritarianism.
30. https://www.populismstudies.org/hindutva-civilisational-populist-bjps-enforcement-of-digital-authoritarianism-in-india/.
31. https://www.asiapacific.ca/publication/indian-election-use-of-ai-political-campaigns-voter-engagement.
32. https://www.thehindu.com/elections/lok-sabha/from-it-bots-to-ai-deepfakes-the-evolution-of-election-related-misinformation-in-india/article68015342.ece.
33. https://internetfreedom.in/.
34. https://www.chathamhouse.org/2024/04/how-indias-democracy-shapes-its-global-role-and-relations-west/risks-horizon.
35. https://datasociety.net/research/media-manipulation/.
36. https://www.ncbi.nlm.nih.gov/pmc/articles/PMC8156576/.
37. https://www.jstor.org/stable/26530801.
38. https://freedomhouse.org/article/ahead-landmark-elections-indias-government-silences-dissent.
39. https://www.tandfonline.com/doi/full/10.1080/13600834.2023.2249780.
40. https://m.thewire.in/article/law/the-strangling-grip-of-uapa-silencing-arundhati-roy-and-the-voices-of-dissent.
41. https://www.ncbi.nlm.nih.gov/pmc/articles/PMC8139392/.
42. https://www.ncbi.nlm.nih.gov/pmc/articles/PMC10106894/.
43. https://www.bbc.com/news/world-asia-india-53165436.
44. https://ggr.hias.hit-u.ac.jp/en/2024/02/26/how-disinformation-erodes-the-worlds-largest-democracy/.
45. https://www.trtworld.com/magazine/how-disinformation-fake-news-and-ai-threatens-indias-electoral-process-17837049.
46. https://newlinesinstitute.org/strategic-competition/the-killing-of-hardeep-singh-nijjar-diaspora-politics-and-the-future-of-indian-allyship/.
47. https://www.reuters.com/world/us/us-charges-indian-national-with-conspiracy-assassinate-sikh-advocate-2023-11-29/.

48. https://www.hrw.org/news/2023/12/15/india-investigate-alleged-overseas-murder-plots.
49. https://theconversation.com/alleged-assassination-plots-in-the-u-s-and-canada-signal-a-more-assertive-indian-foreign-policy-218907.
50. https://www.bbc.co.uk/news/world-us-canada-67570007.
51. https://www.theguardian.com/world/2023/nov/30/contrary-to-government-policy-india-responds-to-us-assassination-plot-claims.
52. https://www.reuters.com/world/how-alleged-india-plots-kill-sikh-separatists-us-canada-unfolded-2023-12-01/.
53. https://www.washingtonpost.com/world/2024/04/29/india-assassination-raw-sikhs-modi/.
54. https://www.independent.co.uk/asia/india/india-us-pannun-assassination-plot-analysis-b2456185.html.
55. https://www.icct.nl/publication/india-canada-rift-sikh-extremism-and-rise-transnational-repression.
56. https://www.bbc.co.uk/news/world-us-canada-67582825.
57. https://www.justice.gov/opa/pr/us-attorney-announces-extradition-indian-national-charged-connection-foiled-plot-assassinate.
58. https://www.abc.net.au/news/2024-06-17/modis-indian-government-accused-of-spying-silencing-critics/103974414.

CHAPTER 14

Virtual Reality: An Amplifier for Disinformation

Virtual reality (VR) has a rich history that can be traced back to the 1930s. In 1935, Stanley Weinbaum's science fiction story 'Pygmalion's Spectacles' introduced the concept of a goggle-like device that could transport the wearer to a fictional world, stimulating their senses and creating an immersive experience. This early vision laid the foundation for the development of VR technology.[1]

The concept of stereoscopic vision, which is crucial for creating a sense of depth and immersion in VR, was first described by Sir Charles Wheatstone in 1838. Wheatstone's research led to the construction of the stereoscope, a device that combined two slightly different images to create the illusion of three-dimensional depth.

Over the following decades, various pioneers contributed to the advancement of VR technology. In the 1950s, Morton Heilig patented the Sensorama, a multi-sensory device that combined 3D video, audio, vibrations, and even smells to create an immersive experience.[2] In the 1960s, Ivan Sutherland and his student Bob Sproull developed the first head-mounted display (HMD), known as the 'Sword of Damocles', which could display simple wire-frame shapes.

The 1980s and 1990s saw the development of VR gaming systems by companies like Sega and Nintendo, although these early attempts had limited success. It wasn't until the 2010s that high-quality VR headsets

T. Singh, *Digital Psychological Warfare*,
https://doi.org/10.1007/978-3-032-15294-7_14

leveraging powerful graphics and motion tracking technology were introduced by companies like Oculus and HTC Vive, reigniting interest in VR.

In recent years, VR technology has experienced a resurgence, driven by advancements in hardware and software. Major tech companies like Meta (formerly Facebook), Sony, Samsung, and Apple have invested heavily in VR, pushing the boundaries of what is possible.[3]

One notable trend is the shift towards standalone VR headsets, which do not require a separate computer or console to function. Devices like the Oculus Quest 2 and the upcoming Meta Quest 3 have made VR more accessible to consumers by eliminating the need for additional hardware.

Another significant development is the integration of augmented reality (AR) and mixed reality (MR) capabilities into VR headsets. The Apple Vision Pro, announced in 2023, is a mixed-reality headset that combines VR and AR, allowing users to seamlessly transition between virtual and real-world environments.

Furthermore, the incorporation of artificial intelligence (AI) into VR experiences is becoming increasingly prevalent. AI-powered VR environments can analyse user behaviour and preferences, adapting the virtual world to individual needs and creating more personalised and intuitive experiences.

Weikmann et al. (2024) argue that virtual reality (VR) may be used to foster false beliefs through disinformation by displaying an entirely false reality.[4]

Beyond gaming and entertainment, VR is finding applications in various industries, such as healthcare, education, architecture, and engineering. Surgeons can use VR to practice complex procedures, students can explore virtual environments for educational purposes, and architects can create immersive walkthroughs of buildings before construction.

As VR technology continues to evolve, we can expect to see further advancements in areas such as display resolution, processing power, and tracking capabilities, as well as the development of new input methods and haptic feedback systems to enhance the overall immersive experience.

Virtual Reality (VR) is a powerful medium that can create immersive and realistic experiences, but there is a growing concern that its persuasive capabilities may be exploited to spread misinformation and disinformation.[5] The vivid and perceptually convincing nature of VR experiences can potentially lead to misperceptions about the real world, a phenomenon referred to as 'mis-experience'.[6]

The concept of *affordances* is crucial in understanding how VR technology's features can shape human beliefs and behaviours in non-deterministic ways. Immersive features like field-of-view and haptic touch pertain to the medium's technological aspects, while content features such as embodiment and persistence relate to the information conveyed about users or other actors in the environment. This affordance-based approach recognises the potential persuasive power of VR features and a user's psychological experience of those features in influencing their beliefs or behaviours.

Given the relative difficulty of creating and sharing misinformation in VR compared to social media, it is likely that misinformation in VR is created by manipulative actors with the intent to spread false information using VR, rather than naive actors who unknowingly spread VR misinformation. This suggests that misinformation in VR should be considered disinformation, a subset of misinformation where the spread of false information is known to be deliberate and with the intent to cause harm by creating misperceptions.

Chaturvedi (2024) contends that virtual reality and mixed reality are soon going to become mainstream and only time will tell how this will impact the field of journalism. As the lines between reality and not reality begin to merge it will begin to become harder to identify disinformation.[7]

To illustrate the potency of VR in creating mis-experiences, consider a simulation developed by a group of Stanford University students. The experience starts on the moon, with a panoramic moonscape seen through the eyes of an astronaut. However, as the viewer turns around, they are stunned to see a large warehouse with movie cameras, set lights, and a catering table for the crew, implying that the lunar landing in 1969 was a Hollywood fake. Perceptually, the teaching staff experienced the awe of being on the moon. But then a sound, spatialised to emerge from behind them, caused them to turn their heads around, where they saw the movie crew. Walking around in the warehouse and then looking back at the 'staged' lunar lander and the US flag through the warehouse windows completely reframed their initial experience of awe. For the teaching staff, it was a jarring experience of how the features of VR could be used to produce such potent misinformation, in this case, that the lunar landing in 1969 was a Hollywood fake.[8] This experience demonstrates how VR can be used to foster false beliefs. While this particular example was created for educational purposes, it highlights the potential for VR to be used as a tool for spreading disinformation and manipulating perceptions of reality.

It is important to note that exposure to misinformation in VR does not automatically lead to misperceptions. Several behavioural and psychological aspects can play a role in whether VR features used to create an immersive misinformation experience will actually lead to belief change. However, the unique affordances of VR and its ability to create direct 'mis-experiences' raise concerns about its potential for amplifying misinformation and disinformation.

Psychological effects must be considered. Users express positive perceptions about the use of VR in healthcare settings, identifying potential use cases such as pain and stress reduction, assisting bed-bound individuals, supporting women during labour, and aiding patients undergoing chemotherapy, dialysis, radiation, or imaging procedures. However, many also voiced concerns that should be acknowledged, including radiation exposure, infection risks, motion sickness, and an overreliance on technology.[9]

VR interventions can induce dissociative symptoms like depersonalisation (perceived disconnection from self) and derealisation (perceived disconnection from the environment). This is primarily attributed to the mismatch between the visual and vestibular (balance) systems when users perceive motion visually but remain stationary. Such adverse effects predict poorer treatment outcomes and increased nausea, underscoring the importance of measuring and addressing them.[10]

There is a consistent 'trust gap' between how much people trust information from traditional news media and how much they trust news found via social media, search engines, and messaging apps, with the latter being viewed more sceptically. Despite these concerns, many users still find digital platforms enjoyable or helpful in their daily lives.[11]

Negative perceptions about journalism are widespread, with people across some countries believing journalists manipulate audiences to serve powerful politicians' agendas or prioritise attention over factual reporting. Those who use digital platforms are also more likely to encounter criticism of the news media.

Virtual reality (VR) experiences can create potent misinformation by leveraging the medium's unique features to produce immersive 'mis-experiences' that foster false beliefs about the real world. The ability to construct an entirely fabricated reality in VR, while intended to display the truth, can be exploited to spread disinformation.[12]

Deepfake technology has made it possible to manipulate not only photographs but also facial movements, voice imitations, and video alterations, adding complexity to manipulated media by enabling deception across multiple sensory levels. This renders deepfakes particularly powerful drivers of false information in VR.

Moreover, the emergence of immersive deepfakes is considered dangerous due to their potential to create mis-experiences. Misexperience highlights the experiential and immersive nature of false information presented in VR.

VR has the potential to bring about significant positive change in the world by fostering connectedness, creating communities, and serving as a tool for education, collaboration, and psychological exploration. However, as VR stands on the cusp of widespread adoption, we should seek to avoid repeating the same mistakes that traditional social media platforms made a decade ago. Especially since some of those same social media companies are also primarily driving VR: 90% of all VR headsets were sold by either Meta or ByteDance in 2022.

There is growing concern that the same properties of VR that create realistic and persuasive experiences can be used for manipulation. One of the core threats of VR to trust and safety is the potential for VR to amplify misinformation. Given the potency of immersive VR for novel experiences that go far beyond text, image, and video, the potential for manipulative persuasion using misinformation is particularly alarming.

The rise of synthetic content and AI-generated media, particularly deepfake images, audio, and videos, has both opportunities as well as risks. The question is not whether deepfakes will be maliciously deployed to spread disinformation, but rather how effectively will Governments, the media, technology companies, and the general public respond to their use by malicious actors. Deepfakes and advanced synthetic media serve as amplifiers of existing threats, including deceptive campaign ads, mis and disinformation, voter suppression, and attacks on election workers.[13]

The proliferation of deepfakes introduces challenges to democratic processes because they can deprive the public of the accurate information needed to make informed decisions in elections. However, the deeper concern lies in the emergence of the 'liar's dividend' – a phenomenon where the very existence of generative AI engenders an atmosphere of mistrust. The fear is that the sheer volume of AI-generated content could make it challenging for people to distinguish between authentic and manipulated information. Furthermore, the boom in large language models, and text-to-speech, or text-to-video software, also speed up the creation of content. The erosion of trust in election information becomes a pervasive issue which requires a collaborative, cross-sector response.

There is a scarcity of research examining VR and misinformation specifically. While a few studies have demonstrated source confusion, in that people will sometimes subsequently remember virtual simulations as if they were real memories, we are unaware of any research that deliberately tests misinformation in VR. We expect that the power of VR to create direct 'mis-experiences' is likely to have powerful persuasive effects on how misinformation presented in VR can influence misperceptions, but we note that there is little research that directly tests this hypothesis.

At the centre of this work is the idea that VR provides an experience that skews closer to an actual one than a mediated one, perceptually and psychologically. VR researchers focus on presence, which refers to the psychological impact of VR experiences that make them feel real to users. Direct experiences translate to higher memory retention and impact beliefs and behaviours differently than indirect experiences. With direct experiences, individuals more quickly form strong convictions surrounding the experience and more confidently display behaviours consistent with those convictions after the experience. The power of VR to create direct 'mis-experiences' is likely to have powerful persuasive effects on how misinformation presented in VR can influence misperceptions, but there is little research that directly tests this hypothesis.

To combat the proliferation of deepfakes and synthetic media, companies are investing in robust AI detection tools, employee training, authentication mechanisms, and collaborative efforts with industry peers. By taking proactive measures to detect, prevent, and respond to deepfake threats, businesses can maintain their reputation, protect their stakeholders, and contribute to a safer digital ecosystem.[14]

Furthermore, generative AI could worsen manipulation in immersive environments, creating endless streams of interactive media personalised to be as persuasive or deceptive as possible.[15] To deliver the promise of VR for its audiences, the news industry needs to work together and present a united front when lobbying tech platforms to ensure a frictionless user experience, making VR an appealing mass-market media proposition.[16]

The 'immersive internet' is expected to be the next stage in the evolution of the online environment, moving beyond flat web pages, images, and videos to create more engaging and interactive experiences. This will include technologies such as augmented reality (AR) and virtual reality

(VR). While the term 'metaverse' has become heavily hyped, the emphasis will be on immersive experiences that enable users to interact and engage with each other in far richer ways.[17]

Generative AI is expected to play a significant role in producing environments, artwork, and other assets that make up digital worlds, as well as creating realistic characters and dialogues. Mark Zuckerberg himself has acknowledged the potential for generative AI to reduce the time it takes designers to build 3D environments.

The convergence of VR and AR technologies will create blended mixed-reality environments where the barriers between the real and the digital are blurred. For example, a live concert could have a parallel virtual event, with virtual attendees visible to in-person attendees through AR glasses.[18]

As these technologies continue to evolve, we can expect to see more powerful, versatile, or lighter devices being developed, with some focusing on offering new experiences, while others aim for a more refined, high-end experience. Simultaneously, there will be a focus on lightness and simplicity to address the barrier of size and weight for current headsets.

Given the potential for VR to amplify misinformation and disinformation, there is a growing concern about the need to address these technologies in this context. Deepfake technology has made it possible to manipulate not only photographs but also facial movements, voice imitations, and video alterations, adding complexity to manipulated media by enabling deception across multiple sensory levels. This renders deepfakes particularly powerful drivers of false information in VR.

Moreover, the emergence of immersive deepfakes is considered dangerous due to their potential to create 'mis-experiences'. It is argued that VR may be used to foster false beliefs by displaying an entirely false reality, although being inherently meant to display the truth.

As generative AI continues to advance, it is expected to transform how VR scenes are produced, including 3D models, dialogue among embodied agents, and contextual scenes. This could allow VR content production to scale in a manner similar to social media, potentially exacerbating the spread of misinformation and disinformation.

Kumar et al. (2024) argue emerging tactics could identify manipulations in virtual reality (VR) and augmented reality (AR) settings. Detection techniques could be developed to halt mis-experiences.[19]

techUK members, ranging from start-ups to established industry leaders, are at the forefront of research and development to detect and prevent deepfake proliferation. Recognising the complexity of the challenge, these members are actively collaborating to share knowledge and insights. Some examples of detection technologies that have been developed in recent years and are being used by members include biological signals, phoneme-viseme mismatches, facial movements and recurrent Convolutional Models.

Additionally, members are fostering partnerships with government, law enforcement, financial services, and other tech companies to address the issue collaboratively. These collaborative efforts contribute to understanding the deepfake challenges, technological advancements, and potential solutions.

As immersive technologies like virtual reality (VR) and augmented reality (AR) gain widespread adoption, there is a need for clear and meaningful privacy and ethical safeguards to mitigate the risks associated with AI in these environments. Policymakers must pass strong privacy laws that safeguard users' data, prevent unanticipated uses of this data, and give users more control over what is collected and why.

Until formal regulations are introduced, companies should collaborate with experts to develop best practices for handling user data, governing advertising on their platforms, and designing AI-generated immersive experiences to minimise the threat of manipulation. As these technologies continue to evolve, it is critical for individuals to become educated on how they work, the data they collect, how that data are used, and what harm they may cause to individuals and society.

References

1. https://virtualspeech.com/blog/history-of-vr.
2. https://program-ace.com/blog/virtual-reality-trends/.
3. https://www.iberdrola.com/innovation/virtual-reality.
4. Weikmann, T., Greber, H. and Nikolaou, A., 2024. After Deception: How Falling for a Deepfake Affects the Way We See, Hear, and Experience Media. *The International Journal of Press/Politics*, p. 19401612241233539.
5. https://media-and-learning.eu/type/featured-articles/misinformation-in-virtual-reality/.
6. https://www.forbes.com/sites/forbesbusinesscouncil/2023/11/09/the-evolution-of-virtual-reality-exploring-the-past-present-and-future/.

7. Chaturvedi, S., 2024. Building Trust in Digital Journalism: Countering Fake News, Misinformation and Disinformation. In *Handbook of Digital Journalism: Perspectives from South Asia* (pp. 517–528). Singapore: Springer Nature Singapore.
8. https://vhil.stanford.edu/sites/g/files/sbiybj29011/files/media/file/brown_vr.pdf.
9. https://www.ncbi.nlm.nih.gov/pmc/articles/PMC5750416/.
10. https://www.ncbi.nlm.nih.gov/pmc/articles/PMC10199391/.
11. https://reutersinstitute.politics.ox.ac.uk/trust-gap-how-and-why-news-digital-platforms-viewed-more-sceptically-versus-news-general.
12. https://www.researchgate.net/publication/370575726_Misinformation_in_Virtual_Reality.
13. https://www.techuk.org/resource/deepfakes-and-disinformation-what-impact-could-this-have-on-elections-in-2024.html.
14. https://www.techuk.org/resource/synthetic-media-what-are-they-and-how-are-techuk-members-taking-steps-to-tackle-misinformation-and-fraud.html.
15. https://www.wired.com/story/immersive-technology-artificial-intelligence-disinformation/.
16. https://reutersinstitute.politics.ox.ac.uk/our-research/vr-news-new-reality.
17. https://www.forbes.com/sites/bernardmarr/2023/10/13/the-10-biggest-ar-vr-and-immersive-internet-trends-in-2024/.
18. https://www.cjr.org/tow_center_reports/virtual_reality_journalism.php/.
19. Kumar, R., Khan, S.A., Alharbe, N. and Khan, R.A., 2024. Code of silence: cyber security strategies for combating deepfake disinformation. *Computer Fraud & Security*, *2024*(4).

CHAPTER 15

Conclusion: Moderating Disinformation Through a Human-Centred Approach

Misinformation does not consider the intent behind spreading false information.[1] It simply refers to any kind of wrong or false information.[2] Some examples of misinformation from reliable sources include statements like 'Over the years, QAnon has demonstrated some of the dangers of letting misinformation flourish online' and 'Consumers are becoming more and more aware of the dangers of misinformation and bias on the web'.[3]

Misinformation leads to the spreading of false information regardless of intent. Disinformation refers to false information that is spread with the *intent* to mislead or deceive. Disinformation is often used in the context of large-scale deception, such as disinformation campaigns by governments targeting populations of other countries.

Disinformation has spread rapidly with the rise of social media, with over 40% of people surveyed in different regions of the world concerned that it has caused increased polarisation and more foreign interference in politics.[4]

Disinformation can confuse and manipulate citizens, create distrust in international norms, institutions, or democratically agreed strategies, disrupt elections, or feed disbelief in key challenges such as climate change. As this phenomenon expands globally and becomes more multifaceted, it is necessary to address not only the content dimension of disinformation but simultaneously the tactics of manipulative influence

T. Singh, *Digital Psychological Warfare*,
https://doi.org/10.1007/978-3-032-15294-7_15

that accompany it. It is also important to understand the motivations for disinformation – political, financial, or reputational (to build influence) – so that these can be addressed.

Fake news (FN) on social media (SM) rose to prominence in 2016 during the US presidential election, leading people to question science, true news (TN), and societal norms. FN, although unvetted, has a credible and professional appearance, ensuring that people cannot always distinguish it from true news (TN). The majority of FN is targeted at a specific sample of the population with the aim of promoting a certain ideology by stimulating strong beliefs and polarising society.[5]

Balčytienė et al. (2024) argue to empower journalists to challenge disinformation, journalism education needs to focus on collaborative learning, believing these leads to fact-checking practices that anticipate the development of epistemic capacities and self-efficacy, crucial for resilient journalistic professionalism.[6]

FN is increasingly affecting societal values, changing opinions on critical issues and topics, as well as redefining facts, truths, and beliefs. The effects of FN cut across society, for example, the spread of FN on SM determines how governments, organisations, and people respond to events in society.

FN has become a major part of SM, raising doubts about information credibility, quality, and verification. Studies investigating the influence of FN on SM have appeared in various fields such as digital media, journalism, and politics; however, in-depth analyses of the impact of FN on society remain scarce. Despite the growing body of research on FN and SM – a significant factor in the fight against FN – an adequate review of the impact of FN in SM on society is also lacking.

To make the different kinds of disinformation that appear on the internet clear, we refer to the useful differentiation by First Draft News. Satire or Parody has no intention to cause harm but has the potential to fool. False Connection occurs when headlines, visuals, and captions don't support the content. Misleading Content involves the misleading use of information to frame an issue or individual. False Context refers to genuine content shared with false contextual information. Imposter Content involves the impersonation of genuine sources. Manipulated Content refers to genuine information or imagery manipulated to deceive. Fabricated Content is entirely false, designed to deceive and cause harm.[7]

It becomes obvious then that the question of whether the information is 'true' or 'false' is not enough to distinguish 'trustworthy' news from 'malicious' news. More important is the intention of the authors behind a story: do they want to inform or deceive the audience?

Disinformation is false or misleading information spread with the intention to deceive or cause harm. It can appear in the form of fabricated or deliberately manipulated audio/visual content, intentionally created conspiracy theories, or rumours spread to harm or cause distrust. When disinformation is shared without the intent to manipulate people, it is called misinformation. The last type is mal-information: the deliberate publication of private information for personal, corporate, or political interests, rather than public interest, such as revenge porn or leaking certain emails to damage someone's reputation.[8]

Information fabrication is not new. As Guardian columnist Natalie Nougayrède has observed: 'The use of propaganda is ancient, but never before has there been the technology to so effectively disseminate it'. Misinformation, disinformation, and propaganda have been features of human communication since at least the Roman times.[9]

Policy makers in some countries deploy history to guide their regulatory approaches. For instance, German policy makers refer frequently to the Nazi and Stasi pasts to justify their actions, while Finnish policy makers invested early in media literacy because of long experiences with Russian and Soviet disinformation. Understanding when disinformation became a mass phenomenon raises the crucial question of causality. Did disinformation cause something, or is it more prevalent for other reasons? The work by Thomas Rid and others undermines the classic narrative of technology as the main driver of disinformation, showing that disinformation in the USA existed long before 2016.[10]

Tackling misinformation is a complex challenge due to various factors. Most investigations focus on examining methods to combat misinformation, as social media platforms are still discovering new tools and techniques to mitigate it from their platforms.[11] This calls for research to understand their strategies. The issue is multifaceted, with cognitive, social, and affective drivers contributing to the formation of false beliefs and truth judgments.

Cognitive biases play a significant role in the spread and persistence of misinformation. Anxiety is one of the primary reasons behind the spread of misinformation. When people fail to receive information from official sources, they tend to gather information from their peer circles or informal sources to control social tension. This tendency is fuelled by confirmation bias, where individuals support information that reinforces their pre-existing beliefs and neglect opposing viewpoints.

The echo chamber effect, driven by confirmation bias, increases the believability and shareability of content that coincides with people's pre-existing beliefs. Platforms' algorithms contribute to this effect by providing users with content that matches their existing beliefs, thus creating echo chambers ripe for manipulation.

Moreover, misinformation can continue to influence people's thinking even after they receive a correction, a phenomenon known as the continued influence effect (CIE). The CIE is attributed to cognitive factors like the use of intuitive thinking, memory failures, and the coexistence of misinformation and corrective information in interconnected memory networks.

Socio-affective factors, such as source credibility, worldview, and emotions, also influence the CIE. Corrections attacking a person's worldview can be ineffective or backfire, while misinformation conveying negative emotions like fear or anger might be particularly likely to evoke a CIE.

Education plays a crucial role in combating misinformation by equipping individuals with the necessary skills and knowledge to critically evaluate information and recognise potential misinformation. Several educational interventions and initiatives can contribute to this effort. Media literacy courses aim to equip people with skills to help them critically evaluate content, recognise content that may be misinformation, and reduce susceptibility to believing and sharing such content. The national curriculum falls short of teaching primary and secondary school children about the broader digital environment, as well as how their digital skills and knowledge can be used to identify misinformation. Notions of information literacy and critical literacy refer to the skills and knowledge that are crucial for accessing and understanding information critically. While they overlap with media literacy and digital literacy, in an age where (mis)information is highly mediated by digital technologies, children cannot be expected to become critically literate unless they know how to use digital media and understand the context where information circulates.

The Computing curriculum places little emphasis on evaluating online content, or understanding the internet as embedded within wider socio-political and economic forces. It overlooks how the internet facilitates, for instance, political participation but also misinformation. Instead, it focuses narrowly on how to engage practically with digital media, how to code, and how algorithms function, in isolation from how they contribute to misinformation by maximising the visibility of popular content through online sharing, or creating information bubbles that expose users only to online content that is aligned with their pre-existing beliefs.

The Government and Department for Education (DfE) should acknowledge that, although the national curriculum was revised a few years ago, it needs further revision to promote digital literacy. As online (mis)information is mediated by the internet, textual analysis and evaluation skills are not enough. While traditional subjects are crucial for promoting critical thinking, the Citizenship curriculum should teach students not only about the role of the press and traditional media bias, but also about misinformation and the broader digital environment – in particular the forms which disinformation can take and how it is targeted at particular groups via social media. The Computing curriculum, furthermore, should focus not just on practical digital skills and how the internet functions but also on the ability to evaluate online content along with knowledge about the internet's implications for society.

Educational organisations, charities, the media industry, and internet corporations such as Google should develop resources and lesson plans for traditional subjects as well as Computing and Citizenship in ways that focus more closely on identifying misinformation. Besides consisting of handouts, worksheets and multimedia content, their resources should encourage students to use the internet and digital technologies to evaluate online content by comparing, for instance, websites and running searches in synergy with knowledge of what these technologies afford and the internet's implications for society.

Inoculation games, which are short games that people of all ages can play online, aim to help them learn common signs of misinformation.

Self-help resources aim to allow individuals to investigate the truthfulness of a claim or gather additional context relating to something they have seen online. However, a study found that the majority of the public are unaware of participatory interventions like inoculation games and self-help resources, while the proportion of people who had used any of them was less than 8% – and as low as 3% for some. Even when people had been told about the interventions, only a small proportion indicated they would take a media literacy course (14%) or play an inoculation game (18%) in the future, while for self-help resources the proportion was higher (33%) but still a minority.

Media literacy education is crucial for adults as well as children. It's not something that you learn once and then you're done. It's about both practical skills, and just as importantly about knowledge and awareness of the digital environment and how it operates. In this sense, it is a life-long process as digital and media environments are constantly evolving. Raising general media literacy levels will increase the public's resilience to online disinformation, even if this is not the direct target of an intervention.

Public awareness campaigns can be impactful. Disinformation actors employ various tactics to influence and manipulate others, often aiming to sow division and cause harm. Understanding these tactics can increase preparedness and promote resilience when faced with disinformation.

Strategies can counter disinformation in public awareness campaigns. Understanding how disinformation actors leverage manipulative tactics to push their agenda is crucial. Be wary of content that tries to divide or polarise opinions. Critically evaluating content and its origin is essential to determine its trustworthiness. Research the author's credentials, consider the outlet's agenda, and verify the supporting facts. Conduct a thorough, unbiased search into contentious issues by consulting credible sources and considering multiple perspectives. Rely on reputable sources of information, such as government sites. Slow down and avoid immediately clicking to share content seen online. Check the facts first, as some of the most damaging disinformation spreads rapidly through shared posts that elicit emotional reactions, overpowering critical thinking. Have private, respectful discussions with friends and family when you see them sharing potential disinformation. Be thoughtful about what you post on social media.

Successful public awareness campaigns often employ multimodal approaches, combining verbal, written, and visual elements to effectively communicate important messages to diverse populations. The 'Know Your Lemons: Worldwide Breast Cancer' campaign is a prime example, using visually modified fruit (with a texture and shape similar to a woman's breast) to raise awareness about breast cancer in a way that transcends language and literacy barriers.

Another noteworthy campaign is the 'Ice Bucket Challenge, Every Drop Adds Up' campaign for ALS (Amyotrophic Lateral Sclerosis). This campaign, which involved pouring ice-cold water over one's head, garnered significant attention and participation from public figures and celebrities, raising over $115 million in the United States alone.

Public awareness campaigns can also focus on effectively utilising healthcare resources. For instance, campaigns that use colour-coded charts and symbols can help patients determine when to seek medical help from a doctor's office, urgent care facility, or emergency department, potentially saving time, money, and valuable resources.

Experts suggest that public awareness campaigns are most successful when they foster openness to seeking help from various sources, a positive attitude towards change, curiosity, vulnerability, and a commitment to problem-solving.

Technology can help in combating misinformation by providing innovative solutions and tools to detect, monitor, and counter the spread of false or misleading information. Several successful tech solutions have emerged. Projects like the collaboration between the Spanish startup AyGLOO and the news agency Europa Press aim to design tools that leverage XAI to detect fake news.[12] XAI involves using AI and machine learning methods to help users understand the reasoning behind AI results, improving transparency and fairness. Journalists can use such tools to verify information circulating online and understand why the system deems it true or false. Natural Language Processing (NLP) techniques enable AI systems to analyse the text of news stories and alert journalists or fact-checkers to potential falsehoods. By understanding the context and meaning of text, NLP can streamline current verification processes.

Tools like TinEye, a reverse image search engine, allow users to search the internet for matches based on an image. This helps identify unauthorised use of images or verify the authenticity of visual content.

Platforms like Whois enable users to look up information about a domain's registration data, facilitating the review of a website's veracity, duration, and updates.

Google's Fact Check Tools, comprising the Fact Check Explorer and Fact Check Markup Tool, provide a scanner with a check markup to help users identify potential misinformation.

Fake news evaluation network focuses on retrospective, large-scale analysis of fake news to quantify the problem, extract patterns, and share the derived knowledge.[13] It emphasises measuring the level of responsibility of news providers, publishers, and social media platforms, aiming to educate, raise awareness, and influence corporate social responsibility strategies.

AI agents can identify the core elements of a story (named entities, events, occasions, timelines, etc.) and find cross-posts, newer versions, references, and user discussions from various sources and languages. This enables a comprehensive evaluation of the reliability of stories and their variants.

An immutable content store can permanently store labelled content, assessments, publisher scores, and metadata as part of global history, preventing deletions and ensuring transparency.

While technology offers powerful tools to combat misinformation, there are limitations and ethical considerations to address. Advancements in deepfake technology and synthesised speech make it increasingly difficult to distinguish real from artificially generated content, posing challenges for detection and verification. AI systems can inherit biases from their training data or the inherent biases of their creators, leading to potential discrimination or unfair treatment of certain groups.[14]

Some AI models have been found to inadvertently generate sensitive personal information from their training data, raising privacy violation risks.[15] Sophisticated language models like ChatGPT can be misused for spreading misinformation, impersonating identities, generating spam, or creating fake content.[16] While AI-generated content may appear original, it often lacks true innovation as it is limited by the scope of the training data. Additionally, excessive reliance on AI for problem-solving may hinder the development of critical thinking and creativity. The ease of generating text with AI models like ChatGPT has raised concerns about academic plagiarism, leading some institutions to ban their use. ChatGPT's training data are limited to a specific cutoff date, potentially leading to the generation of outdated or inaccurate information.[17] AI models may struggle to understand the nuances and context of information, leading to the generation of content that appears reasonable but is factually incorrect or nonsensical.

To address these limitations and ethical concerns, ongoing research, responsible development, and collaboration between technology providers, policymakers, and stakeholders are crucial. Striking the right balance between leveraging technology's potential and mitigating its risks is essential for effectively combating misinformation while upholding ethical principles and safeguarding individual rights.

Civil society is increasingly being mobilised around the world to fight against disinformation, often through a primary focus on human rights and building democratic capacity at the local level. There is a growing number of practical examples from around the world that offer best practice templates for how the counter-disinformation and human rights agendas can not only be aligned with each other but also be mutually reinforcing. Such examples offer valuable reference points and provide guidance on ways through which the EU should direct its counter-disinformation efforts, in tandem with external support, so as to pursue human rights and democracy. These emergent practices highlight the importance of collaboration between European institutions and civil society as the indispensable basis for building societal resilience to disinformation.[18]

Local leaders play a crucial role in combating misinformation and promoting climate action. The UK100, a network of local leaders, has outlined key commitments, including prioritising climate action above party politics, supporting evidence-based discussions to counter misinformation, and working in partnership with the government, businesses, and civil society to deliver inclusive solutions. Additionally, local leaders have committed to engaging residents, civil society, and businesses in co-designing local climate action plans, and to continuously scrutinising climate action efforts to improve delivery.

UK100 emphasises that local authorities need to serve as trusted sources of information and drivers of tangible progress in order to tackle challenges such as wavering government support and the spread of misinformation. With the 2024 local elections poised to be a defining moment for climate action, now is the time for local authorities to send a clear message that they are leading the way for a better climate debate.

Dragomir et al. (2024) argue that a society's information resilience can be viewed as a combination of structural characteristics, features of its knowledge-distribution institutions including its media system, and the activities and capabilities of its citizens. International or intranational strategies do not uniformly strengthen national resilience against disinformation. Anti-disinformation strategies need to be anchored in targeted assessments of the state of information resilience at the national level to be more effective.[19]

Policy and regulation are a very powerful driver, particularly in changing the behaviour of Big Tech companies like Twitter/X, Google or Meta. The European Union has implemented several policies and initiatives to tackle the challenge of disinformation. The Code of Practice on Disinformation, first introduced in 2018, was a pioneering effort to bring together industry players and establish self-regulatory standards to combat disinformation. This voluntary code aimed to achieve the objectives outlined in the Commission's Communication on tackling online disinformation.[20]

In June 2022, a strengthened Code of Practice on Disinformation was signed and presented by 34 signatories, with ten more joining later. The revised code aims to achieve the objectives set out in the Commission's Guidance from May 2021, setting a broader range of commitments and measures to counter online disinformation.[21]

The 2022 Code of Practice is the result of collaborative work by the signatories, who decide which commitments they sign up for and are responsible for ensuring the effectiveness of their implementation. While the Commission does not endorse the Code, it considers that, as a whole, the Code fulfils its expectations.

Signatories have committed to taking action in several domains, including demonetising the dissemination of disinformation, ensuring transparency of political advertising, empowering users, enhancing cooperation with fact-checkers and providing researchers with better access to data.

The Code establishes a permanent Task Force to ensure it remains future-proof and a strengthened monitoring framework based on qualitative reporting elements and service-level indicators. Signatories have also set up a Transparency Centre to provide a clear overview of their policies and regularly update relevant data.

The revised Code of Practice will become part of a broader regulatory framework, combined with the legislation on Transparency and Targeting of Political Advertising and the Digital Services Act (DSA). For signatories that are Very Large Online Platforms under the DSA, the Code aims to become a mitigation measure and a Code of Conduct recognised within the DSA's co-regulatory framework.

While the Code of Practice on Disinformation represents a significant step forward, there are several areas where further improvements could be made such as encouraging more industry players, particularly smaller platforms and emerging technologies, to join the Code and commit to its principles. Another improvement is exploring mechanisms to ensure signatories effectively implement their commitments, potentially through independent audits or regulatory oversight. Increasing transparency around the implementation of the Code's measures, including regular public reporting and independent verification of data provided by signatories. Regularly review and update the Code to address new forms of disinformation, such as deepfakes and synthetic media, as well as evolving tactics used by malicious actors. Promote closer collaboration between signatories, fact-checkers, researchers, and civil society organisations to share best practices and develop coordinated responses to disinformation campaigns. Ensure the Code of Practice aligns with and complements other initiatives, such as the European Democracy Action Plan and the COVID-19 disinformation monitoring programme. Incorporate measures to enhance media literacy and critical thinking skills among the general public, particularly in the digital realm, to increase resilience against disinformation.

By continuously improving and adapting the Code of Practice on Disinformation, the European Union can strengthen its efforts to combat this complex challenge and promote a more informed and resilient digital ecosystem.

Misinformation and disinformation pose significant challenges that are deeply rooted in human behaviour and psychology. A human-centric approach recognises that individuals play a crucial role in the origination, spreading, and virality of false information. This approach aims to understand and address the human factors that contribute to the adoption and circulation of misinformation stories.

Fake news spreading is strongly connected to human involvement, as there are always humans hiding behind technologies as puppet masters. There are also humans on the receiving end where individuals tend to fall for, adopt, and circulate misinformation stories. A deeper study of user roles and profiles is necessary, as behavioural human-centric variations significantly impact the overall fake news lifecycle.

Recent research has explored the role of user profiles and characteristics in misinformation spreading. Studies have focused on factors such as gender, personality, psycho-linguistic features, sentiment, and emotions expressed in users' text, which correlate with the probability of being a fake news spreader.

Explainable machine learning (ML) is a state-of-the-art approach employed in fake news detection. It incorporates techniques that aid in understanding why a news post is labelled as fake, providing human-understandable explanations.

A human-centric approach focuses on detecting user profiles that are suspicious of misinformation spreading based on their profiles. By uncovering fake news spreaders' social and psychological characteristics, explanations can be offered to expose their implicit behavioural patterns and traits.

A human-centric approach aims to provide a mechanism that informs users about their or others' tendency to spread fake news. This awareness can empower individuals to make more educated decisions regarding real and false information.

Putting a human approach at the heart of any strategy is crucial to bridge polarised communities and address the emotional factors that contribute to the spread of misinformation. Understanding the role of human emotion in consuming and accrediting information is essential.[22]

Promoting compassion and understanding: approaching the problem of misinformation with patience and compassion for friends, family, neighbours, and fellow citizens is vital. Condescension should be avoided, and individuals should learn how to recognise misinformation and discuss it constructively with those who believe it.

By adopting a human-centric approach, efforts to combat misinformation can address the underlying human factors that drive its spread, fostering a more informed and resilient society. Deradicalisation programmes can help support victims that have fallen prey to extremist propaganda.

We must also acknowledge Western capitalism is built on corporations that make huge profits from war overseas whether through the sales of weapons, infrastructure reconstruction, sales of resources such Oil and refinancing countries that have been propped up or forcefully taken over. Big Tech firms are just more corporations in the midst of this, selling use of their algorithms to the highest bidder.

International co-operation is needed by global actors, such as through the UN in order to tackle the underlying politics that give rise to the proliferation of technological weapons of mass disinformation.[23] International agreements are needed on regulating the development of AI or emerging technologies to ensure ethical frameworks are incorporated. International agreements are needed over the regulation of Big Technology firms. Binding treaties are needed to bring about peaceful settlements achieved through mutual empathy, mutual respect for human rights and agreements. This is the only way to dismantle the propaganda machines.[24]

Where it is impossible to bring about and end to disinformation than technological means are available. Countries in the West will need to learn to invest deeper into the use of emerging technologies before they can be weaponised by enemies.[25]

For example, we know Quantum Computing could be used both to support AI for even greater Digital Disinformation. It could also be used to detect disinformation.[26] The advancement of quantum computing poses a significant risk to our classical approaches to data security.

Quantum computing's exceptional computational power and AI's data analysis capabilities present a promising alliance that can revolutionise industries. One particularly intriguing application is the use of quantum computing to detect AI-generated content within various media, such as writing, images, and other products. Quantum computing can analyse patterns, linguistic nuances, and semantic structures that are beyond the reach of classical computing. By leveraging quantum algorithms like Grover's algorithm, researchers can enhance the accuracy and efficiency of identifying AI-generated text, making it an invaluable resource for content verification. Additionally, quantum computing's unparalleled processing capabilities can enable advanced image analysis, discerning minute discrepancies that arise from AI algorithms. Techniques like quantum pattern recognition can facilitate the identification of subtle features indicative of AI involvement, providing a powerful means of validation.

This is where QADI (quantum-assured data integrity) is useful. Quantum-assured data integrity is a new method that uses the properties of quantum mechanics to allow unmatched data security. This method uses quantum phenomena, including entanglement, superposition, and qubits to protect the integrity of our data.

QADI begins its mission by encoding the data into a quantum form. Instead of using traditional bits (0 s and 1 s), data are transformed into qubits. These qubits harness the unique property of superposition, meaning they can represent multiple states simultaneously. This complex encoding is the foundation of QADI's data protection, as it makes data highly resilient to unauthorised access and tampering.

At the centre of QADI's secure data handling are quantum gates. These are the tools that enable complex quantum operations on the data qubits. Quantum gates use the data's quantum properties to perform encryption and entanglement. The encryption process is like encoding a message in a secret language that only quantum computers can understand, making it virtually impossible for anyone else to decipher without the quantum key.

Once data are quantum-encrypted, it's ready for distribution. But here's the trick: QADI ensures secure data transfer by taking advantage of quantum entanglement. If anyone tries to intercept or tamper with the data during transmission, the quantum state is disrupted. This disruption is like setting off a digital alarm, indicating that someone is trying to breach the data's integrity. For enhanced security, the distribution can also utilise quantum key distribution channels.

On the recipient's end, a quantum processor equipped with quantum gates is used to verify the integrity of the received data. If the data pass the integrity check, the quantum key is employed to decrypt the qubits, revealing the original information. However, if tampering is detected during the verification process, the data remain encrypted, ensuring that only authorised parties can access and decrypt it.

To maintain transparency and accountability, QADI logs every step of the process. This includes records of quantum states, quantum key usage, and integrity checks. These logs serve as a digital trail, providing insight into the data's history and any potential security breaches.

QADI, with its quantum essence, possesses distinctive advantages that redefine data security. Its quantum resilience empowers it to stand firm against the advancing tide of quantum computing. In contrast, classical encryption methods could wane in the face of quantum adversaries. This quantum stronghold amplifies the protective barrier provided by QADI. Real-time tampering detection emerges as another defining feature of QADI. By capitalising on the entanglement of qubits, QADI affords an immediate alert system that outpaces traditional security paradigms. Traditional methods may identify breaches only after the fact, while QADI offers the assurance of real-time vigilance.

The very crux of QADI's value proposition lies in its ability to enhance data integrity. Quantum principles intertwined with data encoding processes elevate the assurance of data preservation and unaltered states during storage and transmission. However, the synergy between QADI and traditional data security is not to be underestimated. Traditional systems are deeply rooted in established infrastructure, and QADI complements them by offering a supplementary layer of quantum security. The coexistence of classical and quantum security creates a dynamic approach that harmonises with the intricacies of current practices. From a broader perspective, employing both classical encryption and QADI unfolds as a prudent risk management strategy. This diversification acts as a safeguard against data vulnerability by securing information at both classical and quantum layers, adapting to the evolving threat landscape in an era where quantum computing continues to evolve.

Quantum computing promises to revolutionise the fight against digital disinformation by harnessing its exceptional computational power and AI's data analysis capabilities. One innovative solution is the integration of quantum machine learning techniques to develop algorithmic methods that can effectively detect fake news and deepfakes. Researchers are actively exploring this approach, such as Tian et al.'s proposed fake news detection system utilising quantum K-Nearest Neighbours.

Quantum computing's ability to process vast amounts of data at unprecedented speeds could lead to groundbreaking advancements in deepfake detection. By leveraging quantum algorithms like Grover's algorithm, researchers can enhance the accuracy and efficiency of identifying AI-generated content within various media, including writing, images, and other products. Quantum computing's unparalleled processing capabilities can enable advanced image analysis, discerning minute discrepancies that arise from AI algorithms, providing a powerful means of validation.[27]

Furthermore, the synergy between quantum computing and AI could yield revolutionary outcomes in combating disinformation. Platforms like Google's TensorFlow Quantum, one of the first quantum-AI hybrid platforms, take the search for patterns and anomalies in huge amounts of data to the next level. Combined with quantum computing, AI could potentially lead to even more transformative solutions than the AI sentience that critics have been warning about.[28]

While the integration of quantum computing and AI in combating digital disinformation is still in its early stages, several case studies highlight the potential of this approach. For instance, researchers have explored the use of quantum machine learning techniques to detect fake news and deepfakes. Tian et al.'s proposed fake news detection system utilising quantum K-Nearest Neighbours is a notable example of this effort.[29]

Another case study involves the use of quantum computing for advanced image analysis to identify AI-generated content. By leveraging quantum algorithms and techniques like quantum pattern recognition, researchers can discern subtle features indicative of AI involvement, providing a powerful means of validation. This approach could be particularly useful in detecting deepfakes, which often rely on AI-generated images and videos.

While these case studies demonstrate the potential of quantum computing in combating digital disinformation, it is crucial to address the potential risks and challenges associated with this technology. As the quantum community has emphasised, regulatory failure could lead to issues similar to those experienced with AI, such as algorithmic bias, the spread of conspiracy theories, and attacks on democratic institutions fuelled by AI-generated fake news and social media posts. Addressing these concerns through urgent regulatory action is essential to ensure the responsible and ethical development and deployment of quantum computing solutions in this domain.

References

1. https://www.dictionary.com/e/misinformation-vs-disinformation-get-informed-on-the-difference/.
2. https://www.apa.org/topics/journalism-facts/misinformation-disinformation.
3. https://www.dictionary.com/browse/misinformation.
4. https://www.nature.com/articles/s44159-021-00006-y.
5. http://eprints.lse.ac.uk/101083/6/Misinformation_digital_literacy_and_the_school_curriculum_updated_Sept_2019_.pdf.
6. Balčytienė, A., Kasparaitė, R. and Lenčiauskienė, P., 2024. A human-centric approach to countering disinformation: Fostering epistemic agency via collaborative partnerships and digital source verification interventions. *Observatorio (OBS*), 18.*
7. https://www.turing.ac.uk/blog/public-worried-about-online-misinformation-are-tools-we-have-fight-it-working.
8. https://edmo.eu/areas-of-activities/media-literacy/the-importance-of-media-literacy-in-countering-disinformation/.
9. https://www.cisa.gov/sites/default/files/publications/tactics-of-disinformation_508.pdf.
10. https://h1.co/blog/medical-public-awareness-campaigns-examples-and-effectiveness/.
11. https://www.ncbi.nlm.nih.gov/pmc/articles/PMC8853081/.
12. https://www.telefonica.com/en/communication-room/blog/technology-to-combat-fake-news/.
13. https://www.theinnovationmode.com/the-innovation-blog/misinformation-online-a-solution-powered-by-state-of-the-art-tech.
14. https://connect.comptia.org/blog/ethical-issues-in-technology.

15. https://www.gp-digital.org/a-human-rights-based-approach-to-disinformation/.
16. https://www.ncbi.nlm.nih.gov/pmc/articles/PMC8747866/.
17. https://www.europarl.europa.eu/RegData/etudes/STUD/2019/624278/EPRS_STU(2019)624278_EN.pdf.
18. https://www.europarl.europa.eu/RegData/etudes/STUD/2021/653635/EXPO_STU(2021)653635_EN.pdf.
19. Dragomir, M., Rúas-Araújo, J. and Horowitz, M., 2024. Beyond online disinformation: assessing national information resilience in four European countries. *Humanities and Social Sciences Communications*, *11*(1), pp. 1–10.
20. https://digital-strategy.ec.europa.eu/en/policies/online-disinformation.
21. https://digital-strategy.ec.europa.eu/en/policies/code-practice-disinformation.
22. https://odi.org/en/insights/how-to-tackle-misdisinformation-with-a-human-centred-approach/.
23. https://www.europarl.europa.eu/RegData/etudes/STUD/2021/653635/EXPO_STU(2021)653635_EN.pdf.
24. https://helpdesk.rsf.org/digital-security-guide/online-disinformation/types-of-disinformation/.
25. https://commonslibrary.org/disinformation-and-7-common-forms-of-information-disorder/.
26. https://www.cigionline.org/articles/disinformation-its-history/.
27. https://www.insidequantumtechnology.com/news-archive/inside-quantum-technologys-inside-scoop-quantum-detection-of-ai-generated-content/.
28. https://foreignpolicy.com/2022/08/21/quantum-computing-artificial-intelligence-ai-technology-regulation/.
29. https://www.researchgate.net/publication/362008472_Quantum_Machine_Learning-based_Detection_of_Fake_News_and_Deep_Fake_Videos.

Index

T. Singh, *Digital Psychological Warfare*,
https://doi.org/10.1007/978-3-032-15294-7

FSC
www.fsc.org
MIX
Papier | Fördert gute Waldnutzung
FSC® C083411

Kolibri 360 GmbH
Ferdinand-Jühlke-Straße 7
99095 Erfurt, Deutschland
produktsicherheit@kolibri360.de